I0202513

Beat the Drum Ecclesiastic

BEAT THE DRUM ECCLESIASTIC

GILBERT SHELDON AND THE SETTLEMENT OF ANGLICAN ORTHODOXY

HEATHER D. THORNTON

Westphalia Press
An Imprint of the Policy Studies Organization
Washington, DC
2020

BEAT THE DRUM ECCLESIASTIC

All Rights Reserved © 2020 by Policy Studies Organization

Westphalia Press
An imprint of Policy Studies Organization
1527 New Hampshire Ave., NW
Washington, D.C. 20036
info@ipsonet.org

ISBN: 978-1-941472-26-2

Cover and interior design by Jeffrey Barnes
jbarnesbook.design

Daniel Gutierrez-Sandoval, Executive Director
PSO and Westphalia Press

Updated material and comments on this edition
can be found at the Westphalia Press website:
www.westphaliapress.org

For Brandon, for all the reasons you already know.

ACKNOWLEDGEMENTS

Writing is never an easy task and I owe many thanks to a great many people. My advisor, Dr. Victor Stater, read everything at least twice and offered great criticism and advice when I wanted to give up entirely. Dr. Nicholas Tyacke and Dr. Kenneth Fincham gave me early feedback at the Institute of Historical Research and encouraged me regarding the worthiness of Sheldon as a topic. Dr. Steven Gunn and the other participants of the Early Modern Britain Seminar at the University of Oxford welcomed my participation in Michaelmas 2007 and Hilary 2008.

I offer great thanks to the excellent librarians at the Duke Humphrey's Library at the Bodleian Library, Oxford, as well as to the very helpful staff and cheap tearoom at Lambeth Palace Library, London. The British Library staff was also prompt and courteous in answering questions and finding materials.

For my friends, who remained as I lost myself in the past—you know who you are—thanks for pulling me back to the present. In particular, Dr. Carolyn Day, Dr. Matthew Hernando, Dr. Sarah Hyde, and Dr. Marc Patenaude are due a great deal of thanks as we navigated our separate ways into the next chapter of our lives. Thanks my friends, Himes Hall would not have been the same without you.

TABLE OF CONTENTS

ABSTRACT

The subject of this work is Gilbert Sheldon, Archbishop of Canterbury 1663-1677. This project provides an overview of his life and the pivotal points in history where his actions and activities impacted the survival of the remnant of the church during the interregnum and its settling during the Restoration. This project seeks to reconstruct his role in the settlement of a definite Anglican identity during his tenure as archbishop and his legacy in handling the turbulent political and religious climate of late seventeenth century England.

CHAPTER 1

INTRODUCTION

The Restoration of the monarchy and church in the late seventeenth century remains of interest to scholars of the period. The re-establishment of the clerical and political establishment after decades of unrest and civil strife fascinates both professional and amateur scholars. This project is an introduction and re-evaluation of one man who impacted the settlement of the church and left his mark on the world in which he lived. Gilbert Sheldon was the Restoration Bishop of London 1660-1663 who was raised to Archbishop of Canterbury in 1663; in that position, he presided over one of the most tumultuous periods in the history of the Church of England until his death in November 1677. He enabled the church to come back into its own against incredibly long odds as an episcopal-based institution.

Sheldon appears in historical records of the proceeding centuries as either a great villain or a great saint, depending largely upon the political and religious viewpoint of the author. These impressions, however, do not leave a modern scholar or student with an accurate representation of the man and his life. Sheldon was first and foremost a loyal and devoted servant of the Church of England and the monarch of the turbulent three kingdoms of the British Isles. The aim of this larger project is to shed some light on Sheldon and place him in a less biased framework than his Whiggish detractors and Tory hagiographers have done in past centuries.

My own interest in the erstwhile archbishop developed in the reading and preparation for my MA thesis on late seventeenth-century dissent. Sheldon appeared in the secondary sources, usually quoted from his correspondence, and had definite ideas of what should be done to enforce religious uniformity. His personality and appearance intrigued me. I then discovered that very little had been written about the archbishop, which was all the more surprising considering the number of contemporary clerical figures who have multiple volumes devoted to their life and times. One only needs to search for John Tillotson or Richard Baxter to discover this. Historical scholarship, like much in this world, has fashionable and unfashionable subjects of inquiry and study. Sheldon's views have long been out of fashion in historical study in favor of the more moderate voices within the Church of England and the great number of voices outside the church after the religious upheavals of the seventeenth century. The shadows cast by nineteenth century historical giants are slow to recede, even with the light of new generations of researchers and students. Therefore, the aim of this work is to restore some balance and perhaps offer a few opinions and perceptions about a man that the early twentieth century rector Thomas Archer Turner of Ickford said was, "... one whom the world at large had forgotten to commemorate."[1]

Sheldon was a man of many labels. He was a Laudian who publicly disagreed with the then archbishop and Chancellor of Oxford. He was an Arminian who often disagreed with Arminian theologians and recognized the problems they caused his church. He was Warden of All Souls College, standing up for the university's rights over the Parliamentary Visitation of 1648 and lost his position for doing so. He was a loyal friend, even for those on opposite sides of the political spectrum from himself. He was a devoted royal servant, advising two kings on personal, religious, and political issues. He was supposedly irreligious, yet devoted in making prayers, concerned for the catechizing of both the young and old, and in extending charity to all who asked as part

---

1 Thomas Turner, *Gilbertus Sheldon*. 1903. Bucks Pamphlets # 8 1867–1905, 8 43 (11), 3. Turner's work is the eleventh pamphlet in this collection and this quote is from the third page of Turner's work on Sheldon.

of a Christian's duty. He was a generous benefactor, giving money to causes as distinct as university buildings, the augmentation of poor livings, and for those in great need due to personal loss. He was a politician who stated his mind, even though it meant falling out of favor, and he resisted compromising his views out of political pragmatism. He was erudite and a man of letters, although not well published like his contemporaries, leading some to question his scholarship. To the aforementioned could be added persecutor, royalist, master, dean, uncle, and so on. Sheldon in many ways was and remains a man hard to categorize because his actions and the labels adhered to him do not always coalesce well. In my view, he was all of the above and more, changed and tempered in the conflict of the mid-seventeenth century. Sheldon never forgot the impact of "a world turned upside down," to borrow Christopher Hill's phrase, and the lessons learned in the Civil War and Interregnum shaped his viewpoint and colored his legacy in both religious and political spheres.

His contemporaries set the tone for much of what has been written or assumed about the archbishop, although they often had little to say. Gilbert Burnet's *A History of My Own Time,* written to explain and perhaps justify the events of the last decade of the seventeenth century, casts a very long shadow. The Bishop of Salisbury's remarks about the late archbishop were less than complimentary. Burnet wrote of the man:

> Sheldon was esteemed a learned man before the wars: but he was then engaged so deep in the politics, that scarce any prints of what he had been remained. He was a very dexterous man in business, had a great quickness of appreciation, and a very true judgment. He was a generous and charitable man. He had a great pleasantness of conversation, perhaps too great. He had an art of treating all that came to him in the most obliging manner: but few depended much on his professions of friendship. He

seemed not to have a deep sense of religion, if any at all: and spoke of it most commonly as of an engine of government, and a matter of policy.[2]

The greatest ring of untruth in these words is Burnet's disregard for the archbishop's professions of friendship. Burnet petitioned the then archbishop, while still a cleric in Scotland, without great success. Sheldon apparently did not trust him. Sheldon's long-time friend, the former Lord Chancellor of England and first Earl of Clarendon, wrote:

> Of Doctor Sheldon, there needs no more to be said in this place ... than that his learning, and gravity, and prudence, had in that time raised him to such reputation, when he was chaplain in the house of lord keeper Coventry ... and when he was afterwards warden of All Souls' college in Oxford, that he then was looked upon as very equal to any preferment the church could [yield] or hath since yielded unto him; and Sir Francis Wenman would often say, when the doctor resorted to conversation at the lord Falkland's house, as he frequently did, that 'Dr. Sheldon was born and bred to be archbishop of Canterbury.'[3]

Sheldon and Clarendon came into conflict more than once over their long friendship and their relationship cooled in the politically and religiously charged first decade of the Restoration, with one advocating uniformity/conformity and the other limited toleration. Despite the difficulties late in their friendship, Sheldon

---

2   Gilbert Burnet, *A History of My Own Time,* vol. 1, ed. Osmond Airy (Oxford: Clarendon Press, 1897), 313.

3   Edward Hyde, Earl of Clarendon, *Characters and Episodes of the Great Rebellion selected from the History and Autobiography of Edward, Earl of Clarendon,* ed. G. D. Boyle (Oxford: Clarendon Press, 1889), 300. This comment was no doubt colored by events as they unfolded. Sheldon, pre-civil war, looked to have a comfortable career as an Oxford don and as a royal chaplain. He lacked the positions normally necessary for advancement to such a see.

abstained from voting for the Chancellor's impeachment. The comment of being born and bred to be archbishop commonly appears in the secondary sources that introduce Sheldon to the reader. Clarendon's highly colored account of the goings on at Great Tew, while they were both young men, cast as much of shadow as Burnet's account. Both Burnet and Clarendon were writing for posterity to present themselves in a better light. One wrote to defend a lifetime of service to king, church, and country, the other to defend the reshuffling of the dynastic deck. Both accounts offered a particular bias and both saw their writings used to paint Sheldon as either villain or saint. Burnet's work was a starting point for writing about Sheldon in the Whig-influenced histories of the succeeding centuries.

Other contemporaries also mentioned the archbishop in the numerous autobiographies that appeared in print in the early decades of the eighteenth century. Samuel Parker, Bishop of Oxford and one of Sheldon's former chaplains, and skilled debater in his own right, wrote of his former master and patron.

> But as this matter had required me to speak of so great a Man, I cannot pass him by, till I have in a few Words, laid open his good natural Temper, the Firmness of his Courage, the Sweetness of his Disposition ... as that he was a Person of great Virtues, whom Posterity should imitate. And that I may begin with his excellent good Qualities, as a Prelate, he was a Man of manifest Piety. But though he was often, and very assiduous at Prayers, yet he did not set so great a Value on them, as others did; neither did he so much regard Worship, as he did the Use of Worship. He wisely placed the chief Point of Religion in Leading a good Life: In his daily Discourse it was his Custom to caution those about him, not to deceive themselves with an half Religion, nor to think that all Forms of divine Worship was restrained within the Walls and Railes of

the Church: The chiefest Part was without Doors, and consisted in being conversant with Mankind.[4]

Parker's critical examination offered the first praise and critique of the man together and one of the last. Sheldon's historical image might have been quite different if all one had to choose from was Parker's work; Parker owed his position to the patronage and friendship of the archbishop. One of Parker's sons was named Gilbert after all. Sheldon's personal views of religious expression avoided extremes, holding firm to the traditional via media between Rome and Geneva, but especially Geneva. The traditional via media first espoused by Richard Hooker and others of the church being broad enough and vaguely defined to encompass many different viewpoints was one of the great casualties of the mid-century unrest. The Church of England, once restored, differed from its Elizabethan and Early Stuart counterpart as it sought to redefine itself distinctly after being outlawed.

The biography of another contemporary, Bishop Seth Ward of Salisbury, commented upon the primate and his personality. "Wilkins, was out of favour, both at Whitehall and Lambeth, for his Marriage ... upon that account Archbishop Shelden, who had the Keys of the Church for a great time in his power, and could admit into it and keep out of it whom he pleas'd."[5] Walter Pope, Seth Ward's biographer and former personal chaplain, was not aware of the friendly communication between the archbishop and bishop. If Ward had bad feelings about a friend being passed over for promotion supposedly for making an ill-advised marriage, those feelings diminished in light of his own need for Sheldon's support in his diocese.

---

4   Samuel Parker, *Bp Parker's History of His Own Time*, vol. 1 (London: H. Currl, 1728), 28–29.

5   Walter Pope, *The Life of the Right Reverend Father in God Seth Lord Bishop of Salisbury* (London: William Kebelwhite, 1697), 53. Pope implies that Wilkins was out of favor due to his marriage to a blind woman.

Sheldon was one of a number of prominent clerics mentioned in John Walker's reply to Edward Calamy's work on Baxter. Like many others in the period, Sheldon lost his clerical possessions and his great loves, the Church of England and the University of Oxford, which was a training ground for like-minded young men to preserve the church and state status quo. "For I find very few if any Instances, of any single Clergyman, who was once taken in hand by the Parliament that afterwards escaped Sequestration. The greater Part of them were indeed turn'd out of their Prefer-ments, before they were out of their several Confinements."[6] Sheldon, like many others, lost his livelihood during the visita-tion of the universities and for his service to his royal master.

> About this same time he became Chaplain to his Majes-ty, and was by him de[s]igned for the Mastership of the Savoy, and the Deanery of Westminster, had not the Re-bellion prevented it. During which he adhered steadfast-ly to the Royal Cause; and when the Oxford Visitation came on, strenuously Opposed it. March 27, 1648, he Honestly and Boldly told the Visitors, That he could not with a safe Conscience submit to them; for which three days after they deprived him of his Wardenship, and substituted in his room one John Palmer, a bachelor of Physick; tho' it was directly contrary to the statutes of the College ... After this they Broke open the Lodging Doors, put Palmer in Possession, and then Hurried the Doctor to Prison; who as he passed the Streets, had a thousand Prayers and Blessings from the people. In this Durance he continued above Six Months, and then the Reform-

---

6   John Walker, *An Attempt towards the Recovering of the Numbers and Sufferings of the Clergy of the Church of England, Heads of Colleges, Fellows, Scholars, &c. who were Sequester'd, Harass'd, &c in the Late Times of the Grand Rebellion: Occasion'd by the Ninth Chapter (Now the Second Volume) of Dr. Calamy's Abridgement of the Life of Mr. Baxter* (London: W.S. for J. Nicholson, 1714), Part I, 59.

ing Committee set him at Liberty (October 24, 1648) on Condition, that he should immediately depart Five Miles from Oxon; that he should not go to the King in the Isle of Wight; and that he should Give Security to appear before them, at Four Days Warning whenever cited.[7]

Sheldon's dismissal and forced removal from All Souls in April 1648 appeared in many accounts of the period. Anthony à Wood's *Annals of the History of Oxford University* provided a place to illuminate the courage of Sheldon and many others who disagreed with the parliamentary visitation and the course of events in England at the time. Essentially, Parliament provoked the University's ire by issuing an ordinance in May 1647 "to visit the several Colleges and Halls" and "to enquire of all offences, abuses, disorders, and other lawful and statutable matters of visitation whatsoever, and to proceed therein as any other Visitors, by whatsoever authority, might proceed."[8] In addition the visitors had authorization "to enquire by oath concerning all that neglect to take the Solemn League and Covenant, and the Negative Oath, and that oppose the execution of the Ordinances of Parliament concerning the Discipline and Directory."[9] The new oaths proved rather problematic for the clerics who swore an oath of loyalty upon their ordination to the head of the Church of England.[10]

The visitors conferred and decided upon a course of action and took the Buttery Book, to "dash out Dr. Sheldon's name, and enter that of Dr. Palmer in its place. Which done, they sent for Dr. Sheldon to deliver up the keys of his Lodgings; he refuses; they

---

7 Ibid., Part II, 98.

8 Anthony à Wood, *A History of the Visitation of the University of Oxford by a Parliamentary Commission in the Years 1647, 1648,* abridged (Oxford: J.H. Parker, London: J.G. and F. Rivington, 1837), 1

9 Ibid., 1.

10 Swearing an oath to the monarch remains a condition upon ordination into the Church of England to the present day.

break them open, and give Dr. Palmer possession; and for Dr. Sheldon's contempt (as they worded it) forthwith commit him to prison."[11] Sheldon, Henry Hammond, a notable theologian, and Samuel Fell, Dean and Head of Christ Church, all went to prison for various lengths of time for their contempt of parliament. Fell, Hammond, and Sheldon served the king in Oxford and resisted the visitation of the university. Sheldon, along with Hammond, among others, spent the next decade as a central figure in the complicated network of royalists in England and abroad working to preserve the remnants of a banned episcopate and the inheritance of an exile, the young king in waiting. However, his detractors and defenders usually gloss over this part of his life, despite the fact that it gave him the credibility to emerge at the Restoration as one of the men most likely to shape ecclesiastical policy.

Salamon's *The Lives of English Bishops from the Restauration to the Revolution* attempted very early on to rehabilitate High Churchmen from their eighteenth century Low Church and Latitudinarian detractors. He implied that those outside the High Church tradition would never be convinced of the archbishop's good works because their own bias blinded them to the good a committed High Churchman could accomplish. "The Part Dr. Sheldon had in supporting the Honour of Religion and an establish'd Church, proves his deep sense of Religion, if anything can do it to Lovers of Liberty and Moderation."[12] However, Salamon's ardent defense of Sheldon and others like him was a lone voice in a crowded room and easily ignored or overlooked by those following the more dominant trends.

The two great diarists of the seventeenth century also offered opinions on the archbishop. John Evelyn, a committed Church

---

11 A. à Wood, *A History of the Visitation*, 28.

12 N. Salamon, *The Lives of English Bishops from the Restauration to the Revolution* (London: J. Roberts, 1733), 16.

of England man, was joyful at the Restoration and expected great things. He agreed with the passage of the Act of Uniformity and the need for the church and state to work together. He was not above criticizing the leadership, however, "The truth is our *Bishops* slipt the occasion; since had they held a steady hand upon his Majesties restuaration, as easily they might have don, The Church of England had emerg'd & flourish'd without interruption."[13] Samuel Pepys also recorded his encounters and rumors about the archbishop. Pepys was impressed by a luncheon at Lambeth Palace, recalling that "the Bishop [was] mighty kind to me, particularly desiring my company another time, when less company there."[14] Pepys, however, was not above recording juicy (and false) rumors about the archbishop's bedmates.

Other diarists recorded instances of Sheldon's generosity. John Milward, MP for Derbyshire, recorded, "... that the present Archbishop of Canterbury had built a public structure in Oxford for the public service of the university."[15] Elias Ashmole, the founder of the Ashmolean Museum at the University of Oxford, was known to Sheldon from their shared time in Oxford. Ashmole sent a request to his old friend for a license to practice medicine for William Lilly. Ashmole requested, "... of his Grace Doctor Shelden then Lord Archbyshop of Canterbury, a Lycense for the practice of Phisick ... and producing a Testimoniall under the hands of two Phisitians of the Colledge in London on Mr:

---

13 John Evelyn, *The Diary of John Evelyn*, vol. 3, ed. E. S. De Beer (Oxford: The Clarendon Press, 1955), 609. March 12, 1672.

14 Samuel Pepys, *The Diary of Samuel Pepys*, vol. 9, ed. Robert Latham and William Matthews (Berkeley: University of California Press, 1970-83), 554. May 14, 1669.

15 John Milward, *The Diary of John Milward, September 1666 to May 1668*, ed. Caroline Robbins (Cambridge: Cambridge University Press, 1938), 231. March 18, 1668. This statement was in response to the accusation that the bishops raised great sums of money with the benefit of charitable work resulting from monetary largess.

Lillys behalfe, he most readily granted."[16] Ashmole also recorded Sheldon's passing, "The 9th of Nov: about 6H: PM Gilbert Sheldon Archbishop of Canterbury dyed at Lambeth. The 16 of Nov: following he was buried at Croyden, with litle Solemnity, for soe he desired."[17] It was also interesting to note the diaries that have no comment whatsoever on Sheldon. Richard Baxter's autobiography *Reliquae Baxterianae* made no mention of Sheldon while Bishop of London or later in his career. Ralph Josselin, a partially conforming Church of England minister, offered no opinion on the person or policies of this archbishop. Noted non-conformist diarist William Morrice had nothing to say about Sheldon, despite his interest in religious and political debates of the period.

Nineteenth-century historians were quick to follow the pattern of the previous centuries when writing about the archbishop. In Lord Macaulay's influential *The History of England,* his description of the restored church echoed the accusations of those who saw Sheldon as irreligious and overly political. "The Church of England was not ungrateful for the protection which she received from the government. From the first day of her existence, she had been attached to monarchy. But, during the quarter of a century that followed the Restoration, her zeal for royal authority and hereditary right passed all bounds."[18] Following this largely Whiggish trend in historical writing, Peter Bayne's historical essay prefacing *Documents Relating to the Settlement of the Church of England by the Act of Uniformity in 1662* painted an unflattering caricature of a High Churchman.

---

16 Elias Ashmole, *His Autobiographical and Historical Notes, His Correspondence, and Other Contemporary Sources Relating to his Life and Work,* vol. 3, ed. C.H. Josten (Oxford: Clarendon Press, 1966), 1197. October 8, 1670.

17 Ashmole, *His Autobiographical and Historical Notes,* vol. 4, 1496. November 9 and 16, 1677.

18 Lord Thomas Macaulay, *The History of England* (London: George Routledge and Sons, Ltd, 1849), 155.

Sheldon, the ruling mind on the Episcopalian side, was an admirable representative of the school of high and dry Churchmen, which flourished during the reign of Charles II ... He had none of the intensity, sincerity, narrow gloom, or fanatical enthusiasm, of Laud. Princely in his liberalities, eminent in the discharge of those hospitable duties which belong to a bishop's function, with neither the reality or affectation of saintliness, but with the courtesy, urbanity, and manner of one who shone in society, his feelings in reference to the Puritans appears essentially to have been that their earnestness, their zeal, their insistence upon personal piety, were disturbing elements in the great social and political institution of the Church of the throne and aristocracy. He was, what a frank reviewer of our own day has pronounced to be ideal perfection of a bishop, —a thorough man of the world.[19]

Montagu Burrows, historian of All Souls, attempted to correct the opinions held about the former warden of his institution in the frustrating and often cumbersome *Worthies of All Souls: Four Centuries of English History*. Burrows viewed Sheldon as a great man, and his writing evoked the specter of the great man as a historical subject. Burrows wished to rehabilitate views on Sheldon, starting with his religious viewpoint. He stressed that Sheldon was a man who knew his own beliefs and thoughts and was not easily swayed by displays of power or convincing arguments from the other side. For Burrows, Sheldon's true reputation was not available from those who disliked his policies or his church, but those who respected him, which narrowed the field to his own work almost exclusively.

---

19 Peter Bayne, "English Puritanism: Its Character and History," in *Documents Relating to the Settlement of the Church of England by the Act of Uniformity in 1662*, ed. Rev. George Gould (London: W. Kent and Co, 1862), 120.

The history of Gilbert Sheldon, the most distinguished on the roll of the Wardens of All Souls, is in many respects, before and after his forcible expulsion from his post, the history of the College. No man was more influential in promoting his views of Church and State within his University. No man was more fully in the confidence of Charles the First during the later years of that monarch's life. No man had a greater share in keeping his party together during their adversity. No man exercised more authority than Sheldon in the re-settlement of affairs at the Restoration. Consequently no man's memory has been more bitterly attacked by the opponents of his principles.[20]

J.H. Overton's *Life in the English Church 1660-1714* offered a slightly different interpretation of the archbishop and tried to give a balanced description, and his work on the archbishop appeared less overtly biased than some others. However, Overton's final judgment was that Sheldon's admirable qualities in no way made up for his personal involvement in the persecutory policies and practices of the Restoration.

> On certain points all are agreed. His munificence was unbounded ... He was a man of undaunted courage; he stayed manfully at his post at Lambeth all through the Plague; he did not shirk from rebuking his royal master, thereby forfeiting the king's favour, which he never regained ... He had obviously the gift of attaching his friends most devotedly to him. He was emphatically a strong man, with a firm will of his own, perfectly straightforward and candid, without a particle of cant. A man of whom all this can be said has strong claims on

---

20 Montagu Burrows, *Worthies of All Souls: Four Centuries of English History* (London: Macmillan and Co, 1874), 142.

our regard. But on the other hand we can gather, even from his panegyrist's accounts and from his own record-ed acts and words, that he was more a statesman than a divine, that spiritual mindedness was, to say the least, not a conspicuous trait in his character, that he took a leading part in the persecution of nonconformists, and that his disgust at hypocrisy led him, like many others in the anti-puritanical reaction of the time, far too much in the opposite direction.[21]

These viewpoints all have one thing in common. None of them sought to write a life of Archbishop Sheldon. He appeared in lists of clergymen sequestered during the Interregnum, in lists of the lives of bishops of the late Stuart church, or as a figure on the periphery of the life story of other clerical or political figures of the period. Even the recent *The University of Oxford: A History* falls into this category: Sheldon is a benefactor of the university with the theatre that bears his name.[22] No one attempted to rea-son why Sheldon and others reacted in the way that they did or believed in what they believed about church and state.

Sheldon's life attracted the attention of two biographers in the twentieth century, Vernon Staley and Victor Sutch. Both books have problems. Staley's book approached the topic as if writing hagiography and Sutch's scholarship was not as thorough as it might be and was thus prone to errors. Sheldon's life spans a pe-riod of intense activity and a thorough knowledge of the key po-litical, cultural, and theological debates and trends is essential to contextualizing the archbishop's life and times with any measure of success. This is by no means an easy task and any scholastic work needs to rely on both political and religious events to create

---

21 J.H. Overton, *Life in the English Church 1660-1714* (London: Longmans, Green, and Co, 1885), 19–20.

22 L.W.B. Brockliss, *The University of Oxford: A History* (Oxford: Oxford University Press, 2016).

a framework for the life of an intriguing man. The volume of correspondence Sheldon received showed him to be a man of definite ideas, interested in the religious life of his diocesan bishops and at the parish level. His advice was sought on a wide variety of problems from unruly students at Oxford to nonconformity, both clerical and lay, to problems of conflict within the church itself. During his primacy, serious conflict between the deans and chapters occurred in no less than four dioceses, which none of his biographers follow through the letters sent from both sides to the archbishop in the largely underused Tanner Manuscripts in the Bodleian Library.

In 1914, Vernon Staley, Rector of Ickford and Canon of St. Andrews, Inverness, published *The Life and Times of Gilbert Sheldon*. Staley hoped to write a life of the man who lived more than 250 years before he did. His impetus for writing was to correct an omission of this "great man's" life and contributions to the church. As such, Staley's work falls into that category of late nineteenth century histories, which, while enjoyable to read, have little critical examination of events within them. Staley relied heavily upon Burrow's and Clarendon's accounts of events when writing his work. The Sheldon that appeared in these pages served the church with great love and devotion and worked with political figures, especially Clarendon, to restore church and monarchy. His real attempt to redeem the character of the man from historical assassination came in the concluding chapter aptly titled "Sheldon's Character." Staley's clerical background was apparent in how he phrased the question. "Who among men knoweth the things of a man, save the spirit of a man, which is in him? And, in the present instance, the attempt to read aright the personal characteristic traits of Gilbert Sheldon has its own peculiar difficulties."[23] Staley's work used only published accounts

---

23 Vernon Staley, *The Life and Times of Gilbert Sheldon* (London: Wells Gardner, Darton & Co, 1914), 179. Biblical reference I Corinthians 2:11

and no manuscript sources, which was surprising, since his home base was not that far removed from the documents held within the Bodleian. Staley's narrative was not chronological, but thematic, and consequently jumps back and forth between decades and events without ever presenting a clear sequence. Sheldon's activities were then compartmentalized as separate things that intersected infrequently, which in the past, as in the present, is never the case.

Victor Sutch's work *Gilbert Sheldon: Architect of Anglican Recovery*,[24] published in 1973, has its own problems. Sutch's work criticizes Staley's disuse of archival material, but does not actually do much with it either. He skims from the Tanner manuscripts using five volumes and four volumes of the Harleian manuscripts, primarily focusing on one volume containing 150 letters. He also made little use of the resources at Lambeth, including official correspondence and the royal commission for the review of the prayer book. These might help his argument that Sheldon was the "architect of Anglican survival." He attempted to make Sheldon the dominant figure wherever he appeared in the historical record, which suggested a limited understanding of the political and ecclesiastical world in which the archbishop lived. Sheldon played a large part in the survival of the Church of England, but not the only one.

Sheldon appeared in the histories that tell the story of the resettlement of the Church of England after its 1660 restoration. However, these volumes for the most part adhere to the supposition that Sheldon was a politician of consummate skill, but of little real religiosity. Keith Feiling wrote "the masterful spirit of Restoration Churchmen was admittedly Gilbert Sheldon ... Bred in a College, All Souls, which Laud as Visitor had done his best to weld in a

---

24 Victor Sutch, *Gilbert Sheldon: Architect of Anglican Recovery* (The Hague: Martinus Nijhoff, 1973).

rock for Church and King."[25] Feiling connected Sheldon to Laud, following a familiar historical trend. Sheldon, in Feiling's work, held to narrow policies despite diverse friendship and showed himself as a masterful politician. Feiling was writing a history of the Tory party and Sheldon played a part in its origins by organizing churchmen into a political block in parliament. However, his tone seemed regretful in writing of the former master of his own institution; "Strength not charity, must cover his faults, and strength we find in all his actions."[26]

Robert Bosher agreed with Feiling's assessment of Sheldon, deeming his analysis the fairest in the histories written about the Restoration.

> Sheldon is a more enigmatic figure, grave and reserved in religious matters, yet withal an accomplished courtier. His administrative ability and single-minded devotion to the Church have never been questioned; but in general historians have fixed on him the character of a worldly ecclesiastic and callous persecutor. Against such charges must be set the fact that he enjoyed the intimate friendship of some of the noblest men of his time, and that in the days of his obscurity he was much loved and trusted by his fellow clergy.[27]

Bosher's thesis on the Restoration of the Church of England placed Sheldon as one of the major players in the settlement reached in 1662. Despite his claim that Sheldon enjoyed friendship with a wide assortment of people, the Sheldon in his work conformed largely to the trend of skilled politician, not devout

---

25 Keith Feiling, *A History of the Tory Party 1640-1714* (Oxford: The Clarendon Press, 1924), 126.

26 Ibid., 127.

27 Robert S. Bosher, *The Making of the Restoration Settlement: The Influence of the Laudians 1649-166.* (New York: Oxford University Press, 1951), 29.

churchman. The question begs to be asked, if Sheldon was such a skillful politician, why during the age of personal monarchy did he oppose and anger the monarch?

Ian Green presented Sheldon as a royal servant while arguing against Bosher's main points. Green wrote of the committee work undertaken by Sheldon, George Morley, and John Earle to fill vacancies created by the upheaval in the church. Green believed "it was natural for the king to turn to three episcopalians who had wide acquaintance of their fellow churchmen through their own university and cathedral backgrounds."[28] Green's settlement narrative focused on politics and less on the religious aspects. Sheldon, because of his perceived association with Laud, was a less important figure and only one of many clerical types working to restore the church.

John Spurr's *The Restoration of the Church of England*[29] painted the most complete picture of Sheldon from modern histories. Sheldon as represented by Spurr was both consummate politician who: "in the 1660s ... set a group of clerical pamphleteers to work to defend uniformity and thwart any move towards the 'comprehension' or toleration of Dissent."[30] His Sheldon was also a churchman who warned "the bishops against ordaining those who were 'to the scandal of the church and dissatisfaction of good men.'"[31] Good men in this instance being those who agreed in large part with the Cavalier Parliament's agenda in the early days of the Restoration.

In other narratives of the Restoration or of the seventeenth century Church of England, variations of Sheldon as a loyal church-

---

28 I.M. Green, *The Re-Establishment of the Church of England 1660-1663* (Oxford: Oxford University Press, 1978), 54.

29 John Spurr, *The Restoration of the Church of England, 1646-1689* (New Haven: Yale University Press, 1991).

30 Ibid., 48.

31 Ibid., 182.

man and adroit politician emerged. Paul Seaward referred to Sheldon as both a moderate bishop in the Lords and as an intractable opponent to those who wished to offer a moderate religious settlement on the Privy Council of Charles II, both referring to the debates about the Act of Uniformity.[32] Tim Harris recalled a Sheldon who opposed the Declaration of Indulgence and despite the insistence of the king of his right to issue it and refused to "forbid his clergy to preach in defence of a religion they believed in [while the king] said he was of it."[33] Patrick Collinson viewed Sheldon as the driving force behind the Restoration Church, though he only mentioned Sheldon three times in his work on the archiepiscopate.[34] Norman Sykes offered a picture of Sheldon that showed him as both a capable politician and a cleric concerned with the regulations and statues of the church.[35] Kenneth Fincham and Nicholas Tyacke placed Sheldon in the Arminian and Laudian camp, but wrestled with the terminology at the Restoration and chose the term High Churchman instead. Sheldon fit into their definition of High Churchman, "a convenient shorthand for a group drawn together by a set of shared views and objectives about issues of conformity, ritual and theology, but representing neither a single party nor a factional interest."[36] Other works barely mention Sheldon, including J.R.H. Moorman's *A History of the Church of England,* first published in 1952, and the 2017 *The Oxford History of Anglicanism Volume I and II.* Moor-

---

32 Paul Seaward, *The Cavalier Parliament and the Reconstruction of the Old Regime, 1661-1667* (Cambridge: Cambridge University Press, 1989), 175–176, 180.

33 Tim Harris, *Restoration* (London: Penguin Books, 2005), 69–70.

34 Patrick Collinson, *From Cranmer to Sancroft* (London: Hambledon Continuum, 2006), 181.

35 Norman Sykes, *From Sheldon to Secker* (Cambridge: Cambridge University Press, 1959). See Chapter 1 for most of his comments on Sheldon.

36 Kenneth Fincham and Nicholas Tyacke, *Altars Restored* (Oxford: Oxford University Press, 2007), 307.

man mentions Sheldon a total of four times and the two volumes of the *History of Anglicanism* mention Sheldon a dozen times.[37] Interestingly enough, the most positive review of Sheldon in recent work comes from a more popularly geared work *Not Angels but Anglicans,* where the archbishop is praised as a champion of orthodoxy in a brief write-up.[38]

What of the man? Gilbert Sheldon was born June 19, 1598 in Stanton, Staffordshire and died November 9, 1677 at Lambeth Palace. His birth and status have been misrepresented in his only biographies and corrected in a review by R.A. Beddard and the new *Oxford Dictionary of National Biography* article by John Spurr. Sheldon was named for his godfather, Gilbert Talbot, Seventh Earl of Shrewsbury, who employed his father as bailiff and man of affairs. His other godfather was Robert Sanderson, father of the later bishop of the same name. He was born an Elizabethan, came of age as a Jacobean, and served the church as a Carolinian divine.

What of Sheldon? If nothing more, his life and work deserve consideration among the next generation of scholars to help fill a void in the picture of seventeenth century religious and political life. I find myself in agreement with Dr. Beddard's assessment of the situation, "it must still be said that the restored Church and the two major figures of Restoration hierarchy, Sheldon and Sancroft, have an importance of their own, and in consequence an independent claim on the historian's attention."[39] Sheldon, as I

---

37 J.R.H. Moorman, *The History of the Church of England,* 3rd ed. (Harrisburg, PA: Morehouse Publishing, 1980). Anthony Milton, Ed, *The Oxford History of Anglicanism,* vol. 1, *Reformation and Identity, c. 1520-1662* (Oxford: Oxford University Press, 2017). Jeremy Gregory, Ed, *The Oxford History of Anglicanism,* vol. 2, *Establishment and Empire, 1662-1829* (Oxford: Oxford University Press, 2017).

38 Henry Chadwick, Consulting Ed., *Not Angels but Anglicans: A History of Christianity in the British Isles* (Norwich: Canterbury Press, 2000), 172.

39 R.A. Beddard, "An Unpublished Memoir of Archbishop Sheldon," in *The*

plan to argue elsewhere, was neither the great villain Burnett's history portrays nor the great political and religious *bon homme* of Clarendon's account. He was the sum of all these myriad and contradictory opinions. I believe he was a man motivated to do what he believed the best for his beloved church and the peace of his nation and for my part, I agree also with Dr. Spurr, who credited Sheldon's hand on the tiller that steered the Church of England through stormy waters and ensured its survival.

Bodleian Library Record, vol. 10, *1978-1982* (Oxford: Eric Buckley, 1982), 41.

CHAPTER 2

CHANGING TIMES,
THE 1620S AND 1630S

The history of seventeenth-century England and the greater British Isles intrigued those who lived through the tumultuous decades of the century and continues to intrigue those who follow them. The discussion of any aspect of this part of English history requires an overview of the events of this era. This chapter deals with the broad political and religious narrative of events largely in England, but also some events in Great Britain. The pivotal events of seventeenth century British history are the Civil Wars and the eventual Restoration of the Stuart monarchy, culminating in the alteration of the succession in the Glorious Revolution. Any discussion of an individual or event needs placement within its larger historical context.

The theological battles of the early to mid-seventeenth century raged across European cities and churches. English divines watched with interest as the Arminian position lost out to the unyielding orthodoxy of Calvinism at the Synod of Dort held the Netherlands in 1619. Arminians remained a viable force in England, however, and in isolated pockets on the continent. Arminianism as a doctrinal system evolved from the writings of Dutch theologian Jacob Hermann Arminius. Arminius held similar views to Calvin on human depravity and the need for grace to effect salvation. Arminianism was much more than just the belief that Christ died for all men, not just the elect. For example, God's knowledge of future acts of free agents is mediate and Adam's original state was one of innocence, not holiness, with Adam's will in precarious balance between good and evil.[1] Atonement

---

1   Alan Cairns, Ed., "Arminianism," in *Dictionary of Theological Terms*, 2nd ed.

was universal, but not universally efficient, because not all men chose to follow God. The sacrifice was for all.[2] In this system, God's sovereignty and omniscience appeared to be limited, not in actual intent, but in the impression others received.

Calvinism is associated with the theology and practices of John Calvin and the Reformed Churches associated with his methodology. Calvinists believed and continue to believe in God's sovereignty and in the use of the scriptures as the most logical guide in Christian teaching and life. Calvinism involves five points of orthodoxy: total depravity, unconditional election, limited atonement, irresistible grace, and perseverance of the saints.[3] The central focus of Calvinist worship was the pulpit, not the altar—preaching over the sacraments. The English observers at Dort returned to their homes convinced that without the king's support, such Arminian notions would never make inroads into the universities or the Church of England under their watch.

Calvinism in England and Calvanism in Scotland differed a great deal in manners and mode of church governance. England's Calvinists supported a church governed by bishops, who believed in the benefits of liturgical books, as well as a preaching ministry. These bishops funded places in cathedrals and other large churches for preaching ministries. They also allowed ministers to adapt the basic frame of the prayer book and use fewer liturgical tools, like vestments, which some found objectionable. The English Calvinists tried to keep the broad consensus, a legacy of the Elizabethan settlement, intact. The *via media* settlement and the Thirty-Nine Articles had multiple interpretations that few sought

---

(Belfast: Ambassador-Emerald International, 1998), 39. Arminianism has its own five points: conditional election, unlimited atonement, total depravity, resistible grace, and the possibility of apostasy. These points were offered by the Dutch Remonstrance in 1610.

2   Hillel Schwartz, "Arminianism and the English Parliament, 1624-1629," *The Journal of British Studies* 12 (1973): 42.

3   Cairns, "Calvinism," 73.

to reconcile. The only real exception to this statement involved those who wished to purify (i.e., the Puritans) the church from perceived popish practices, i.e., vestments, liturgies, and bishops. Scottish Calvinists were much more austere. The church in Scotland had bishops, but the real power lay with the preaching ministers. These ministers viewed the church in England as needing further reformation and were eager to aid and to encourage the work of the Puritans south of their border. Puritans in England and a majority of the clerics of Scotland wished to end the power of bishops or abolish them all together. Throughout the 1620s and 1630s, Calvinist positions in parliament and often the press became more and more Puritan in viewpoint. The Calvinist bishops and ministers who held the same doctrinal foundation lost their natural allies. This minority became powerful, and as time passed, supporting episcopacy was enough to have an individual labeled an Arminian. The perception of being an Arminian was enough to cause those in parliament to see a grave threat and to react accordingly.[4]

---

4 For more on Arminianism and its influence in England, see Jean-Louis Quantin, *The Church of England and Christian Antiquity* (Oxford: OUP, 2009), especially Chapter 3. Carl Bangs, "'All the Best Bishoprics and Deaneries': The Enigma of Arminian Politics," *Church History* 42 (1973): 5–16. Jonathan Atkins, "Calvinist Bishops, Church Unity, and the Rise of Arminianism," *Albion* 18 (1986): 411–427. Peter McCullough, "Making Dead Men Speak: Laudianism, Print and the Works of Lancelot Andrewes, 1626-1642," *Historical Journal* 41 (1998): 401–424. Dan Steere, "'For the Peace of Both, for the Humour of Neither': Bishop Joseph Hall Defends the Via Media in an Age of Extremes, 1601-1656," *Sixteenth Century Journal* 27 (1996): 749–765. For work on Puritans, see John Spurr, *English Puritanism* (London: Palgrave, 1998), especially Chapters 6-9. John Coffey, "The Toleration Controversy in the English Revolution," in *Religion in Revolutionary England* (Manchester: Manchester University Press, 2006). Philip Gorski, *The Disciplinary Revolution* (Chicago: University of Chicago Press, 2003). Anthony Milton, *Catholic and Reformed* (Cambridge: Cambridge University Press, 1995), 395–447. Ann Hughes, "'Popular' Presbyterianism in the 1640s and 1650s: The Cases of Thomas Edwards and Thomas Hall," in *England's Long Reformation 1500-1800* (London: University College London Press, 1998).

Gilbert Sheldon came into the world June 19, 1598 in the waning years of the reign of Elizabeth I. Sheldon inscribed this date into his personal bible.[5] He was the youngest son of Roger Sheldon, who made his living serving as bailiff to Gilbert Talbot, seventh Earl of Shrewsbury. The earl stood as one of Sheldon's godfathers at his baptism on June 22 and the infant was named after him. His other godfather was Robert Sanderson, father of the future bishop and friend to Sheldon with the same name.[6] Little is known of Sheldon's early life other than the name of his older brother, Ralph, and the assumption that he received some sort of grammar school education because of his arrival at the University of Oxford in 1614. He matriculated at Oxford July 1, 1614 and graduated BA from Trinity College November 27, 1617. He furthered his education with his incorporation at Cambridge in 1619 and received a MA June 28, 1620. He returned to Oxford in November 1621 when he became a probationer of All Souls College; he received admittance as a fellow January 14, 1623.

James I and VI was undoubtedly a Calvinist in matters of faith, but not everyone promoted by him was as orthodox in their beliefs. James's own hope for a new Christendom, in which a divinely ordained king ruled aided by godly bishops, faced two threats: Papists and Puritans. James walked a fine line pulling in moderates from both sides, excluding the more radical members, thus stripping them of their power (perceived or actual) to disrupt the state and church. The Church of England, headed by James, required evangelical Calvinists devoted to both a preaching ministry and episcopacy.[7] Few men met both criteria, which led to the appointment of a diverse range of men to influential positions in the church. The courtly prelates and bishops of James

---

5   MS English Bible 1648 d 3.

6   John Spurr, "Gilbert Sheldon," *ODNB*, 1.

7   Kenneth Fincham and Peter Lake, "The Ecclesiastical Policy of King James I," *The Journal of British Studies* 24 (1985): 187. See especially Section IV.

I included both Arminian and Calvinist stalwarts. The orthodox Calvinist position galvanized around George Abbot, Archbishop of Canterbury, aided by John King (London) and James Montagu (Winchester). Bishop Richard Neile of Durham, later Archbishop of York, promoted and protected a group of young Arminian churchmen, including a future archbishop and bishops: William Laud (Canterbury), Matthew Wren (Ely), and John Cosin (Durham). These men developed their ideas and churchmanship, drawing from the work and ideas of Lancelot Andrews (York). Neile was to the Puritans the type of bishop "whom all the pious, as well as private men as ministers" believed "would do the most mischief."[8]

Neile's support for Richard Montague showed the division between Calvinist and Arminian churchmen. Montague was a religious controversialist who made his first dramatic entry with a never finished history intended to refute the work of Cardinal Baronius's Catholic history *Annales Ecclesiastici*. Baronius's work gave the history of the church from the birth of Christ through 1198. Montague's planned work was suppressed by then Archbishop George Abbot for bearing an outward similarity to another history commissioned by the archbishop. Montague's history intended to argue for the historical continuity of the Church of England and defend it from its two enemies: Popery and Puritanism. Thus deterred from history, Montague wrote against a Catholic tract that appeared in his parish of Stanford Rivers in Essex. *A New Gagg for an Old Goose* (1624) was an anti-Catholic work aimed at stopping Catholic missionary activities in the area and answering the latest Roman Catholic apologetic. With the support of the Durham House group, Montague published his most "dangerous" book, *Apello Caesarem: a Just Appeale from Two Unjust Informers* (1625), in response to those who attacked *A*

8   Nicholas Tyacke, *Anti-Calvinists: The Rise of English Arminianism* (Oxford: The Clarendon Press, 1987), 107.

New Gagg. In this work, Montague refuted the claim that he was a papist or an Arminian.[9] The House of Commons accused Montague of a litany of sins, ranging from disrespect to the memory of James I to disrespecting the honors and privileges of parliament. Charles I authorized a panel of five bishops to review *Apello Caesarem*; they found that it was not contrary to the doctrine and practices of the Church of England. Lancelot Andrewes led the conference, which met at Winchester House January 16, 1626.[10] Bishops John Howson of Oxford, John Buckeridge of Rochester, and William Laud of St. David's certified Montague's orthodoxy, influenced no doubt by the patronage of Neile.[11] Neile aided the aforementioned men in gaining places of influence in the university of Oxford and at court. The winds of religious change were blowing, and few predicted the changes that were soon launched with the support of the king and the eager enthusiasm of a group of divines. One of the main functions of a university education in this era was to funnel the right sort of men into the church and the right sort of men would be of interest to Sheldon during the Restoration as well.

Religious beliefs or ideas about religious belief underpinned many of the bigger issues that would ultimately lead to the mid-century revolution. Religion was a bone of contention and both sides watched and waited to advance their version of orthodox faith. However, by the waning years of James's life, religious policies and ideas had shifted, coalescing around the person and beliefs of Charles, Prince of Wales. Charles was a devout man, but he was no Calvinist, especially since his initial spiritual tutor was Lancelot Andrewes.[12] Under his support and promotion, the Ar-

---

9 See Ibid., Chapter 6 for a fuller treatment of Montague.

10 John S. Macauley, "Richard Montague," *ODNB*, 2–5.

11 Tyacke, *Anti-Calvinists*, 108.

12 Richard Cust, *Charles I* (Harlow, UK: Pearson Longman, 2005), 82. For more on Charles's religious beliefs, see also 133–147.

minians within the Church of England began to rethink the way the public worship of God occurred throughout England.

One of the prime players in the change of religious experience and worship in England was William Laud. Laud's elevation was no surprise to those watching religious patronage in the early years of Charles I. Laud came into his own under the tutelage of Bishop Richard Neile's Arminian nursery at Durham House. Laud made his mark scholastically by arguing against popery on the continent, in particular against Cardinal Bellarmine's *Disputations*. Laud's clerical career began with his ordination as both a deacon and priest in the twilight years of Elizabeth I's long rule. He left the university and gained the notice of James and the court bishops by his turns in the preaching rotations before the king. His first major promotion was to the see of St. David's in 1621; he was translated to Bath and Wells in 1626, and replaced the recently elevated Bishop George Montainge of London in 1628.[13]

Laud was, however, more than just a divine: he served as a member of Charles' privy council from 1627 and gathered enemies for his religious ideas and his unwavering support for unpopular royal programs. Laud's policies as primate provoked a range of responses: they were loved, reviled, or ignored throughout his tenure. He promoted "the beauty of holiness" orderly and ceremonial worship throughout his jurisdiction. In some places, eager acolytes, like Bishop Matthew Wren of Norwich and later Ely, worked to implement the archbishop's policies. At the University of Oxford where Laud sat as Chancellor from 1630 to 1641, he implemented programs encouraging the beautifying of the collegiate chapels, bringing them in line with his overall scheme.

---

13 Anthony Milton, "William Laud," *DNB*, 3–11. See also "William Laud," *Clergy of the Church of England Database*, www.theclergydatabase.org.uk (afterwards CCeD), Person ID: 2801 and Hugh Trevor-Roper, *Archbishop Laud 1573-1654*, especially Chapter 8 on his dealings with Oxford. For more on the "beauty of holiness" see Ian Atherton, "Cathedrals, Laudianism, and the British Churches," *The Historical Journal* 53, no. 4 (2010): 895–918.

Evelyn noted in his diary "then was the University exceedingly regular under the exact discipline of William Lawd."[14] Many of the colleges collected funds to beautify the chapels of their respective enclaves.

Gilbert Sheldon, by this time Warden of All Souls,[15] kept a record of the donors to the new chapel in his own hand, writing, "The names of such worthy benefactors who have contributed to the beautifying on All Soulse Colledge in Oxon: and the re-establishinge of the Quire in the same left by the ffounder."[16] During his tenure as warden, the college had a leader capable of weathering the storms and disputes within the Church of England; the appointed Visitor of the college was Laud, although Sheldon stood against Laud over irregularities regarding the election of fellows. In particular, the election of a Cambridge man, Jeremy Taylor, was against the college's statutes.[17] Sheldon objected to Taylor on a technicality, as only college members could nominate fellows. Perhaps he was trying to limit Laud's interference at All Souls. At least some of the money collected during Sheldon's wardenship went towards chapel carpentry and joinery—perhaps altar rails or other additions for the beauty of holiness.[18] Sheldon's promotion to warden came quickly upon the heels of his DD June 25, 1634. He argued against the idea that the pope had the power or authority to depose Christian princes and that clerics

---

14 Evelyn, *The Diary of John Evelyn*, vol. 2, 19.

15 Sheldon became Warden in March 1635, according to the *ODNB*, or March 1636, according to CCeD record id 135047.

16 MS DD All Souls c 259, Exhibition [6]. The records in the book are brief and only four contributors are named: John Hamner Bp of St. Asaph, Thomas Cruyem, Arthur Duck, and William Stede. All but Stede, who promised 50, pledged 100 pounds.

17 Kenneth Fincham, "Oxford and the Early Stuart Polity," in *The History of the University of Oxford*, vol. 4, ed. Nicholas Tyacke (Oxford: Clarendon Press, 1997), 208–209.

18 Scott Mandelbrote, "All Souls from Civil War to Glorious Revolution," in *All Souls Under the Ancien Regime* (Oxford: Oxford University Press, 2007), 56.

have exemption from obedience to secular rulers by God's law. He also argued that it was perfectly acceptable to oblige obedience by oath from England's Roman Catholic population. These arguments were not nearly as novel as the argument Sheldon put forward six years earlier for his BD, when he denied the Calvinist position that the pope was the antichrist.[19] Before becoming Warden, Sheldon went into the church as a Deacon ordained by John Howson, Bishop of Oxford at Dorchester Parish Church in Oxfordshire, May 23, 1624. He became a priest shortly thereafter and received his first clerical living. Sheldon became a chaplain in service to Lord Keeper Thomas Coventry sometime in the mid-1620s. It was in this position that Sheldon received a letter from Stephen Goffe detailing the difficulties of ministering to the English merchant community in Delft.

> The merchants have been used to hear "three extemporary sweating sermons every week" .... unless he brings them at least two sermons, he shall never be reckoned a preacher amongst them, and he cannot see how it is possible to perform that, unless he should descend to their unconscionable fashion in talking whatsoever offers itself. Besides he must abandon his studies which he has been hitherto able to carry on, making use of the University and such learning as might be found there. In Delft he shall be penned up in one narrow corner among men that hate him, and do not love our church.[20]

The opinions voiced in these letters left a less than favorable impression of the Puritans. The Puritan position of equating pop-

---

19 John Spurr, "Gilbert Sheldon," 1. See also Milton, *Catholic and Reformed: The Roman and Protestant Churches in English Protestant Thought, 1600-1640.*, 117. Some of Sheldon's living included Vicar: Hackney, Middlesex May 2, 1633, Rector: Oddington June 2, 1636, resigned June 29, 1639, and Rector: Newington com Broghtwell May 28, 1639. All taken from the CCeD Person Id: 15373.

20 *CSPD* CI, vol. 260, February 3/13, 1634. Stephen Goffe to Gilbert Sheldon.

ery with Arminianism directly affected Sheldon. As an advocate for the Laudian program, Sheldon was subject to the same suspicions and charges. Sheldon was no papist and disliked being labeled as such by Calvinists living either at home or abroad, due to his circle of friends and colleagues at Oxford. Sheldon's DD defense would have been enough for Dr. John Prideaux, Regis Professor of Divinity, to believe ill of the new warden of All Souls. The lingering effects of the Synod of Dort and the Dutch reactions to the innovations in English religion made the Low Countries a difficult place for many to minister. Goffe complained of people mistaking him for either a papist or some other kind of troublemaker. Writing to Sheldon about his experience in Amsterdam among the English there, he fretted that:

> for the zeal of his pious countrymen makes all men believe that the wri[t]er is nothing less but a papist in his heart, and sent thither underhand by the Bishops of England (which to Dutch ears by them is made an odious name,) to bring in Episcopal government, or else to make the King angry with the States, that so they may fall out, which is much desired, (as our countrymen tell the Dutch,) in England.[21]

The religious complexities of the continent were difficult at the best of time and in the period of the last major religious war, distrust and suspicions ran very high.

Sheldon's service to Coventry introduced him to the king's notice and attention. Sheldon was named one of Charles's chaplains sometime between the achievement of his BD in 1628 and his becoming Warden of All Souls.[22] Sheldon was a chaplain-in-ordinary and the king had plans to place Sheldon at the Savoy and

---

21 *CSPD* CI, vol. 286, April 1-17, 1635, April 16, 1635. Stephen Goffe to Gilbert Sheldon.

22 Beddard, "An Unpublished Memoir," 45.

as Dean of Westminster so that he would be close enough for easy consultation.[23] As a chaplain-in-ordinary, Sheldon would have had semi-regular to regular contact with the king and been obligated to offer religious services in the Chapel Royal for one month of the year.

While Sheldon corresponded with those within and without England's boundaries of the two institutions dearest to him, the Church of England and the University of Oxford, he was entering a dangerous period. Laud's policies brought him into conflict with moderate Puritans who were happy under the broad-based church of James I. The ceremonial aspects that caused the most anger involved the placement and railing of the communion table and the requirement of proper clerical dress for divine service. This change to the communion table evoked the specter of popery and an unhappy portion of the Church of England waited for a further and complete reformation. Furthermore, Charles and Laud worked to implement a desire of James I in Scotland in 1637: an Anglicized liturgy. The introduction of the Scottish Book of Common Prayer was a disaster that would ultimately involve all three of Charles's kingdoms in warfare and that is addressed later in this chapter.

The period preceding the outbreak of open war was probably one of the most pleasant of Sheldon's life. He was at home in Oxford, serving as Warden in his beloved college of All Souls and engaged in earnest academic and religious debates within the circle that met at Lucius Cary, Lord Falkland's estate of Great Tew. The members of the Great Tew Circle became influential in political and religious settlements both during and after the civil war. Falkland and his friends tried to create a utopian vision in which union and harmony (in any subject) came about using reason and criticism.[24] Edward Hyde, later Earl of Clarendon,

---

23 Ibid., 47.

24 Sarah Mortimer, "Great Tew Circle," *ODNB*, 4.

reminisced fondly in his history of the company and conversation present at the estate. The estate "being within ten or twelve miles of the University, looked like the University itself by the company that was always found there. There were Dr Sheldon, Dr Morley, Dr Hammond, Dr Earles, Mr Chillingworth, and indeed all men of eminent parts and faculties in Oxford, besides those who resorted thither from London."[25] Chillingworth was the author of *The Religion of Protestants,* Hammond was a notable theologian and royal chaplain, and the others served as royal chaplains and later as bishops in the restored Church of England. The library and conversations at Great Tew may have provided respite from unwelcome advances in clerical and political conformity. The men of Great Tew, despite differences in religious and political opinions among them, sided with the king and the church in the Civil War. The alumni of Great Tew became vital religious mentors and caretakers of the exile's church and were important in the volatile political climate.

Religious changes sparked the initial shots of the Civil Wars, but Charles and his parliaments had a rocky relationship from the outset of his reign. In 1625, the king, with broad popular support and the help of his favorite George Villiers, first Duke of Buckingham, attempted to intervene in world events by showing support for the beleaguered Protestant forces in the Thirty Years War (1618-1648). A badly planned and executed military expedition to aid the French Protestants and their Dutch allies resulted in the loss of the ill-equipped and ill-trained English army. It also illustrated the fact that the English were not yet capable of playing on the world stage as many had assumed. Charles's marriage to Louis XIII's sister, Henrietta Maria, undertaken while in the midst of military disasters, cost the king his early popularity.[26] Parliament

---

25 Hugh Trevor-Roper, "The Great Tew Circle," in *Catholics, Anglicans and Puritans Seventeenth Century Essays* (London: Secker and Warburg, 1987), 168.

26 G.M. Trevelyan, *England Under the Stuarts* (London: Routledge, 2002); see

wanted Buckingham's head, but to protect his favorite, the king prorogued it, which caused him to look beyond parliamentary means for war funds. Charles turned to a "forced loan" to raise the money necessary to continue to fight. The forced loan was essentially a tax. An individual's worth resulted in a set subsidy to the government's coffers, much like an early income tax. The forced loan was collected between October 1626 and December 1627 and was very successful. The difference was that this tax was not parliamentary in origin. The Commons and the king argued even before this period about whether taxation was a principle protected by law and therefore needed parliament. James I had not believed in this and neither did his successor.[27] The forced loan was a political disaster on par with the loss of an army, but it was a fiscal success. Charles called his third parliament, which presented him with the *Petition of Right* on June 7, 1628. The petition said, "... it is declared and enacted, that from thenceforth no person shall be compelled to make any loans to the King against his will, because such loans were against reason and the franchise of the land."[28] Charles feared rightly that the Commons was preparing another remonstrance over the issue of the revenue of tonnage and poundage traditionally granted to the king. The fear of stopping the coins coming into the royal coffers was troubling to Charles, but more troublesome were the complaints about the religious modes preferred by the head of the church. Charles was not going to give into parliament's request to review/reform religious practices as that imposed upon his royal prerogative.

The parliamentary leaders of the late 1620s disliked the king's religion. The Calvinist Members of Parliament (MPs) who were in-

---

Chapters 5 and 6 for a stirring narration of these events in the grand Whig school of history.

27 Cust, *Charles I*, 65.

28 S.R. Gardiner, *The Constitutional Documents of the Puritan Revolution, 1625-1660*, 3rd ed. (Oxford: Clarendon Press, 1906), 66. Petition of Right, June 7, 1628.

fluenced by a strict interpretation of religion from Geneva found much in the Church of England lacking. The king's forced loan seemed a step toward arbitrary government and all that it represented; to the Puritan MPs, this meant popery. Arminianism to the parliamentary leaders held three basic positions: "a doctrinal laxity that admitted the validity of certain Roman Catholic teachings, political and religious reliance on the royal prerogative, and disrespect for other avenues of English law, especially parliamentary sources."[29] The Arminian religious leaders around the king supported his actions and the support of episcopacy began to seem like popery to the extreme Puritans of the 1620s. Anti-Arminian sentiment ran high in the Commons and simmered for the decade that Charles ruled without summoning a parliament. Charles prorogued parliament, reminding the MP's "... for none of the House of Commons, joint or separate, (what new doctrine soever may be raised) have any power either to make or declare a law without my consent."[30]

Charles was a sincere and devout man, but his devotional practices differed from a vibrant and vocal sub-group within his own church. The king's religion was Arminian at best and Protestant popery at worst, according to his most vocal detractors. Charles sought to soothe religious anxieties by reissuing the articles of religion. The articles of religion were statements of doctrine and practice of the Church of England, which every cleric subscribed to formally, although not always in reality. Charles acknowledged that questions could arise about religion as authorized by law, but only a select group had the ability to judge in matters of faith. For the king, only bishops and select lower clerics sitting in a duly authorized Convocation had authority to judge in these matters, with the king's leave and permission to do so. Charles

---

29 Schwartz, "Arminianism and the English Parliament," 67.

30 Gardiner, *The Constitutional Documents*, 74. The King's Speech at the Prorogation of Parliament at the end of the Session of 1628.

reaffirmed his governorship of the church and reminded his readers and hearers "... that if any difference arise about the external policy, concerning the injunctions, canons, and other constitutions whatsoever, the Clergy in their Convocation is to order and settle them."[31] Convocations met customarily when parliaments sat under the seal and authority of the king. Charles refused to acknowledge the complaints of parliament about innovations in religion. The sub-committee on religion from the House of Commons in the parliament of 1628 looked at the state of religion to produce an argument for defense of true religion in England. One of the most dangerous threats to the Protestant Churches at home and abroad was Catholicism, "the mighty and prevalent party, by which true religion is actually opposed and the contrary maintained."[32] Popery was the great shadowy threat to Protestantism in the seventeenth century, and popish practices invited trouble home to roost.[33] The target of the committee was the new practices of the newly empowered Arminians within the Church of England.

> The subtle and pernicious spreading of the Arminian faction; whereby they have kindled such a fire of division in the very bowels of the State, as if not speedily extinguished, it is of itself sufficient to ruin our religion; by dividing us from the Reformed Churches abroad, and

---

31 Ibid., 75. The King's Declaration prefixed to the Articles of Religion, November 1628.

32 Ibid., 78. Resolutions on Religion Drawn by a Sub-Committee of the House of Commons, February 24, 1628/9.

33 For a more detailed discussion of the fear of popery in England, see Caroline Hibbard, *Charles I and the Popish Plot* (Chapel Hill: University of North Carolina Press, 1983). For more on the political climate, see Ethan Shagan, "Beyond Good and Evil: Thinking with Moderates in Early Modern England," *Journal of British Studies* 49, no. 3 (2010): 488–513 and Noah Millstone, "Evil Counsel: The Propositions to Bridle the Impertinency of Parliament and the Critique of Caroline Government in the Late 1620s," *Journal of British Studies* 50, no. 4 (2011): 813–839.

separating amongst ourselves at home, by casting doubts upon the religion professed and established; which, if faulty or questionable in three or four Articles, will be rendered suspicious to unstable minds, in all the rest, and incline them to Popery.[34]

The fear of popery was a recurrent theme throughout the seventeenth century in the British Isles. When the first petition met with little success and the Commons issued a Protestation, the king dissolved parliament and entered the period of personal rule without meeting or resolving any of the concerns of the assembled MPs. Its words about religion were more forceful: "Whosoever shall bring in innovation of religion, or by favour or countenance seem to extend or introduce Popery or Arminianism, or other opinion disagreeing from the true and orthodox Church, shall be reputed a capital enemy."[35]

Charles disregarded these religious grumblings and continued with his own preferences in religious matters. The Arminian bishops reached their height of influence and the austerity of Reformed Protestantism lost out to the more elaborate ceremonials at the center of Laud's program for the beauty of holiness, an ornamented and ritualized form of divine service that seemed to the Puritans within in the church as popery writ large. Further divisions between the king and a portion of the population became apparent with the reissuing of the "Book of Sports." In this declaration, the king argued that games and sports on Sundays were beneficial, stressing that the church saw no harm in honest recreation and fun. Sundays after divine service was an appropriate time for the populace to enjoy their day of rest from their labors. The other argument stated simply that regular games and sports kept men in shape for war whenever the occasion called.

---

34 Gardiner, 79.

35 Ibid., 82–83. Protestation of the House of Commons, March 2, 1628/9.

The declaration also called for the clergy and church wardens to be "... careful and diligent, both to instruct the ignorant, and convince and reform them that are misled in religion, presenting them that will not conform ... to our Judges and Justices ... to put the law in due execution against them."[36] Charles and his bishops acknowledged the need for proper catechism as both a means of ensuring conformity and a tool to reclaim those lost to Catholic teachings.

Charles added fuel to the fires of religious discontent by allowing and encouraging Laud's program to re-orient the altars in English churches. This decision to make communion rather than preaching the central aspect of divine service displeased portions of the English church-going population and made clear for once and all that Charles' religion was not the broad consensus achieved under his father. The re-orienting of the altars caused several churches and parishioners to seek redress at law. In London, St. Gregory's church brought a petition before the Privy Council in November 1633. St. Gregory's was under the jurisdiction of the Dean of St. Paul's by virtue of its close proximity to the cathedral church and chapter. The details of the case presented before the king and the archbishop stated that five parishioners attempted to change the position of the altar by appealing to the Court of Arches. The Arches was the highest ecclesiastical court for those living under the jurisdiction of Canterbury. They appealed to the Book of Common Prayer and the Eighty-Second Canon, arguing that the table must be in a place of convenience. They reiterated the canon's instructions that "the Minister may be more conveniently heard of the Communicants in his Prayer and Administration, and the Communicants also more conveniently, and in more number may communicate with the said Minister."[37] The

---

36 Gardiner, 101. *The Declaration of Sports,* October 18, 1633.

37 Charles II, *Constitutions and Canons Ecclesiastical* (London: John Norton for Joyce Norton and Richard Whitaker, 1633), not paginated. Canon LXXXII.

table's replacement at the upper end of the chancel instead of the middle of the church was due to an order of the then Dean of St. Paul's, Thomas Winniffe, translated to Lincoln in 1642, and two ordinaries of St. Gregory's, then serving as prebends of the cathedral. The Dean and ordinaries argued that nothing new or innovative occurred, but rather a return to the practices of antiquity. The changes proposed by Laud's program were couched in arguments that insisted on a return to ancient forms, not innovations. Charles declared "his dislike of all innovation in religion ... especially in matters concerning ecclesiastical order and government."[38] The petitioning parishioners left without having their goal granted. The king and council supported the actions of the ordinaries in placing the altar where it now "standeth in the said cathedral and mother church (as also in all other cathedrals and His Majesty's own chapel), and is constant to the practice of antiquity."[39]

Winniffe, like others of his generation, stood boldly against the hostilities of others while the king was alive. Winniffe and his brethren, however, retired and left the leadership of the church to others when it was in great danger. This inaction earned them the contempt of younger men like Sheldon and a network of lesser clerics, who worked ceaselessly to preserve a remnant of the church against great adversity when its natural leaders failed. The majority of these younger leaders held positions at either Oxford or Cambridge during the 1620s and 1630s. As a rule, the collegiate chapels, with a few exceptions, followed the proscribed reordering more quickly than their non-collegiate counterparts did. Even Sheldon, who quarreled with Laud on more than one occasion, used his position as warden to enforce uniformity in his college. Under Sheldon's guidance, All Souls participated in raising funds to beautify and reorient its chapel.

---

38 Gardiner, 104. *Act of the Privy Council on the Position of the Communion Table at St. Gregory's*, November 3, 1633.

39 Gardiner, 104.

However disgruntled the Puritans, the MPs and others were with the king's policies; the actions that began the ball rolling toward civil war occurred in the northern kingdom. The introduction or attempted introduction of a prayer book in Scotland met with fierce resentment and outright rebellion. The religious problems north of the border were not new. Since the reign of James VI and I, and continuing unabated under his son, the Scots disliked the anglicizing tendencies of the crown over the church and other polices. This was a source of major aggravation, one not helped by an absentee king or the Scottish Privy Council. One early and lingering religious contention came in the form of the *Five Articles of Perth,* reluctantly agreed to in 1618 and even more reluctantly ratified by the Scottish parliament in 1621. The five articles included directives for kneeling at communion, private baptism, private communion for the sick/infirm, confirmation by a bishop, and observance of Holy Days. The most contentious of these articles was kneeling for the Lord's Supper.[40] The Scots charged that the king was "badly counseled" and were quick to point to the bishops who supported an unpopular religious program as evidence. The Scots were ready to aid their lawfully ordained king in finding "good counselors" in religious matters: they wished to call a general assembly and parliament. Charles was not willing to accept a remedy from below that assaulted his authority and prerogative. An assault on kingly authority in any form was treason in Charles's mind.

The introduction of a Scottish liturgy in 1637 accomplished a long dormant dream of James VI and I, but at the cost of peace that this king found so appealing. The fiercely independent Presbyterian Church, or kirk, demanded a revocation of the prayer book and took up arms to defend their way of worship. The riots

---

40 Peter Donald, *An Uncounselled King: Charles I and the Scottish Troubles, 1637-1641* (Cambridge: Cambridge University Press, 1990), 12. See also Jacqueline Rose, "Kingship and Counsel in Early Modern England," *The Historical Journal* 54, no. 1 (2011): 47–71.

that broke out in Edinburgh at St. Giles Cathedral in the summer of 1637 were only a taste of the problems to come. The signing of the national Solemn League and Covenant in February 1638 and preparations to repel an armed invasion illustrated the divisiveness of Charles's policies. Scotland was divided over religion—whether Scotland would have an episcopal-based church or something else. The something else won out, and with the signing of the Covenant, Scotland's people signed in favor of a Presbyterian-based national church.

> We all ... do protest, that after long and due examinations of our own consciences in matters of true and false religion, we are now thoroughly resolved of the truth, by the word and the spirit of God; and therefore we believe with our hands, and constantly affirm before God and the whole world, that this is the only true Christian faith and religion ...[41]

Charles attempted throughout the late 1630s to suppress the Scottish rebellion, but was unsuccessful in the so-called Bishops Wars. The Covenanters and their supporters believed the king to be "deluded, and seduced, and made a Baby," although it was Charles who allowed "Coblers Sonnes, and the Sonnes of Meckanicks, to be privy Councellors and Bishops."[42] The king required their aid to escape from the clutches of evil advisors, especially clerical ones.

Charles's plan was simple, at least on paper. He issued a summons requiring his supporters to offer aid and military support. The troops raised by the king were ill-trained and largely undisciplined. However, both the king and the Covenanters received aid from men returning from military service on the continent.

---

41 Gardiner, 124. The Scottish National Covenant, February 27, 1638.

42 Mark Fissel, *The Bishop's Wars: Charles I's Campaigns against Scotland, 1638-1640* (Cambridge: Cambridge University Press, 1994), 7.

Charles also hampered the military movements by his own decision not to call a parliament to raise money for his military expenses. The Covenanters prepared and planned better than the king, effectively organizing the revenues of the counties and supplying the additional logistical needs of an army. The fighting was back and forth, with the best Scottish commanders appearing on the side of the Covenanters under Montrose. The Scots defeated the English for the first time since the Battle of Bannockburn in the course of the fighting. The Covenanters claimed not to be fighting against their legitimate and legal king, but against episcopacy and the impure religious influences around their king. This argument was a recurrent one in the early years of the Civil Wars. The disastrous military adventures north of the border forced Charles into an action he had long avoided, the calling of a parliament and a religious convocation alongside it.

The decisions made by Sheldon's royal master in these fateful days changed his life and experiences in ways he had yet to fathom in the spring of 1640. Sheldon, like many of his colleagues and friends, experienced upheaval in his personal and private life in the two decades that followed. The lessons Sheldon learned over the Civil War and the Interregnum remained with him until his death in 1677.

CHAPTER 3

UNIVERSITY MAN, THE 1640S

The Short Parliament sat briefly in the late spring of 1640. Parliament convened on April 13 and Charles dissolved it May 5. Among the leading members of the House of Commons who remained from the fractious parliaments of the 1620s were Sir Francis Seymour and John Pym. Seymour and Pym had very different agendas. Pym worked to ensure that parliaments defended the true religion as established by law. Seymour believed that parliaments had authority beyond merely rubber-stamping the monarch's program, especially in regards to taxation. Seymour was the more moderate of the two remaining leaders, but it was Pym who led the Commons and that fact alone was indicative of the changing political climate. The newly chosen Lord Keeper Sir John Finch opened the meeting urging the members gathered to grant a quick subsidy for the settlement of affairs in Scotland. Finch urged "that you will for awhile lay aside all other debates, and that you would passe an Act for such and so may subsedyes as you in your hearty affecions to his Majesty and to the common good shall think fitt and convenient for so great an accion."[1] The Commons was not alone in dealing with controversy. The House of Lords disputed with Laud over his belief that the bishops constituted a third estate in parliament and their presence was necessary to make the proceedings legitimate.[2]

---

1   Conrad Russell, *The Fall of the British Monarchies 1637-1642* (Oxford: Clarendon Press, 1991), 102.

2   Elizabeth Read Foster, *The House of Lords 1603-1649* (Chapel Hill: University of North Carolina Press, 1983). See section two of this book for more on the Lords and the controversies within it throughout the early seventeenth century.

Adding fuel to the fire was the presence of the barred Roger Manwaring. The Lords forbade Manwaring from ecclesiastical preferment in 1628, but during the personal rule, he advanced into the see of St. David's. Bishop Joseph Hall of Exeter defended Manwaring, protesting "that if they dealt so with the bishopps they would show themselves to be like unto the Coventanters in Scottland."[3] Laud argued for the right of the church to introduce decisions regarding religion without the counsel of the laity and place it before parliament for confirmation or refusal.

> I will not dispute it here, what power a lay assembly (and such as a Parliament is) hath to determine matters of religion, primely and originally by and of themselves, before the Church hath first agreed upon them. Then, indeed, they may confirm or refuse ... to take this power over religion into lay hands, is that which hath not been thus assumed since Christ to these unhappy days.[4]

The MPs' attempt to rework religious matters was an affront to the bishops and their historic privileges working within the parliamentary process.

In the Commons, Pym and his stepbrother Francis Rous dominated the brief discussion by working as a duo. Rous spoke on religious issues especially, playing on fears of reuniting the Church of England with Rome. Rous defended the ministers who had been deprived due to their failure to read the Book of Sports; as a Calvinist, he believed the Sabbath was holy and set apart and admired men of like conscience. Pym touched on religious matters, especially parliament's role in defending his definition of Protes-

---

3   Russell, *The Fall of the British Monarchies,* 104.

4   Paul E. More and Frank L. Cross, Ed., *Anglicanism: The Thought and Practice of the Church of England, Illustrated from the Religious Literature of the Seventeenth Century* (London: SPCK, 1935), 689. *The Answer of the Most Reverend Father in God William, Lord Archbishop of Canterbury, to the Speech of Lord Saye and Sele, Touching the Liturgy,* n.d.

tantism. Pym's Protestantism focused on the need for evidence of godliness in the church, especially among the clergy, and the Laudian church fell far short of this type of excellence in his opinion. In civil matters, Pym repeated a litany of charges against the king raising money and fines outside the parliamentary sphere. Pym argued that the only way to cure these ills of state was by calling annual parliaments. The end of April saw the Commons entering into the debate surrounding the church. Edward Hyde and Robert Harley offered differing opinions on Laud's policies surrounding the revised placement of the altar. Hyde argued, "that it is not contrary to the rubrick that the communion table stand altar wise," which caused Harley to reply "the forme of religion trenches upon religion. All our ancestors suffered for these words, *hoc est corpus meum*, and are not wee almost brought to idolatry, in bowing to that?"[5] No one was in the mood to compromise, and Charles ended parliament on May 5, determined to continue fighting the Scots on his own.

The Bishops' Wars were a conflict between Charles I and the episcopal leadership of England led by Laud and the members of the Presbyterian kirk of Scotland, both lay and clerical. The first Bishop's War lasted from March to June 1639 and the second Bishop's War lasted from June to August 1640. These brief military encounters illustrated the divisions in England and the lack of understanding that Charles and his ministers had of the northern kingdom of the British Isles. Ultimately, the Bishops' Wars were an unmitigated disaster and proved to members of the dissolved Short Parliament that something was terribly amiss around the king. It was two of Charles must trusted advisors, Laud and Thomas Wentworth, Earl of Strafford, who faced the ire of the Long Parliament once it came into being.[6]

---

5   Russell, *The Fall of the British Monarchies*, 114.

6   See Fissell, *The Bishops' Wars*, for detailed accountings of the events in Scotland at this time.

As was customary, the Convocation of the Church of England met while parliament sat. Convocations were internal bodies made up of clergymen that ensured that standard doctrines and practices were in use throughout the kingdom. Usually these two bodies met at the same time and if one dissolved, so did the other. Both parliaments and convocations used their own practices and procedures governing the experience. Both had long traditions of meeting and contributing in political and religious spheres due to the close relationship between the church and the instruments of government after the Reformation. However, the convocation that met in tandem with the Short Parliament continued to sit and debate, despite questions within its own membership about its legality. Two future bishops, John Hacket and Ralph Brownrigg, argued against continuing, unless new writs were forthcoming; these men realized that irregular actions would most certainly provoke parliamentary wrath. The environment outside the meeting was tense and it was in this atmosphere that on May 15, orders arrived from the king authorizing the continuation of Convocation. Moreover, the king stated that any member who left would lose his favor. Laud spoke to the Dean of Exeter, William Peterson, "in a very sharpe and severe manner if (he) did further mention (his) departure."[7]

The Convocation of 1640 endorsed seventeen canons. The canons touched upon popery, the Royal Supremacy, rites, jurisdiction, and clerical behavior, to name a few. Laud and others among the upper clergy were concerned with the charges of popery and/or popish affectation attributed to them. The Canons of 1640 increased the power of the church to prosecute recusants. This renewed effort to prosecute Roman Catholics indicated that churchmen, Arminian or not, were not crypto-Catholics, as their detractors claimed. However, Charles was reluctant to enforce

---

7   Julian Davies, *The Caroline Captivity of the Church* (Oxford: Clarendon Press, 1992), 255.

the laws already enacted against recusants and any type of pleading from the Convocation to enforce them would have been ignored. The most contentious canon that came out of the Convocation proceeded from the king and entered the books as canon 6. The canons of 1640 were questionable on several accounts: the convocation that issued them flirted with illegality and widened the theological divide present between a vocal and angry laity. Canon 6 included the et cetera oath, which forbade innovation in religion. Most controversial were the words "nor will I ever give my consent to alter the government of this church by archbishops, bishops, deans and archdeacons, etc, as it stands now established and as by right it ought to stand."[8] Canon 6 quickly provoked responses. Nathanael Fiennes wrote strongly, "as to the matter of this new Oath, it is wholy illegall. It is against the Law of this Land, it is against the Law and Light of Nature, it is against the Law of GOD, it is against the Lawes of this KINGDOME."[9] Canon 5 redefined sectaries and it proved to be long-lasting—absence from the established church for more than a month marked an individual as a sectary.

The men tapped to attend the controversial convocation included a long list of notables and many who would be so. Several future bishops sat in various positions in the lower house of convocation. Gilbert Sheldon served as procurator for the chapter of Gloucester. He was a canon of that cathedral. Charles I provided Sheldon with the position on January 29, 1633 and he was first installed by proxy on February 26. He took his oaths in person August 1.[10] The final men promoted by Charles I also attended Thomas Winniffe, Dean of St. Paul's, Accepted Frewen, Dean of Gloucester, Henry King, Archdean of Colchester (London),

---

8 Russell, *The Fall of the British Monarchies*, 138.

9 Nathanael Fiennes, *A Second Speech of the Honorable Nathanael Fiennes, Touching the Subjects Liberty against the Late Canons, and the New Oath* (London, 1641), 11–12.

10 *FEA*, vol. 8. Canons of Gloucester, 49–64.

and Ralph Brownrigg, Archdeacon of Coventry (Lichfield and Coventry). Restoration era bishops who sat in the lower house included John Hacket, Gilbert Ironsides, and Benjamin Lany. These men occupied the sees of Lichfield and Coventry, Bristol, and Ely while working with Sheldon first as Bishop of London and later as primate in Canterbury. Other notables attending were theologian Henry Hammond, Dean Samuel Fell of Christ Church, future Dean of Canterbury Thomas Turner, religious controversialist William Chillingworth, and historian Peter Heylyn.[11]

Sheldon's activities during the Convocation were not notable; he only stayed for one session. While sympathetic to the king's views, he may have been dubious about the legality of its continued sitting after the dismissal of the Short Parliament. While at the Convocation, Sheldon met men like John Hacket, who worked closely with Sheldon to enforce conformity in his future diocese. In fact, the later correspondence between Hacket and Sheldon was extremely friendly, even gossipy, with Hacket's reports of his family and children. Hammond and Sheldon's association during the 1650s was vital to the survival of the underground church during the Interregnum and it was possible that the Convocation meeting drew these two men closer together. One might argue that the beginnings of Sheldon's vision of the codependence of church and monarchy began here, despite his unease with the procedural abnormalities. Sheldon was at this point more than likely unaware as to the heights he would eventually attain in the church or the difficulties he would face in the next twenty years.

The fighting continued in the north and disaster after military disaster forced Charles once again to call parliament. The Long Parliament, named thus because it sat in some form or another for over a decade, convened in London with many members still smarting at their dismissal earlier in the year. In November 1640,

---

11 Davies, *The Caroline Captivity of the Church*, Appendix, 319–326.

both houses reconvened at Westminster and were quick to make their displeasure known about matters ecclesiastical and civil. The Canons of 1640 were unpopular and the Commons wasted no time in offering up an opinion about religious matters aided and abetted by Londoners. The inhabitants took great pains to present the higher clergy as subversive to the kingdom by accusing them of holding to *jure divino* authority as opposed to secular authority. They beseeched the Commons to abolish episcopal government of the church. "That the said government with all its dependencies, roots and branches, may be abolished, and all laws in their behalf made void, and the government according to God's word may be rightly placed amongst us."[12] The petition listed twenty-eight disagreeable procedures and practices used by the clerical establishment. A sampling of the complaints included the publication of Arminian and popish books and tracts and the growing numbers of Roman Catholics in and around London. It also harshly condemned the Canons of 1640 and Laudian policies related to divine service in England. The petition concluded with the dire warning that the conflict between Scotland and the king would continue and "also increase to an utter ruin of all, unless the prelates with their dependences be removed out of England."[13]

The Long Parliament began with the premise of working toward a consensus with the king. The Lords wanted to settle with Charles and were more prepared to compromise. The Lords wanted a compromise and devised one that required a ministerial scapegoat. They selected the king's friend and advisor, Thomas Wentworth, Earl of Strafford. Theologically, the peers in the Lords were moderate Episcopalians with varying degrees of loyalty to Calvinist positions. The Bishops seated in the Lords also varied from moderate Calvinists, like Bishop Thomas Morton of Durham, to the soon imprisoned Matthew Wren of Ely, a Lau-

---

12 Gardiner, 138. The Root and Branch Petition, December 11, 1640.

13 Gardiner, 144.

dian protégé. The bishops as a group condemned ship money and upheld the privileges of their order. Bishops had sat in parliament since before the Reformation and they guarded this privilege against all who dared question the right of spiritual leaders to weld temporal power. The Commons was not going to cooperate with the king just for a return to the non-parliamentary world of the 1630s. The Commons also shared the Lords' desire to punish the guilty and/or misguided ministers around the king and insert their own (proper) choices around him. The Commons moreover wanted a reformation of religious life in England, which brought it into conflict with the bishops and some of the peers sitting in the House of Lords. Just over a month after sitting, the Commons launched an attack on the Laudian program, directed in large part by Francis Rous and John Pym. Charles wanted to protect Strafford and jealously guarded his royal supremacy in religious matters.

The relationship between the king and parliament deteriorated steadily over the first weeks and months of the Long Parliament's existence, ultimately leading to the withdrawal of the king from his capital and civil war. The parliament passed acts abolishing the Court of Star Chamber and the Court of High Commission. These two acts stripped clerical officials of their traditional role in English temporal affairs, especially in regards to punishment for religious offenses. Religious matters occupied much of the early business of the parliament. The Commons passed a resolution ordering "that the churchwardens of every parish church and chapel ... do forthwith remove the communion table from the east end ... into some other convenient place; and that they take away the rails ... as heretofore they were before the later innovations." [14] Laud and his associate's program promoting the beauty of holiness died with a few strokes of the pen in the Commons.

---

14 Ibid., 197–198. Resolutions of the House of Commons on Ecclesiastical Innovations, September 1, 1641.

The most ardent promoters of these Laudian polices became targets for the parliament's wrath, especially since the archbishop was imprisoned at the passing of this resolution. For example, Bishop Matthew Wren of Ely was an ardent supporter of the king as clerk of the closet and suffered imprisonment for his close association with Laud.

The interim between the renewal of the king's campaign in Scotland and the beginning of the Civil War saw the king and parliament remaining in the same location for only about six weeks from November 25, 1641 to January 10, 1642.[15] This short time was insufficient to allow either side to bridge the vast difference between the king and parliament. A sign that the parliament and the king were at an impasse came in the form of a written account of the ills of the kingdom as perceived by the assembled MPs. The Grand Remonstrance presented on December 1, 1641 argued, "the root of all this mischief we find to be a malignant and pernicious design of subverting the fundamental laws and principles of government, upon which the religion and justice of this kingdom are firmly established."[16] The main perpetrators of the subversion of the laws were Roman Catholics, bishops, corrupt clergy, and councilors and courtiers around the king. According to the Commons, these elements worked to cause discontent between the king and country regarding the use of the prerogative, suppressed the purity of religion, and slandered parliaments to the king. The MPs saw a vast conspiracy:

> To cherish the Arminian part in those points wherein they agree with the Papists, to multiply and enlarge the difference between the common Protestants and those whom they call Puritans, to introduce and countenance such opinions and ceremonies as are fittest for accommodation with Popery, to increase and maintain igno-

---

15 Russell, *The Fall of the British Monarchies,* 400.

16 Gardiner, 206. The Grand Remonstrance, December 1, 1641.

rance, looseness and profaneness in the people; that of those three parties, Papists, Arminians and Libertines, they might compose a body fit to act such counsels and resolutions as were most conducible to their own ends.[17]

Charles took time to respond to the demands of his most recently called parliament. He received the remonstrance almost immediately upon his return to London from Scotland and took nearly three weeks to reply. He offered first a proclamation on religion charging and commanding "that Divine Service be performed in this his kingdom of England and dominion of Wales, as is appointed by the laws and statutes established in this realm."[18] The king's response to the petition and remonstrance expressed his bafflement and incomprehension of the accusations of the MPs. "We say that there are divers things in the preamble of it which we are so far from admitting that we profess we cannot at all understand them."[19] He disagreed with the accusations that the men in places of civil and spiritual authority were corrupt or of undesirable character. Pertaining to religion, Charles offered:

> ... we are persuaded in our consciences that no Church can be found upon the earth that professeth the true religion with more purity of doctrine than the Church of England doth, nor where the government and discipline are jointly more beautified and free from superstition, that as they are here established by law, which ... we will with constancy maintain ... not only against all invasions of Popery, but also from the irreverence of those many schismatics and separatists ...[20]

---

17 Ibid., 207.

18 Ibid., 232–233. The King's Proclamation on Religion, December 10, 1641.

19 Gardiner, 234. The King's Answer to the Petition Accompanying the Grand Remonstrance, December 23, 1641.

20 Gardiner, 235.

The die was cast for a bitter conflict between the king, who refused to limit his belief in his inherent powers, and a parliament, which wanted to advise and to check royal powers—especially in matters religious and financial.

The MPs and the king were at odds and the proverbial straw that broke the camel's back came early in 1642. The king ordered the arrest of five members of the Commons: John Pym, John Hampden, Sir Arthur Haselrig, Denzil Holles, and William Strode. These men "have traitorously endeavoured to subvert the fundamental laws and government of the kingdom of England, to deprive the king of his regal power."[21] In the mind of the king and other conservatives, these men were the leaders of the radical and reform-minded MPs. Instead of impeaching the members, however, the Lords questioned the legality of the king's procedure. It all ended badly, with the king withdrawing to Hampton Court and leaving parliament in Westminster under the protection of an armed band outside of royal control. The pieces were moving into place and the Civil War began in earnest late in the summer of the same year, with the king raising his standard near Nottingham. Ultimately, the king removed to Oxford and used the university facilities as his own. Christ Church became the residence of the king and his closest inner circle.[22]

In the run-up to the outbreak of the Civil War, Sheldon and many of those who would be very involved in later years were expe-

---

21 Ibid., 236. The Impeachment of One Member of the House of Lords, and of Five Members of the House of Commons, January 3, 1642.

22 For details on the Civil Wars, see Ian Gentles, *The English Revolution* (Harlow: Pearson Longman, 2007). Allan Macinnes, *The British Revolution* (Houndmills: Palgrave, 2005). Conrad Russell, *The Causes of the English Civil War* (Oxford: Clarendon Press, 1990). John Kenyon, *The Civil Wars of England* (London: Phoenix Giant, 1996). Trevor Royle, *The British Civil War* (New York: Palgrave, 2004). S.R. Gardiner, *History of the Great Civil War* (London: Longman's, Green and Co, 1905). Ann Hughes, *The Causes of the English Civil War* (Houndmills: Palgrave, 1998).

riencing the great calm before the storm. Neither Oxford nor Cambridge had yet experienced the wrath that parliament would later unleash upon the universities. Sheldon and Hammond were among the royal chaplains present in Oxford to offer counsel to the king, and as things went south, the Oxford dons were favorites of the beleaguered king. Clarendon discussed access to the king after he went into the army's custody:

> All restraint was taken off from Persons resorting to him, and he saw every day the Faces of many who were grateful to him; and he no sooner desired that some of his Chaplains might have leave to attend upon him for his Devotion, but it was yielded to, and they who were named by him (who were Dr Sheldon, Dr Morley, Dr Sanderson, and Dr Hammond) were presently sent, and gave their attendance, and perform'd their Function at the ordinary hours, in their accustom'd Formalities ...[23]

Sheldon, Morley, Hammond, and Sanderson all played a role in keeping a remnant of the Church of England in existence after it was formally dissolved.

The outbreak of fighting caused a reduction in the number of MPs leaving parliament, with a vocal faction calling for reformation in matters religious. The newly proposed mode of English religious practices bowed to pressure from the Scottish allies that parliament made in order to fight the forces of Charles I. The new alliance required adherence to the Solemn League and Covenant, which drew largely from the Scottish National Covenant. The Presbyterians in Scotland and the Puritans in England hoped and worked for a new church settlement. The Covenant stated boldly, "that we shall in like manner, without respect of persons, endeavour the extirpation of Popery, prelacy (that is Church

---

23 Clarendon, *History*, vol. 3, 50. This incident refers to the king's time with the army in Newmarket 1647.

Government by Archbishops, Bishops ... and all other officers dependent upon hierarchy)."[24]

The difficulties of fielding armies in two kingdoms and without any great success on either side made peace negotiations a welcome development. Problems emerged immediately in the discussion of terms. Parliament had a lengthy list of terms: to nullify all declarations made against either house of parliament/ convention in England and Scotland, to have the king swear to the Covenant, to abolish episcopacy, to confirm the Westminster Assembly in place of episcopacy, to thoroughly reform religion in accordance with the direction of the assembly, and to regulate Cambridge, Oxford, and so on.[25] The Westminster Assembly authorized the restructuring of the Church of England along a Presbyterian model, finally completing the final reformation long desired by Puritans. The Westminster Assembly, however, never spoke for the majority within England. John Thurloe, the secretary for the parliamentary members, wrote a proposal for peace. He suggested, "Religion is to be by the power of vote in the several states to be determined, so far as it becomes statute law" and "Liberty, and the fortress thereof the militia, falls under the same notion; which settlement therefore is to be as firm as particular, positive, stated, or fundamental law can make, and beyond this line none to move, upon any occasion, at the utmost perill."[26] Voting for religious and military settlements limited the prerogative of the king and Thurloe's suggestions were not heeded. The recommendations to the king also included a long list of those

---

24 Gardiner, 268. The Solemn League and Covenant, September 25, 1643.

25 Gardiner, 275–277. The Propositions of the Houses Presented to the King at Oxford, and Subsequently Discussed at the Treaty of Uxbridge, November 24, 1644.

26 Thomas Birch, Ed., *A Collection of the State Papers of John Thurloe*, vol. 1, *1638-1653* (London, 1742), 607. Thurloe became secretary to Cromwell's council of state and postmaster, which aided him in his job at intercepting royalist plots during the Interregnum.

ineligible for pardon. A brief sampling illustrated the MPs' distrust of those closest to the king. William Laud, Matthew Wren, and his nephews, Princes Rupert and Maurice, were all on the list of *personae non grata*. Charles's proposals were simple. He wished for the return of his revenue and other possessions taken by force or prevented from his use by force. Additionally, all laws and actions derogatory to the king and the established system of laws needed to be overturned and recalled to prevent such rebellions in the future. He also demanded that all subjects arrested without due process of law and in violation of Habeas Corpus would be released from imprisonment. Those persons named outside the general pardon all deserved a trial to acquit or condemn them. Charles tiptoed around the religious issues, offering a token to the Presbyterians, protecting the Common Prayer, and restating his desire to suppress popery.[27] Sheldon was one of a number of loyal and trusted royal servants sent to Uxbridge to negotiate a settlement in the early months of 1645. The gaps between the positions were too broad to settle without great compromise on either side. Neither the king nor the Presbyterian-influenced parliament wanted to give ground, so the meetings at Uxbridge were over before they actually began. Sheldon returned to the king and continued to work for his monarch.[28]

Laud's execution on January 10, 1645 (during the abortive meetings at Uxbridge) illustrated just how deeply religious tensions were running in Charles' three kingdoms. The further reformation of religion greatly interested the godly in England and their Scottish allies to the north. Parliament called an assembly of divines to further reform the English church and finish in some minds what had been halted since the Hampton Court Conference of 1604. The Westminster Assembly of Divines had the un-

---

27 Gardiner, 286–287. The King's Propositions to be Discussed at Uxbridge, January 21, 1645.

28 Interestingly, little secondary literature covers this abortive meeting in 1645. S.R. Gardiner, *History of the Great Civil War*, vol. 2, Chapter 25.

enviable task of trying to make everyone happy and inevitably, very few were actually satisfied. The problem was that multiple ideas emerged as to what proper worship looked like. The most well-defined and ultimate winner in the legislation were the English Puritans, whose Calvinism lent itself well to a Presbyterian system of church government similar to that of the Scottish Kirk. The breakdown in the traditional religious framework allowed a number of groups to surface or resurface and campaign for religious toleration or full religious freedom. These groups became a problem for the MPs and the new model of worship was exclusionary from its inception, completely breaking with the broad path of English Protestantism since the time of Elizabeth I.

The Church of England was a surprisingly late victim in the conflict of the Civil Wars. The bishops left the Lords, forced to by the passage of the Bishop's Exclusion Act.

> Whereas bishops and other persons in holy orders ought not be entangled with secular jurisdiction, the office of the ministry being of such great importance that their intermeddling with secular jurisdictions hath occasioned great mischiefs and scandal both to Church and state.[29]

The majority of bishops in England retired and lived as quietly as possible years before the office was abolished in 1646. This left the church's defense to clerics associated with the universities and those who chose to live in exile. They were supported by devout members of the laity who chose the Church of England over other emerging options. It was not surprising that the post-1646 leadership fell to university men who were more than capable of picking up the slack. Sheldon, Hammond, and Morley all fell into this category and reached new prominence by refusing to turn away from the liturgical tradition of their faith.

---

29 J.P. Kenyon, Ed., *The Stuart Constitution 1603-1688* (Cambridge: Cambridge University Press, 1986), 237. The Bishops' Exclusion Act, 1641/42.

The Westminster Assembly was to settle the question of religion in England. There was little question as to the type of settlement sought, as the wording used the traditional calls of the Puritan party. Regarding the liturgy, government and practices of the Church of England, "that as yet many things remain ... which do require a further and more perfect reformation than as yet has been attained."[30] The call for the assembly claimed, "government by archbishops, bishops, their chancellors, commissaries, deans, deans and chapters, and other ecclesiastical officers dependent upon the hierarchy is evil, and justly offensive and burdensome to the kingdom."[31] Members of Sheldon's circle, such as theologian Henry Hammond, refused to participate in the remaking of the church. Sheldon, Hammond, and Sanderson all later wrestled with the question of how to modify the prayer book for covert use and whether they actually had the authority to do so. Moderate Calvinists, in the mode of clerics preferred by James I, also stayed away because of their support of episcopacy. The prayer book was the first official casualty, becoming illegal with the establishment of the Westminster Directory of Public Worship in January 1645.

> The Lords and Commons assembled in Parliament, taking into serious consideration the manifold inconveniences that have arisen by the Book of Common-Prayer in this Kingdome, and resolving, according to their Covenant, to reform Religion according to the Word of God, and the Example of the best Reformed Churches, have consulted with the Reverend, Pious, and Learned Divines called together to that purpose; And do judge it necessary, that the said Book of Common Prayer be abolished, and the Directory for the Publique Worship

---

30 Kenyon, *The Stuart Constitution 1603-1688*, 237. The Westminster Assembly, June 12, 1643.

31 Ibid., 238.

of God, herein after mentioned, be established and observed in all the Churches within this Kingdome.[32]

Parliament quickly worked to execute the law and punish those
who remained loyal adherents to the prayer book and liturgy. The
pressing need for more funds to continue fielding the victorious
parliamentary army caused parliament to look to the example of
Henry VIII and to use the resources of the church to finance the
needs of the state.

> For the abolishing of Archbishops and Bishops, and pro-
> viding for the payment of the just and necessary debts
> of the Kingdom, into which the same hath been drawn
> by a War, mainly promoted by and in favour of the said
> Archbishops, and Bishops, and other their Adherents,
> and Dependents; Be it Ordained, and it is Ordained by
> the Lords and Commons in Parliament assembled, and
> by the authority of the same; That the Name, Title, Stile,
> and Dignity of Archbishop of Canterbury, Archbishop
> of York, Bishop of Winchester, Bishop of Duresme, and
> of all other Bishops of any Bishopricks within the King-
> dom of England, and Dominion of Wales, be from and
> after the fifth day of September in the year of our Lord
> God, 1646, wholly abolished and taken away.[33]

---

32 "January 1645: An Ordinance for taking away the Book of Common Prayer,
and for establishing and putting in execution of the Directory for the publique worship of God," in *Acts and Ordinances of the Interregnum, 1642-1660,*
ed. C.H. Firth and R.S. Rait (London: His Majesty's Stationery Office,
1911), 582–607. *British History Online,* accessed September 5, 2018, http://
www.british-history.ac.uk/no-series/acts-ordinances-interregnum/pp582-
607.

33 "October 1646: An Ordinance for the Abolishing of Archbishops and
Bishops within the Kingdom of England, and Dominion of Wales, and for
Setling of their Lands and Possessions upon Trustees, for the Use of the
Commonwealth," in *Acts and Ordinances of the Interregnum, 1642-1660,* ed.
C.H. Firth and R.S. Rait (London: His Majesty's Stationery Office, 1911),
879–883. *British History Online,* accessed September 5, 2018, http://www.

The dismissal of episcopacy as a legitimate form of church government affected not only the great cathedrals of England, but also the deaneries, chapter houses, and collegiate chapels. Selling ecclesiastical properties and renegotiating rental agreements with tenants caused long-term problems that, after the Restoration, often took decades to resolve.

The disestablishment of the church was one slight that Charles would not accept. Characteristically, in the face of parliamentary demands, he refused to remove his support from the liturgy and episcopacy. During this volatile decade, Charles's support for his church was his most consistent position. "And because religion is the best and chiefest foundation of peace, His Majesty will begin with that particular. That for abolishing Archbishops, Bishops, &c. His Majesty clearly professeth that he cannot give his consent thereunto, both in relation as he is a Christian and a King."[34] Charles tied the power of the king to the power of the church, illustrating the fears of parliament regarding the influence of corrupt churchmen on the king—but also demonstrating the old proverb, "No bishop, No king." Charles granted one concession in religious matters. He would have accepted Presbyterian church government for a period of three years, if those who wished to leave Presbyterian congregations would be granted the freedom to do so, implying the return of episcopally governed churches. Charles knew the Presbyterian factions in parliament would not grant de facto toleration to any of the opposing religious movements present in England from the mid-1640s onward. The issue of toleration was complicated, causing no end of debate. The Presbyterians wanted power and to suppress all those who opposed their vision of worship. The army became a potent breeding ground for other religious

---

british-history.ac.uk/no-series/acts-ordinances-interregnum/pp879-883.

34 Gardiner, 328. Letter of Charles I to the Speaker of the House of Lords, September 17, 1647.

groups and the failure of military commanders to enforce adherence to the Westminster Directory created an environment for religious experimentation. Ultimately, England never again experienced monolithic religious observance; dissent from the preferred mode of worship continued, as did suspicion of those outside the established directions for worship.

Sheldon became clerk of the closet to Charles I sometime in early 1646, a further sign of the regard the king held for his chaplain. The clerk of the closet served the king as a religious and personal advisor. He replaced the imprisoned Matthew Wren. In this position, Sheldon served the king and spoke on behalf of the church. Sheldon spearheaded a campaign to solicit religious opinions as to what was permissible to concede to the enemy to make a settlement. Matthew Wren wrote to his successor from the Tower:

> But I pass not for that; As it is shewes you my opinion (whereof take, I beseech you, what you can approve of, & let the rest be refuses) my readiness also both to give you an Answer, & to venture my poor talent in any occasion for the King, or the Church. God preserve them both in his own best time, I am rich in leisure of begging that continually.[35]

Sheldon became a skilled agent in soliciting opinions from leading minds and sending on the orthodox and weeding out the less orthodox opinions presented to him. One question put forth by Sheldon to other clerics was whether the king had a duty to punish those who in their conscience denied the Trinity, but gave no trouble to the authorities or tried to bring others to that way of thinking. Wren replied:

> I clearly conceive that the two conditions annexed, do answer the Question Negatively. For they truly observ-

---

35 MS Tanner 145, f. 4. Matthew Wren to Gilbert Sheldon, August 14, 1647, sent to Hampton Court.

ing the conditions, are to his Majestie, as yf they held
no such opinion. Many others (for ought his Majestie
knows) may be of the same mind, and I doe not conceive
his Majestie obliges to enquire into their thoughts, much
less to punish them yf they do transgress the conditions,
they render themselves liable to the punishment of that
transgression, rather then of their opinion, though they
render him free from his engagement.[36]

Actions, not thoughts, became key in the theological debates
over the following decades, highlighted by the emerging definition of nonconformity. Wren's rather moderate answer to one of
the fundamental tenants of Christian thought offered a model for
Sheldon's own developing ideas about discipline and doctrinal
questions. What a person privately held was not cause for discipline as long as the matter was private. If and when a person
began spouting heterodox or outright heretical ideas, it was time
for intervention, with the full power of both the church and state.

Both Cambridge and Oxford underwent a cleansing for their
loyalty to the king and the church. The universities of the seventeenth century existed for the making of clerics in some degree or
another and the men of these institutions were loyal. Their hopes
and livelihoods needed a church, and the king was the best defender and protector the church possessed. Oxford was divided:
the town supported the parliament and the gown supported, supplied, and lodged the king and his retinue. Charles took lodgings
at Christ Church and Henrietta Maria across the field at Merton.
Lodging within the university depended upon the individual's
own matriculation record and personal connections. Colonel
Richard Spencer returned to Corpus Christi for at least part of
the time; he had matriculated there over thirty years earlier. Sir
Edward Hyde owed his lodging in All Souls to his friendship

---

36 MS Tanner 145, f. 8. Undated, but with a series of correspondence dated
August-September 1647.

with the warden, Sheldon.[37] The colleges were male-oriented and scrambled to make accommodations for courtiers and their families. Ralph Kettel, the elderly and eccentric president of Trinity (Sheldon's first academic home), disliked the teasing manner of the women lodging with him. He infamously retorted to one, "Your husband and father I bred up here, and I knew your grandfather; I know you to be a gentlewoman. I will not say you are a whore, but gett you gonne for a very woman."[38]

Parliament knew it needed to control the information and the supplies coming out of the university towns as prime supporters of the king and the church. "The Civil Wars breaking out, the Effects of them were first felt by the Bishops, and afterwards by the Universities: *Cambridge* suffer'd first, lying in the associated Counties, and subject to the Parliaments Power; *Oxford*, which was then a Garrison, and the King['s] Head-quarters, drank the same bitter Cup some years after."[39] Once the city and university returned to parliament's hands, a reformation of the colleges and its environs began.

> That the said Visitors or any five of them, may enquire by Oath *viva voce*, to be taken before them respectively, of and concerning all the Masters, Schollers, Fellows, and Officers of the respective foundations of all and every the said Halls and Colledges, and of all and every the Officers belonging to them, or to the said University, concerning those that neglect to take the Solemn League and Covenant, and the Negative Oath, being tendred to them by such as are authorized thereunto by Parliament; And

---

37 Nicolas Tyacke, Ed., *The History of the University of Oxford*, vol. 4, *Seventeenth Century Oxford* (Oxford: Clarendon Press, 1997), 702. See Chapter 14 for more info on Oxford and the civil wars. See also Brocklisss, *The University of Oxford*, especially Part II for discussion of this era.

38 Tyacke, *The History of Oxford*, 706.

39 Pope, *The Life of the Right Reverend Father*, 12.

likewise concerning those that oppose the execution of the Ordinances of Parliament concerning the Discipline and Directory, or shall not promote and cause the same to be put in execution, according to their several places and callings.[40]

Sheldon was one of the men selected as a delegate to argue for the traditional privileges of the university and to defend it from the parliamentary visitors. These men created a set of rules for dealing with an unpopular and illegal visitation of the diverse colleges. They decided that no one would appear unless summoned by five different individuals, no one would appear on a holy day, and that upon appearing, the individual would ask by what authority they were summoned and request to see it written, request time to pen a written response, and refuse the oath *ex officio*.[41] The oaths applied to every man over the age of twenty-one, exempting most of the undergraduates, but fell upon all the fellows, professors, wardens, and so forth, and of course the entire cathedral contingent at Christ Church. Additionally, many of the collegiate chapels subscribed in some way to the Laudian programs of the beauty of holiness, including the chapel at All Souls. One of the main driving forces of the visitation was to make the university as a whole subscribe to the Directory and the Presbyterian rule of church government. The men of the university impacted by this ordinance were Church of England men by virtue of their academic lifestyle and most of their private religious feelings. A number of royal chaplains both ordinary and extraordinary had permanent homes at the congenial colleges

---

40 "May 1647: An Ordinance for the Visitation and Reformation of the University of Oxford and the Several Colledges and Halls Therein," in *Acts and Ordinances of the Interregnum, 1642-1660*, ed. C.H. Firth and R.S. Rait (London: His Majesty's Stationery Office, 1911), 925–927. *British History Online*, accessed September 5, 2018, http://www.british-history.ac.uk/no-series/acts-ordinances-interregnum/pp925-927.

41 A. à Wood, 7.

they matriculated from or in which they had secured fellowships. These men were not soldiers, but scholars, and fought with the pen, not the sword.

> We the Masters, Schollars, and other Officers and Members of the said University, not to judge the Consciences of others, but to clear our selves before God and the world from all suspicion of Obstinancie, whilst we discharge our own, present to consideration the true reasons of our present judgment concerning the said *Covenant, Oath,* and *Ordinances:* Expecting so much *Justice,* and hoping for so much *Charity,* as either not to be pressed to conforme to what is required ... further then our present judgments will warrant us; or not condemned for refusing so to do, without cleare and reall satisfaction given to our just scruples.[42]

The convocation of the university placed a well-argued defense of their inabilities to submit to the visitors working article by article through the Covenant, the Negative Oath, and the Directory of Public Worship. They questioned the very birthplace of the covenant, wondering how they should profess to protect the Presbyterian church of Scotland. They opposed adamantly the reworking of ancient modes of church government (episcopacy) and inserting something new in its place. The men of Oxford equated new modes of worship with an increase of popery, schism, and superstition. They also spoke in favor of the lower level episcopal appointments (deaneries and chapter houses), as many of them held positions in one of the cathedrals of the country. Most importantly—and possibly most damning in the eyes of the visitors—the convocation remained loyal to the king. "It is cleare to our understandings, that we cannot without

---

42 Robert Sanderson, *Reasons of the Present Judgement of the University of Oxford* (Oxford, 1647), 1.

disloyalty and injury to Him, and double Perjury to our selves, take upon us without his consent to make any alteration in the Ecclesiastical Lawes or Government, much less to endeavour the extirpation thereof."[43] The visitors worked hard to remove those unwilling to bow to the new authority. The Dean of Christ Church and vice-chancellor of the University, Samuel Fell, had his family forcibly removed from their lodgings in the deanery. This happened while Fell was pleading before the MPs in London about the university's historic rights and privileges and making the case about the illegality of imposing visitors. Fell's family received aid from Hammond and Sheldon, as many did in the coming years. Hammond had lost his position as a prebend of Christ Church due to the stripping of the episcopacy, which was not enforced until the Visitation. Sheldon was also a target for removal for his support of the king and the church. Sheldon's ejection from All Souls had all the elements of a farce.

> At length they sent for Dr. Sheldon the Warden (then walking in his garden), who appearing before them, did with great moderation of mind ask them "by what authority they summoned him?" Upon which the authority was shewn and read. Dr. Sheldon told him that it concerned not him at all, for it was dated March the 8th ... and that he was not so much as then questioned nor voted out of his place till March 30.[44]

Sheldon followed the directions of the university convocation and disputed the wording of the Visitor's Commission and the legality of their actions. Sheldon's replacement, Dr. John Palmer, was waiting in the wings for his new residence and occupation. Sheldon refused to give over his keys and the buttery books in his possession. The visitors broke into the warden's lodgings, took the keys and

43 Sanderson, *Reasons of the Present Judgement*, 12.

44 A. à Wood, 27. April 12, 1648.

installed Dr. Palmer in Sheldon's place.[45] An argument could be made that Palmer's best achievement was simply that he was the warden when Christopher Wren became a fellow in 1653.[46] The visitors were unhappy with his actions "and for Dr. Sheldon's contempt (as they worded it) forthwith commit him to prison with a guard of musqueteers, followed by a great company of Scholars, and blest by the people as he passed the streets."[47] Sheldon and Hammond were imprisoned together and were quite popular with well-wishers. It remains unclear how long Sheldon spent in prison, but various sources put him in Ickford or under house arrest in Oxford.[48] This was despite parliamentary acts to limit the influence of men dangerous or perceived so by the visitors:

> Whereas divers Doctors and others, in the University of Oxford, do still continue their Contempt to the Authority of Parliament, in acting contrary to the Votes and Commands of Parliament, notwithstanding they are some of them convicted, and cast out of their Places upon Conviction; besides, their Continuance in the University may be of Dangerous Consequence, for moving of Sedition and Tumults: Be it Ordained, by the Lords and Commons assembled in Parliament, That the Committee of Lords and Commons for regulating the University of Oxford shall have Power to send for in Custody, and to imprison any such Persons as shall be found to be

---

45 Palmer's tenure as warden was rather unremarkable, and the men promoted by him were seen as unremarkable academically. Between 1648-1652, forty-three men were put into the college, including thirteen from Cambridge. During the Restoration, all but one of these men was removed from the college. www.all-souls.ox.ac.uk/content/The_seventeenth_century.

46 Kerry Downes, "Sir Christopher Wren," *ODNB*, 2.

47 A. à Wood, 28.

48 Spurr, "Gilbert Sheldon," 3. Sheldon was ejected from Ickford in November 1646. If he was under house arrest, he had a five-mile prohibition from the university and the king.

under Contempt of the Authority of Parliament, and to
act contrary thereunto.[49]

Sheldon's imprisonment must have not been too severe, because
by June 30, 1648, he appeared in the entry book for readers at the
Bodleian Library. He used the library again in August, September, and October, and then not again until January 1649, as he
seemed to have left Oxford for the duration of the Interregnum.[50]
Sheldon's library record recorded him reading traditional works
of Christian piety in Latin, Greek, and French. A brief survey of
his reading from January 14, 1648 includes Samuel Page's *The
Allegeance of the Clergie* (1616), *The Office of Christian Parents*
(1616), William Jones's *The Mysteries of Christes Nativitie,* and
Richard Crankanthorp's *Iustinian the Emperor Defender.*[51]

During this period, Sheldon also played a part in the king's ongoing struggles with parliament over religion. The king was a prisoner of either parliament or the army during these months, and
the years of imprisonment threatened to break the king's spirit,
especially in religious matters.

His Majesty bore this constraint so heavily that he writ a Letter
to the House of Peers, in which he inclosed a List of the Names
of thirteen of his Chaplains; any two of which he desir'd might

---

49 "May 1648: Ordinance to Enable the Committee for Oxford University
to Send for Delinquents," in *Acts and Ordinances of the Interregnum, 1642-
1660,* ed. C.H. Firth and R.S. Rait (London: His Majesty's Stationery Office,
1911), 1143. *British History Online,* accessed September 5, 2018, http://
www.british-history.ac.uk/no-series/acts-ordinances-interregnum/p1143.

50 Bodleian library records e. 544. I am grateful to Dr. Mary Clapinson, St.
Hugh's, Oxford for sharing this information with me.

51 Shelf marks referenced against the old library database at the Bodleian. Perhaps Sheldon was reading *The Office of Christian Parents* as preparation for his
role as guardian to the children of Lucius Cary, 2nd Viscount Falkland, who
died in 1643. Personally, I find the most interesting to be *Le combat spirituel
de la patience chrestienne avec tous ses enemis tant visible qu'invisible,* published
in Geneva in 1595. Perhaps it was encouraging to Sheldon, as his world was
full of enemies.

have liberty to attend him for his Devotion. To which, after many days consideration, they return'd this Answer; "that all of those Chaplains were disaffected to the Establish'd Government of the Church, and had not taken the Covenant; but that there were others who had, who if his Majesty pleas'd, should be sent to him."[52]

Surprisingly, the army, home of many religious opinions, allowed the monarch the comfort of having friends attend to his religious needs. The military leaders allowed Charles the small comfort his chaplains. "Yesterday Doctor Sheldon and Doctor Hammond (two of his Majesties Chaplaines) went from hence toward Saint Albans, upon a command sent them to come and attend their Master: a favour which he had longed begged of the two Houses, and hath now (it seemes) obtained it of the Army."[53] Sheldon was with the king at Hatfield and Newmarket in 1647 and served his master by soliciting and compiling opinions on religious toleration to make a treaty possible. William Juxon (Bishop of London) and Brian Duppa (Bishop of Salisbury) wrote:

> ... we cannot conceive in this your majesty's condescension any violation of that oath, whereof your majesty is so justly tender, but that your majesty doth thereby still continue to preserve and protect the church by the best ways and means you have left to you, (which is all the oath can be supposed to require;) and that the permission intended, (whereby, in some men's apprehension, your majesty may seem to throw down what you desire to build up,) is not only by your majesty allowed to that end, but, as your majesty stands persuaded, probably fitted for the effecting it in some measure.[54]

---

52 Edward Hyde, Lord Clarendon, *A History of the Civil War and Rebellion in England Began in the Year 1641* (Oxford, 1712), vol. 3, 39.

53 *A Letter From a Scholar in Oxford to his Friend in the Countrey* (Oxford, 1647), 5.

54 Henry Cary, *Memorials of the Great Civil War in England from 1642 to 1652,*

Sheldon would have been one of first men to read Juxon and Duppa's reply to the king since, due to his service as clerk of the closet, reading and circulating opinions throughout the land was a large portion of his work in the Interregnum. Sheldon's correspondents on the matter of toleration and oaths (however sincerely or insincerely offered) included most of the bishops remaining in England. Robert Skinner (Oxford), Thomas Morton (Durham), and James Ussher (Armagh) all replied to Sheldon about this matter. They offered conflicting advice. Skinner wrote:

> ... that necessity ... which I conceive our gracious sovereign now stands under, for the safety of the crown and dignity, and for the settling of peace, and preserving of the true religion established by law. For these ends, in such a strait, such a toleration is, in my judgment, not only lawful but expedient.[55]

Morton offered a critique of the other religions allowed to come to prominence if toleration were to succeed in making peace. Morton had doubts as to sustaining true doctrine when others competed. He wrote, "because there are some other religions which consist of principles destructive to the state politic, and which patronize the freedom and toleration of all other religions, albeit they ruinate the fundamental doctrines of the faith, to the confusion of all."[56] Ultimately, Morton advised against any attempted toleration due to the danger inherent in such a religious program to the state and church. Ussher allowed for the king to grant toleration because the situation was dire and God granted latitude to monarchs so hard-pressed by outside forces. Ussher reaffirmed the mandate that "... every Christian prince be obliged,

---

vol. 1 (London: Henry Colburn, 1842), 169–170. Juxon and Duppa to Charles I, October 4, 1646.

55 Cary, *Memorials of the Great Civil War,* vol. 1, 329. Robert Skinner to Gilbert Sheldon.

56 Cary, vol. 1, 335–336. Thomas Morton to Gilbert Sheldon.

by all just and Christian ways, to maintain and promote, to his power, the Christian religion in the truth and purity of it."[57] The opinions on the topic of a full or partial toleration varied so much that the idea had little chance of ever succeeding, and parliament was losing its desire to treat any subject with the king. For a growing number of MPs, it was a case of too little, too late. Sheldon and Hammond failed to attend a second permitted visit to their royal master in 1648, because both were in jail due to the Visitation at Oxford. Sheldon offered a final service to his royal master by offering the familiar rituals and rites of the proscribed liturgy the day before Charles's execution.

Forces were now in motion that altered the English experience during the Civil Wars. A select group of members in power in both the army and parliament began to rethink England's political structure. One of the first movements was a vote of "No Addresses" presented to both houses in November 1647. The king was no longer necessary to the business of governing. The Houses of Lords and Commons were cutting the ties that bound them to the monarch by making it a treasonable activity to be in contact with the king without the consent of both houses. They also declared that they would no longer receive any messages from the king or invite any further messages from the king. Over the course of 1648, things deteriorated even further in the relationship between the king and parliament. In 1647, both houses referred to Charles as king; by the beginning of 1649, he was simply Charles Stuart and charged with treason. Parliament charged that all "wicked designs, wars, and evil practices of him the said Charles Stuart, have been, and are carried on for the advancement and upholding of a personal interest of will, power, and pretended prerogative to himself and his family."[58] Within a week a court pronounced a sentence of high treason and issued a warrant stat-

---

57 Ibid., 334–335. James Ussher to Gilbert Sheldon.

58 Gardiner, 371. The Charge Against the King, January 20, 1648/9.

ing, "Whereas Charles Stuart, King of England, is, and standeth convicted, attainted, and condemned of high treason ... [he is] to be put to death by the severing of his head from his body."[59] The king was dead, and his family, friends, and supporters were reeling from the shocking execution, but the struggle that began as a conflict between king and parliament continued, with factions within the army and parliament vying for control. The Civil Wars of the three kingdoms were not over, and the struggle for religious, political, and military dominance of the British Isles continued for another decade.

---

59 Gardiner, 380. The Death Warrant of Charles I, January 29, 1648/9. For more on the regicide see Mark Kishlansky, "Mission Impossible: Charles I, Oliver Cromwell and the Regicide," *The English Historical Review* 125, no. 515 (2010): 844–874.

CHAPTER 4

THE STRUGGLE TO SURVIVE, THE 1650S

The death of the king created a flurry of protests across Europe, but little real action. The execution of Charles I disheartened his supporters at home and abroad. The churchmen had an illustration of the adage "no bishop, no king" presented to them in the clearest way possible. One must assume that this striking event left an indelible mark upon those close to the king and to his cause. The king was dead, his church made illegal, and the following decade saw the only republican rule ever instituted in England. Diarist Evelyn noted of the regicide:

> The Villanie of the Rebells proceeding now so far as to Trie, Condemne, & Murder our excellent King, the 30 of this Moneth, struck me with such a horror that I kept the day of his *Martyrdom* a fast, & would not be present, at that excecrable wickedness; receiving that sad <account> of it by my Bro: Geo: & also by Mr. Owen, who came to Visite this afternoone, recounting to me all Circumstances.[1]

The images of Charles I and Archbishop Laud as martyrs continued to grow among those devoted to the Anglican Church. However, the death of the king was not a soul-shattering event to everyone in the British Isles; opinion varied about the king and the righteousness or reasoning behind his execution. Ralph Josselin was vicar of Earls Colne, Essex from 1641-1683 and his diary was more sympathetic to the new regime than Evelyn. Josselin interpreted the events as perhaps the beginning of a judgment

---

1 Evelyn, vol. 2, 547. See also Clive Holmes, *Why was Charles I Executed?* (London: Hambeldon and London, 2007).

on his country. "The death of the king talked much of, very many men of the weaker sort of Christians in divers places passionate concerning it, but so ungroundedly, that it would make any bleed to observe it, the lord hath some great thing to doe, feare and tremble at it oh England."[2]

Sheldon and his contemporaries had close ties to the monarchy and felt the loss of their king keenly. Henry Hammond wrote of the event to Sheldon, "... I have the addition of that heaviest blow that was ever struck in this nation to chill me, of which, alas, I was kept ignorant till Thursday evening. God hath spit in our face."[3] The members of the scattered Anglican establishment (clerical and lay) viewed Charles I and Laud as martyrs of the faith, especially the king with the anonymous publication of the *Eikon Basilike*. The image of the doomed and saintly king stuck chords across social classes. This image reinforced the king as a martyr and his earnest devotion to the church dismantled by his enemies. The dismissed clerics of the church went into hiding in England and a large number went abroad to serve the exiles, although many returned at some point during the 1650s. The exiled clerics clustered around the royal court in exile hoping to influence the religion and education of the royal heirs of Charles I.

The churchmen had several choices after the execution of the head of their church. One, they could leave England to minister to the English exiles on the continent clustered about the royal relatives of the Stuarts in France and the Low Countries. Two, they could remain out of sight of the new authorities living with well-placed country families as private chaplains and tutors. Three, they could continue their work and use the new policies

---

2   Josselin, *Diary*, 155. February 4, 1648/9.

3   "Illustrations of the Church and State during the Great Rebellion," in *The Theologian and Ecclesiastic* (London: Joseph Masters, 1848), vol. 4, 4. Hammond to Sheldon February 5, 1648/9. Afterward *TE*.

and practices of the Directory and thus maintain their livings and livelihoods. Those of the last group included both time-servers and men who believed that a limited service was better than the alternative in their parishes. This last group was probably the largest number of clerics within England, but their loyalty and adherence to the Directory ranged from full acceptance to partial acceptance to those who memorized the Common Prayer and used it in place of the new Directory. This last feature was true especially of those that needed "extempore" prayers for weddings and funerals. Those that memorized the Common Prayer often used passages from the old liturgy when the directory called for the minister to formulate their own prayers. Many who remained loyal to the Church of England refused to work with the Presbyterian based worship within England, and worked to preserve a remnant of their church despite opposition from many parties. Many put pen to paper to attack the new mode of worship. Bishop John Bramhall of Armagh wrote:

> It is time to let the world see that this Discipline, which they so much adore, is the very quintessence of refined Popery, or a greater tyranny than ever Rome brought forth; inconsistent with all forms of civil government, destructive to all sorts of policy, a rack to the conscience, the heaviest pressure that can fall upon a people, and so much more dangerous, because by the specious pretence of Divine institution, it takes away the sight but not the burden of slavery. Have patience, reader, and I shall discover unto thee more pride and arrogancy through the holes of a threadbare coat than was ever found under a Cardinal's cap or a triple crown ...[4]

---

4   More and Cross, Ed., *Anglicanism*, 80. John Bramhall, *A Fair Warning to take Heed of the Scottish Discipline, as Being of all Others Most Injurious to the Civil Magistrate, Most Oppressive to the Subject, Most Pernicious to Both* (London, 1649).

Even Hammond wrote of his distaste for dealing with the Presbyterians, "I have done with the Presbyters; & have so farr observed your directions without receiving them, that I find not that they have at all hurt my health."[5] Among some, loyalty to the church rejected any form of compromise with any alternative religious denomination. The lack of tolerance showed by the Presbyterians to the episcopal clerics solidified lines in the sand and created an "us and them" mentality that existed long after the Restoration. Loyalty to time honored institutions and rubrics would factor into the leadership of the re-established Church of England. Hammond, Sheldon, Morley, and others followed this policy in years to come, and key positions in the restored church went to men who suffered ejection, suspension, or sequestration for their loyalty.[6]

The leading men of this remnant of the outlawed church formed themselves into a network of mutual aid and support that acted outside of the actions (or more correctly inactions) of the remaining bishops. The task of organizing the fractured and frightened underground church fell largely to university men stripped of their homes and livings by the two universities' visitations. The emerging leaders were men with some personal connection to Charles I and/or connection with Laud. Many of the sequestered bishops simply retreated into retirement and began to die off without replacements. Notable exceptions were Brian Duppa (Salisbury), William Piers (Bath and Wells), and Matthew

---

5   MS Harleian 6942, f. 17. Hammond to Sheldon, April 25, undated but from the early 1650s.

6   For more info on the church and an overview of types of churchmen who survived the Interregnum, see Christopher Dutton and Judith Maltby, Ed., *Religion in Revolutionary England* (Manchester: Manchester University Press, 2006), essay by Judith Maltby, "Suffering and Surviving: The Civil Wars and the Formation of Anglicanism, 1642-60," 158–180, Ann Hughes, "'The Public Professions of these Nations': The National Church in Interregnum England," 93–112 and Kenneth Fincham and Stephen Taylor, "Vital Statistics: Episcopal Ordination and Ordinands in England, 1646-60," *The English Historical Review* 126, no. 519 (2011): 319–344.

Wren (Ely). Wren spent much of the decades the church was under attack in the Tower, so he wrote when able, but was out of the picture much of the time. Duppa was the most active of the bishops working to keep a remnant alive, and he counted on the support of men like Sheldon and Hammond. Fourteen sees between 1643-1660 became vacant due to death, including three archbishoprics: Canterbury (1645), York (1650), and Armagh (1652).[7]

The remainder of the Church of England looked to the leadership and advice of a group of university men to guide them working with the remaining bishops. Gilbert Sheldon, Henry Hammond, and George Morley remained in contact and exchanged letters that covered a broad range of topics, from weighty theological and academic issues to more pragmatic concerns about money and education. These men worked tirelessly to preserve their church and to offer support and aid to those dispossessed by the new regime. Robert Payne, a canon of Christ Church wrote to Sheldon, "Since you went from Oxford I writ to my friend in Paris, and received an answer from him, by which I am assured that Paris is free. He tells me the French—especially the men of the Guard—take the death of our King very much to heart."[8]

One of the theological tasks these men attempted was to defend the office and dignity of the bishop from attacks.

---

7   *Fasti Ecclesia Anglicanae, 1541-1857,* vols. 1-11. See also the Church of England Database, location index, www.theclergydatabase.org.uk. The list of vacated sees included Sodor and Man (1643), Bristol, Hereford (1646), Winchester (1647), Peterborough (1649), Worcester (1650), Carlisle, Chester (1652), Lincoln (1654), Norwich (1656), and Durham, Exeter (1659). James Ussher of Armagh held Carlisle; thus his mention in the text above.

8   *TE,* vol. 6, 165–166. Robert Payne to Gilbert Sheldon, April 25, 1649. Mordechai Feingold, "Robert Payne" *ODNB.* The Friend in Paris in may be Morley, due to a eulogy Morley offered in letter to Sheldon after Payne's death in 1651.

> My endeavour was to vindicate our BB. [Bishops] from that imputation—which I suppose might be done two ways. 1. By granting the B had a power (and by power here I mean not *jus* but *facultatem* in that sense as we say a power of miracles,) not derived from the supreme civil, yet dependent on it for the execution of all acts belonging to that power: or 2. if by power must be meant *jus,* yet that *jus* is not granted to them, but with such limitation as the Bishop, when he ordains a priest, gives him the power to preach the word and administer the Sacraments with this limitation.[9]

Payne offered that the power of the bishop was not just a right; however, it was an ability granted by a higher power, not deriving from the civil government, but dependent upon it for its work. Further, he defined the right (*jus*) as a byproduct of ordination and limited to preaching and the administering of the sacraments. Bishops needed to work within the framework of a civil government supported and aided by the local magistracy. One of the largest charges leveled against the bishops by Puritans and others dealt with their involvement in temporal government, especially involvement in the House of Lords and the ecclesiastical courts: the High Commission and the Star Chamber.

Hammond and Sheldon aimed to figure out in what form or manner they might work to keep the Common Prayer in use. They worried and wondered if their actions were correct or desired at all by the new head of the church, the young exiled king. Those around the king were often just trying to survive on limited incomes and broken dreams. Even Hammond wondered at the legality of their actions:

> ... in pursuance of your directions, have written to the B of W, but besides him have no correspondence with any

---

9   *TE,* vol. 6, 166. Payne to Sheldon, February 4, 1649/50.

other but Sar[um]. I think your proposal is reasonable, and wish you would in your thoughts mould it into such a form as might want nothing more but acting, and then propose it where it may probably take effect: But sure the beginning must be from abroad.[10]

One of the main aims of Sheldon and Hammond was to keep the Common Prayer in practice, using whatever means possible. The use or non-use of the prayer book caused questions about whether or not it was fitting to worship with those who omitted the liturgy. Hammond encouraged Sheldon to write their mutual friend Robert Sanderson, who was wavering. "Certainly he told me he used the Common Prayer; otherwise I wonder not that he that disuses it should think fit to go to their churches that do omit it. When you meet with him endeavour to infuse some courage into him, the want of which may betray his reason."[11] Both men concerned themselves with the continuing debate over vows and the conscience. Sheldon and Hammond agreed that vows to perform any duty were not dispensable even in matters of tender conscience. Hammond wrote, "Such is our vow of baptism, our oaths which bind us to that allegiance which was due to the fathers of the country, under whose dominion they which are born owe a natural allegiance to him."[12] The Bishop of Salisbury lived in a home provided by a friend in Richmond where the bishop lived "as the tortoise doth, by not going out of my shell."[13] Duppa attempted to call a gathering to discuss the state of the church and to preserve what they could of the apostolic succession. Duppa wished both Hammond and Sheldon to attend this gathering to aid him in the task of preserving the use of the prayer book.

---

10 Ibid., 300. Hammond to Sheldon, October 14, 1649.

11 Ibid.

12 Ibid., 301–303. Hammond to Sheldon, March 17, 1649/50.

13 Ian Green, "Brian Duppa, Bishop of Winchester," *ODNB*, 2.

> I am so sorry you are so intangled as you speake, & yet I
> also apprehend your presence very useful at Richmond
> or London at this tyme, where some of our Eccl: affaires
> are now afoote, & by what I heare concerning a report
> made to Bp of Ro: by Dr Jer: T: concerning the Clergyes
> desire to have the Comm: pr: taken of, & some other
> formes made, I cannot but wish you were there to inter-
> pose your judgmt & authority. I heard also from the B: of
> Sa: this week, who much depends upon your coming ...[14]

For unknown reasons, Sheldon never ventured into London or
Richmond despite repeated requests for his presence. He might
have been ill, as he was several times during the 1650s. He might
have remained in place to look after the family and affairs of the
friends he lived with. He may have believed that such meetings
were useless because of the fractured nature of the Anglicanism
in England and it was therefore not worth the risk to travel out
of a safe haven. The churchmen at this point were trying to stir
the rightful leaders to action, not attempting to have new bishops
named or even petitioning the king to name replacements. The
clerics at court tried to stem the wooing of the young king toward
Roman Catholicism, a threat made imperative after a couple of
prominent conversions. They worried more about Rome than
the Presbyterians in Scotland, who alienated the king in the lead
up to the disaster at Worcester.

The clerics who remained in England wondered if they made the
right decision. Should they follow the exiled king and court to
the continent? Sheldon's concern over rumors of possible banishment by the authorities perhaps made him voice questions
about going into exile.[15] Hammond replied:

---

14 Harleian 6942 f. 24. Probably Hammond to Sheldon, May 23. There was a
    meeting at the Richmond home of Duppa in August 1653.

15 For more on the idea or experience of exile, see Nicole Greenspan, "Charles
    II, Exile, and the Problem Of Allegiance," *The Historical Journal* 54, no. 1

What you foresee, as possible, concerning our common condition perhaps may not be far off, yet truly I have not yet considered of it, being much inclined to wait God's providence, and to stay here in or out of prison as long as we may, and when nothing but going beyond the sea will free us from spiritual imprisonment, then to prefer banishment as the less evil ... I am yet more inclined to wish those friends here again, which have gone on those terms, than to follow them; if I had a sufficient stock to support me, and no care of any but myself. But besides, methinks yet a man may do some good here, and I see no way of doing any, anywhere else.[16]

The encouragement worked and both men worked tirelessly to protect and promote their church among the clerical remnant at home and abroad as well as within their communities. Sheldon and Hammond remained on the list of those watched and monitored by the state. Sheldon moved locations several times during this decade. He retired to the Midlands, moving to various locations in the following counties: Derbyshire, Leicestershire, Nottinghamshire, and Staffordshire. Sheldon spent time at Sir Robert Shirley's house at Staunton Harold, with his Okeover relatives at East Bridgford, Nottinghamshire, and with his brother Ralph Sheldon in Stanton, Staffordshire. Sheldon also spent some time with the Coventry, Yelverton, and Pakington families, all of whom were royalists of some degree or another.[17] Sheldon's Bible contained a glimpse of why he sought shelter with the Okeover's in particular—he listed the eight children born to Hum-

---

(2011): 73–103, Timothy Raylor, "The Anglican Attack On Hobbes In Paris, 1651," *The Historical Journal* 53, no. 1 (2010): 153–164, and M.R.F. Williams, "Between King, Faith and Reason: Father Peter Talbot (SJ) and Catholic Royalist Thought in Exile," *The English Historical Review* 127, no. 528 (2012): 1063–1099.

16 *TE*, vol. 7, 119–129. Hammond to Sheldon, October 29, 1650.

17 Spurr, "Gilbert Sheldon," 3.

phrey Okeover and his unnamed wife. Sheldon may have lived with them to help educate some of their children or to prevent more trouble for his brother. He also recorded "Mr Humphry Okeover dyed at London Dec 29 163_."[18] He lived with his cousin's widow and her family and more than likely provided educational and spiritual guidance to that household. He also recorded the little tragedies of his own life. His nephew, Joseph Sheldon, the second son of his brother, received his uncle's foreign post and forwarded it to him. Sheldon recorded, "Gilbert Sheldon borne at London May 4th 1657 between five & sixe of the clock in the afternoon in St. Paul's Churchyard. He dyed there Feb 11. 1657/8 a little before one of the clock in the morning."[19]

It was not an easy thing to remain in England, and many churchmen and/or their families had their property seized by the state for their delinquency. Delinquency in this sense was loyalty to the king, the Church of England, or in many cases both. Sheldon owned property: Cauldon Grange in Staffordshire. He purchased the property from his elder brother, Ralph Sheldon, while Ralph was in a period of financial difficulty and desired the property to stay in the family. Sheldon placed the land in a trust for his brother's seven children in 1638, to aid in providing preferment for his nephews and marriage portions for his nieces. Sheldon's nephews and nieces successfully petitioned the county for the settlement of the land their uncle held in trust for them.[20]

---

18 Eng bib 1648 d 3. Notes in Sheldon's hand pertaining to the Okeover family. The children of the couple were Rowland 1624, Thomas 1626, Katherine 1627, Elizabeth 1629, Martha 1630, Humphrey 1631, Ralph 1632, and Phillip 1639. Humphrey Okeover probably died in 1639 after the birth of his last child, since Sheldon recorded the children's full birthdates.

19 Eng bib 1648 d 3. Notes about Sheldon's immediate family. This bible is the 1638 Authorized Edition with prayer book and apocrypha. Sheldon had several nephews and one great nephew named for him, which gives a glimpse into his family connections. One might imagine Sheldon to be a doting uncle concerned for his namesakes and eager to secure proper places for them, as was evident in his provisions for them in his will and while he was still alive.

20 Mary Anne Everett Green, Ed., *Calendar of the Proceeding of the Committee*

Sheldon and Hammond both raised and filtered money throughout the period to those of their fellow churchmen and their families who were in financial distress. The government was to pay
sequestered churchmen a percentage of the value of their livings,
usually one-fifth, but this small amount, if paid, was a pittance
for men unable to support their families or themselves. Being a
university man and accustomed to the company of collegians,
Hammond came up with a scheme to raise money for a society
of scholars.

> Let me mention to you an hasty undigested phansy of
> mine suggested to me by reading the conclusion of Bp
> Bramhalls, excellent booke of Schisme p. 276.277. It
> is this. What if you & Dr Henchman and I should en-
> deavour to raise 600l per anum: (each of us gaining sub-
> scriptions for 200l) for 7 yeares to maintain a society of
> 20 exiled scollers, and when we discern things feasible
> communicate it to Bp Bramhall, & require of him a cat-
> alogue of 20 such, whose wants & desires of such a re-
> cess in some convenient place (by him to be thought of
> also) might make it a fit charity to recommend to pious
> persons. Next if this be not unreasonable to be endeav-
> oured, then tell me whether it must be privately carryed,
> or may be publickly avowd, & what els you can think of
> to perfect & forme this suddein rude conceit. Which
> when I have also communicated to Dr Hencchman, I
> shall be content to be laughed at by ether of you.[21]

for Compounding, 1643-1660, vol. 4: *Cases, July 1650-Dec. 1653* (London:
Eyre & Spottiswoode, 1892), 2717. This case went through the Reading
court in Feb 1651. For more on compounding and sequestering, see Melanie Harrington, "The Earl of Derby and His Tenants: Sales of Royalist Land
during the Interregnum Revisited," *The Economic History Review* 64, no. 4
(2011): 1195–1217.

21 MS Harleian 6942, f. 18. Unsigned, but internal evidence and handwriting
match Hammond to Sheldon, April 30, undated. Must be after/during 1654,
as Bramhall's book *A Just Vindication of the Church of England from the Unjust*

This scheme of Hammond's never took root and he apologized to his friend, "I importuned you last week with a suddain motion that came into my head."[22] Clerics, even those as reserved as Hammond, might be forgiven their own flights of fantasy, since the decade was awash in such schemes across the religious fabric of the kingdoms of the Commonwealth. Sheldon even assisted those with whom he did not fully agree, illustrating a keen sense of personal fairness. Suffering for loyalty to the church overrode personal differences of theological opinion. One such individual was Jeremy Taylor, who wrote to Sheldon:

> Dear Sir, I received yours dated November 5, in which I find a continued and enlarged expression of that kindness with which you have always assisted my condition and promoted my interest. Two debts you are pleased to forgive me; one of money, the other of unkindness. I thank you for both; but this later debt was contracted when I understood not you, and less understood myself; but I daresay there was nothing in it but folly and imprudence. But I will not do it so much favour as to excuse it. If it was displeasing to you then, it is so much more to mee now that I know of it.[23]

Sheldon was especially eager to aid men with families who had lost their livings; Taylor fell into this group. He filtered money from England to those in distress while living in exile. Sheldon got reports from his contacts about the family of his old friend Sir Edward Hyde. "The truth is, they are, and have been at least seven or eight months, in a very sad condition ... in March last

---

Aspersion of Criminal Schism was published that year. For more on scholarly pursuits of the Anglican clergy, see William J. Bulman, *Anglican Enlightenment: Orientalism, Religion, and Politics in England and its Empire, 1648-1714* (Cambridge: Cambridge University Press, 2015).

22 MS Harleian 6942, f. 21. Hammond to Sheldon, May 9, undated.

23 Burrows, *Worthies of All Souls*, 199. Jeremy Taylor to Sheldon, late 1655.

that is to say, at least L200 in debt, —an old father and mother, an aunt, a sister, and four children, and as many more as come in all to nineteen."[24]

Sheldon's major correspondent abroad was George Morley. Morley was an old friend of Sheldon's from their association in Oxford, among the congenial academic circle of men that congregated at Great Tew. Morley was also a fellow royal chaplain of Charles I and one of the negotiators at the ill-fated Uxbridge meeting. Morley left England in March 1649 and went to the court of Charles II at St. Germain, later moving among the royalists in the Low Countries.[25] Sheldon, Hammond, and Morley had the additional task of sharing responsibility for the estate of Lucius Cary, Second Viscount Falkland. Falkland's estate at Tew was difficult to oversee, due to its entanglement in court battles. More interestingly, these bachelors accustomed to undergraduates were the guardians of Falkland's children. The eldest son and third viscount, Lucius Cary, died in 1649 and passed the title to his younger brother Henry Cary. The newly minted Fourth Viscount Falkland went abroad with his tutor and was not thrilled by the restrictions placed on him by his clerical tutor, while the delights of Europe awaited.

> Now I am farther to tell you that fro[m] Dr Map: I received this week that upon my mention of the dangers of Italy to his yong charge, hee is so convinced that as hee is now tempered, they are not to bee avoyded, that hee (contrary to all his own interests) proposes these 2 things 1. that wee assign him next spring form his returne into Ingland, which is assered to be a way of fixing his unsettled phansy 2. that the space till then be spent to surveying other parts of France, &c: To this I have re-

---

24 *TE*, vol. 7, 125. Morley to Sheldon, November 26, 1650.

25 John Spurr, "George Morley," *ODNB*, 1–2.

turnd to him a letter wch he may shew his young charge, that there are but 2 things wanting to make it reasonable for his freinds heer to prefix a time, One the quiet of this place, (out of all our powers) the other (much in his power) the staydness of the mind that may make him capable of beeing his own sole director.[26]

The guardians of the young Lord Falkland wanted to insure that their great friend and patron's heir had the tools necessary to govern himself and oversee his estate and that of his family. The task of overseeing the teenager was wearing, as Sheldon received word.

Since my last I am by Dr Ma: desired to assigne the Autumn for the yong Lds returne, though he himself meanes not to returne, with him ... Mr Cary also writes earnestly to mee, to send a letter to the Dr wch (in case he cannot perswade him to the contrary) many promise him this liberty, & enclines me to this by asuring me, that nothing but this can stay him so long & if it be denyed, his coming without mony & attendants will bring great hazards with it & signe him his absolute release from all power of any of us over him for the future ... I confess though I conceive this no way to continue our power to his good, yet from Dr Ma: weariness of him I begin also to be weary with wrestling with him to so little purpose. When he comes home we may sojourn with his grandmother & by his uncles help look into his estate & see better acounts made then we yet can. And perhaps he that hath profited so little under restraint, may do better or not so ill without it.[27]

---

26 MS Harleian 6942, f. 3. Probably Morley to Sheldon, April 18, undated. Falkland's tutor while abroad might have been Robert Mapletoft, later Dean of Ely. Falkland's *ODNB* article lists Dr. Thomas Triplett as his tutor.

27 MS Harleian 6942, f. 13. Probably Morley to Sheldon, May 6, undated.

The young man returned to England, eventually married, and became a representative for Oxfordshire in the third protectorate parliament of 1659. He went on to hold office in the restored regime until his death in 1663, holding strong royalist and Anglican sympathies.[28] One cannot help but speculate about the influence of his clerical guardians on his later sympathies. Sheldon counted on men like Falkland to help pass the legislation vital to the re-establishment of the Church of England in the Cavalier Parliament.

Another concern of the churchmen, especially for those living abroad, was the threat of conversion, due to close proximity to those within the Church of Rome. Charles I had warned his own children about the dangers of Catholicism and urged them to remain true to the church of their father, not that of their mother. The disheartened churchmen read reports and heard rumors relating to the conversion of men away from the protestant fold. One such sensational early conversion involved William Chillingworth. Chillingworth was an Oxford man and one of the members of the Great Tew Circle. One of his closest university friends was Sheldon, from their shared experiences at Trinity.[29] He wrote, questioning Sheldon on the doctrine of infallibility and, perhaps more dangerously in Sheldon's mind, inviting him to conversion.

Meane while, lett mee entreate to consider most seriously of these two queries.

1. Whether is be not evident, from Scripture ... from the goodnesse of God, and the necessity of mankind, that these must be some one Church infallible in matter of faith.

2. Whether there be any other society of men in the world besides that of the church of Rome that after

---

28 David L. Smith, "Henry Cary, 4th Viscount Falkland," *ODNB*, 1–2.

29 Warren Chernaik, "William Chillingworth," *ODNB*, 2–3.

can upon good warrant, or indeed [mss missing]
to itselfe, this priviledge of infallibility in matter of
faith.

When you have imployed your most attentive consideration upon these questions, I doe assure my selfe your
resolution will be Assir: in the first, and Ney: in the second and then the conclusion will bee that you will approve and follow that way hereinto I have had the happi-
nesse to enter before you: and should thinke it infinitely
encreased if it would please God, to draw you after.[30]

Chillingworth returned to the church of his baptism, but the
questions that plagued this notable theologian also resounded in
the writing of those less inclined to go to the English seminary
at Douai. His return to the fold brought a gifted polemicist to
the side of the Church of England and his *The Religion of Protestants a Safe Way to Salvation* (1638) was a favorite recommended
reading to those wavering in their orthodox Church of England
Protestantism in the 1640s and 1650s. This volume underwent
reprints in 1664, 1674, and 1684. Extracts of the work against
Catholicism went to press in 1680, as part of the mania around
the Popish Plot.[31] Chillingworth's re-conversion gave strength to
those confronted with conversion away from the Church of England, either to popery or to a sect. Truth in matters religious,
they believed, would triumph, given adequate time and support
from a legitimate magistracy.

Others reported conversions and recovered converts questioned
the idea of infallibility. The idea of one infallible religion among
the plethora in England was something these men and women
wanted. They sought assurance in matters of faith in a time of

---

30 MS Tanner 73, f. 3. William Chillingworth to Sheldon, undated but after his
conversion, probably between 1628-1630.

31 Chernaik, "Chillingworth," 9.

great personal and political instability. Most of those who flirted with Roman Catholicism returned eventually to the church of their baptism. One of Sheldon's correspondents, probably Morley, wrote, "... Mr Pa: Caryes conversion as yet is rather from the Romish, then to the Prot: rel: a seeker he saith he is & unravells & questions all, that he may build infallibly."[32] The horror and dismay at the conversions to Rome ought to have illustrated the Protestantism of these men to their Puritan detractors and enemies, but that was not the case. Puritans and other propagandists used these conversions as proof that the Church of England had too many elements of popish superstitions in it and was thus in need of direction under the hands of the presbyters out of perceived superstitious practices.

Forced out of active ministry, many churchmen turned their talents toward academic defenses of their church and liturgy and the longstanding debates with Catholic controversialists. Jeremy Taylor sent word of such a matter over a debate over the issue of transubstantiation.

> Sir, I have now sent to the presse, but first to my L. Bp. of Salisbury to be perused a discourse of the Real presence, occasioned by my contest with a Jesuit in these parts. It hath pass'd all the Welch censure I could well obtaine for it, & I have put as much care & industry upon the Qu: as I could.[33]

The churchmen also watched as the government structures they long recognized fell to eager new forms promulgated by the destroyers of the monarchy and the church.

The regicides had to work quickly to stabilize the government without a monarch. The first step of the new government was to

---

32 MS Harleian 6942, f. 2. Probably Morley to Sheldon, April 1, undated.

33 MS Tanner 52, f. 7. Jeremy Taylor to Sheldon, April 11, 1653

organize a council of state to oversee the Commonwealth of England. The first in a list of requirements for the members of the council was that they were "authorised and required to oppose and suppress whomsoever shall endeavour to go about to set up or maintain the pretended title of Charles Stuart, eldest son of the late King."[34] This requirement put the men loyal to the exiled young king in a quandary. The parliament moved quickly and abolished the office of the king finding "the office of a King ... is unnecessary, burdensome, and dangerous to the liberty, safety, and public interest of the people."[35] Following the republican leanings of the Rump and the leaders of the Council of State, the House of Lords became the next victim of the winnowing of the government. Parliament declared England a Commonwealth in May 1649, stating:

> Be in declared and enacted by this present Parliament, and by the authority of the same, that the people of England ... are and shall be, and are hereby constituted, made, established, and confirmed, to be a Commonwealth and Free State, and shall henceforth be governed as a Commonwealth and Free State by the supreme authority of this nation, the representatives of the people in Parliament.[36]

Cromwell's goal was to create a stable and godly nation, after nearly a decade of fighting and strife. Time quickly showed that these two goals were incompatible, as divisions and heated discussion developed over the definition of "godly" in the Commonwealth. Many English citizens felt lost and confused by the rapidly changing political and religious climate, which ultimately enabled the Restoration, after various experiments in godly rule failed.

---

34 Gardiner, 381. Act Appointing a Council of State, February 13, 1648/9.

35 Ibid., 385. Act Abolishing the office of King, March 17, 1649.

36 Ibid., 388. An Act declaring England to be a Commonwealth, May 19, 1649.

The religious climate of the newly formed Commonwealth varied among different groups: the army, London, parliament, the gentry, and the country set all wished different things in the charged religious climate. The decades of the Civil Wars and Commonwealth saw an explosion of sects all professing the right path to God, holiness, peace, and ultimately salvation. The only thing most of them agreed on was that whatever their sect promulgated as truth was the only way and all others were wrong. Many of these groups were as intolerant of outsiders as the Restoration churchmen. The most enduring of the new sects that emerged during the political disruption were the Quakers, or Society of Friends. The Quakers emerged from the ministry and itinerant preaching of George Fox. Fox and company followed the prompting of the "inner light" over scriptural traditions. Baptists existed in England since the time of James I, but they flowered in the absence of persecution over religious experimentation. Baptists in England found a safe haven in the army, serving as chaplains and common soldiers. Presbyterians in parliament and within the City of London and its environs distrusted both of these groups as dangerous and heterodox, if not heretical, but Cromwell protected them from the worst discrimination.

More radical were the Ranters. The Ranters flourished in the two years immediately following the execution of Charles I. These individuals followed long-running Antinomian traditions and trends. Antinomians asserted that believers were not under the law, but under grace, and that therefore moral laws were irrelevant. Additionally, a believer may sin without fear of punishment, because grace trumps sin.[37] The Ranters flouted the morality of the Puritans vigorously, especially sexually. Essentially, the Ranters believed that God was in every man and if one acknowledged this truth, an individual could not sin.[38]

---

37 Cairns, "Antinomianism," 29–30.

38 Michael Watts, *The Dissenters*, vol. 1 (Oxford: Clarendon Press, 1978), 182.

The Ranters and Quakers together flouted "the deuteronomic taboos against sex outside of marriage and 'went naked for a sign' offending traditional morality,"[39] reviving the long remembered specter of Anabaptist Munster in the sixteenth century. Seekers believed that the church needed a new breed of apostles to restore the true church. They blamed Roman Catholicism for the corruption of the church. The Seekers were non-violent and many of them eventually ended up in the ranks of the Quakers, swayed by the charismatic preaching of Fox. The Fifth Monarchists worked for the millennial kingdom of God. These individuals wanted to aid in ushering in the New Jerusalem in any way possible, both by supporting the military and the parliament in furthering the reformation of England.

Sheldon's circle focused on Presbyterians as the real enemies of the Church of England. This idea had merit and weight behind it, as the purging of universities and livings led to the replacement of many loyal Anglicans with Puritans or Presbyterian-inclined men. William Sancroft summed up the experience while at Emmanuel College Cambridge in 1650:

> The new nothing, or Presbyterian Commencement, is over; expect no part of the history of it from me; I will never be historiographer to that faction. As I look upon that cursed Puritan faction as the ruin of the most glorious Church upon earth, (in whose faith I still live and hope to die) so I cannot but esteem this late solemnity as a piece of their triumph over us; and my just resentment will not give me leave so diligently to attend it, as to be able to give an account of it to you or any man, any otherwise by my grief and silence.[40]

---

39 Alexandra Walsham, *Charitable Hatred* (Manchester: Manchester University Press, 2006), 47.

40 *TE,* vol. 8, 167.

The government responded to the most radical of these groups by issuing the Blasphemy Act, targeting Ranters and others deviating from standard moral practices. The act passed in August 1650 and stated:

> ... that there are divers men and women who have lately discovered themselves to be most monstrous in their Opinions, and loose in all wicked and abominable Practices ... not onely to the notorious corrupting and disordering, but even to the dissolution of all Humane Society, who rejecting the use of any Gospel Ordinances, do deny the necessity of Civil and Moral Righteousness among men.[41]

When convicted under the Blasphemy Act, an individual's sentence was six months in prison without bail. Under these conditions, many of those accused and convicted slipped into other religious forms, commonly returning to Baptist or other independent congregations. Upon a second conviction, the individual was banished and not allowed to return until licensed by parliament for re-entry to the Commonwealth. The Rump continued its program of religious reform by repealing the laws relating to non-attendance in parish churches, ignoring Holy Days, and not hearing the Common Prayer. Common Prayer services ended officially with the abolition of the institutions of the Church of England in the 1640s. The Rump was not willing to allow an absence of rules regarding church attendance. Non-attendance was for many a step down the slippery slope toward atheism, which was an anathema to the godly MPs.

---

41 "August 1650: An Act against Several Atheistical, Blasphemous and Execrable Opinions, Derogatory to the Honor of God, and Destructive to Humane Society," in *Acts and Ordinances of the Interregnum, 1642-1660*, ed. C.H. Firth and R.S. Rait (London: His Majesty's Stationery Office, 1911), 409–412. *British History Online*, accessed September 10, 2018, http://www.british-history.ac.uk/no-series/acts-ordinances-interregnum/pp409-412.

That all and every person and persons within this Commonwealth and the Territories thereof, shall (having no
reasonable excuse for their absence) upon every Lords-
Day, Days of publique Thanksgiving and Humiliation,
diligently resort to some publique place where the Service and Worship of God is exercised, or shall be present at some other place in the practice of some Religious
Duty, either of Prayer, Preaching, Reading or Expound-
ing the Scriptures, or conferring upon the same.[42]

The passage of this act gave religious toleration for all but the
Anglicans and Catholics. The Anglicans were the largest group
of worshippers in republican England, but for the most part ordinary parishioners remained unaffected by direct action against
them. One example of direct action against Anglican services involved diarist John Evelyn and his family. In 1657, Evelyn and
his family went to London for Christmas services at the chapel
at Exeter House. "Mr. Gunning preaching ... as he was giving us
the holy Sacrament, The Chapell was surrounded with Souldiers:
All the Communicants and Assembly surpriz'd & kept Prisoners
by them, some in the house others carried away."[43] This was the
only instance Evelyn recorded of trouble in pursuing prayer book
rites for major events—his children were christened and his wife
churched after childbirth. Gunning served as a chaplain to Sir
Robert Shirley and Sheldon spent a great deal of time with this
family during the period. Gunning became a model of the type
of man necessary to the return of the church—one with royalist
credentials and prayer book loyalties. The Interregnum govern-

---

42 "September 1650: Act for the Repeal of Several Clauses in Statutes Imposing
   Penalties for Not Coming to Church," in *Acts and Ordinances of the Interregnum, 1642-1660*, ed. C.H. Firth and R.S. Rait (London: His Majesty's Stationery Office, 1911), 423–425. *British History Online*, accessed September 10,
   2018, http://www.british-history.ac.uk/no-series/acts-ordinances-interreg
   num/pp423-425.

43 Evelyn, vol. 3, 203. Peter Gunning later became Bishop of Ely.

ment was eager to suppress those clerics who remained faithful to the prayer book, but many used the full or part of the liturgy in different ministries in private homes and quietly in public events. Stories abounded at the Restoration of ministers memorizing the liturgy's prayers and using them in funerals and other ceremonies at times to the pleasure of their Puritan or Presbyterian congregations until the source became clear.

The religious complexities were but one piece in the backdrop of growing political divisions between the English and the Scottish. The execution of Charles I caused the tensions between the Scottish Covenanters and their English parliamentary allies to worsen. The Scots realized that the forces coming to power in the south lacked the commitment to the Presbyterian program that marked earlier negotiations. The regicides made their decision to execute Charles I without consulting the representatives of Charles's northern kingdom. The young heir to the throne learned of his father's execution in February 1649, and following on the heels of that information, he discovered that the Covenanters led by Archibald Campbell, Earl of Argyll, declared for Charles II as King of Scotland.[44] The problems with this declaration lay within the factional divisions in Scotland between Argyll and James Graham, Earl of Montrose. Charles II sought to use these two factions against one another to give him a position of strength against the parliamentary forces in England. Charles II hoped that using Montrose as a de facto war chief would force Argyll and the Covenanters to offer better terms to him than those offered to Charles I. Montrose, however, acted before Charles II completed the delicate political dance with Argyll. Montrose returned to Scotland and Argyll defeated and captured his rival. Montrose went to the block on May 21, 1650, despite Charles II's effort to save this favorite.[45]

---

44 J.R. Jones, *Charles II: Royal Politician* (London: Allen & Unwin, 1987), 13. Ronald Hutton, *Charles II* (Oxford: Clarendon Press, 1989), Chapters 3 and 4.

45 David Stevenson, "James Graham, First Marquess of Montrose," *ODNB*, 5–9.

The death of Montrose forced Charles II to renew efforts with Argyll and his faction in the Covenanters. Charles II joined Argyll in Scotland on May 24, but the young king's advisors were abhorrent to the godly Scots, who forced their removal. Charles was essentially under house arrest under the aegis of Argyll's son Lord Lorne, commander of the Life Guard. The proclamation of Charles II in Scotland provoked Cromwell to invade Scotland, and the Scottish army lost at Dunbar in September 1650. The presence of the king in Scotland encouraged the royalists to come forward and Argyll began to lose his grasp on the situation. However, Argyll crowned Charles II at Scone on January 1, 1651 and installed him on his throne.[46] Royalists in England and abroad watched with hope, which fell quickly on the heels of disastrous defeats of the Scots by Cromwell's superior military. The young king returned to the continent, leaving via a legendary escape involving a great oak tree and woman's clothing. The royalist clergy opposed forcing the covenant on the king and worried about its lasting effects. The lingering impact of these events in Scotland would play out in the problems over restoring episcopacy and a national church in Scotland. Sheldon, first as Dean of the Chapel Royal and then as Bishop of London and Archbishop of Canterbury, tried to find a solution to the religious divisions in the northern kingdom.

The move of the Scots to crown Charles II went against English parliamentary acts and showed the frailty of the alliance with the other kingdom. Scotland's uprising collapsed on the battlefields of Dunbar and Worcester, leading to a military occupation of the north under the command of former royalist turned parliamentary general George Monck. Cromwell and other parliamentary leaders then turned to the more organized royalist resistance in Ireland under the leadership of James Butler, Marquess of Ormonde. Ireland was a double threat. In addition to harboring roy-

---

46 David Stevenson, "Archibald Campbell, Marquess of Argyll," *ODNB*, 13.

alists, the island nation held a Roman Catholic majority, which made them deadly enemies. The campaigns in Ireland were brutal and efficient. The massacres at Drogheda and Wexford reinforced the brutal images each side held of the other as something less than human. The recurrent military expenditures and the difficulty of trying to placate opposing sides led to the breakdown of the rule of the Rump. The godly republican experiment could not cope with the demands of multiple military expeditions: rival religious groups all clamoring for their right to speak, coupled with the army's emergence as a political force.

By early 1653, the Rump was on its last legs. The Rump failed to deliver a godly government and had many enemies. The great changes expected by those wanting a reform in religion never materialized. Sheldon and the clerics waiting watched the political infighting between the sects with a wary eye. The time to make peace or even compromise with the groups that held the most in common to those men loyal to the Church of England was long past. All that Sheldon and his allies could do was wait until providence and/or political matters made the return of the king possible.

The initial excitement over the acts against blasphemy and for the propagation of the gospel in Ireland and Wales turned sour when the Rump failed to satisfy the numerous groups at work in English political life. Presbyterians disliked the fact that no national Presbyterian church had come into existence. Presbyterian ministers were unhappy with the new oaths and angered in part by the actions of the regicides. Other groups were unhappy that the longed for and expected rule of the saints and further reform of the church was not coming under the rule of the Rump. Cromwell and others realized that the settlement of religious matters required a working settlement of the state. Cromwell's dissolution of the Long Parliament in April allowed him de facto rule of the Commonwealth simply by virtue of his position as head of the army. Cromwell and his officers nominated the replacements for the next experiment in republican rule. Cromwell sought to nominate "divers persons fearing God, and of approved fidelity and honesty"[47]

The Barebones Parliament opened July 4, 1653 to great expectations. However, even a group of like-minded individuals in religious matters could not make the government work. Cromwell realized that whatever was going to happen needed to happen before the population called for the return of all the purged members of the Long Parliament or, worse yet, called for new elections entirely. The great accomplishment of the Barebones Parliament was the creation of a system of civil marriage within England. This act was another in a long line of strikes against the cohesive power of any national ecclesiastical body whether Anglican or Presbyterian. This placed an additional burden on the weary magistrates who were now doing the work of clerics registering birth, deaths, and marriages. The system put in place by the civil marriage act helped increase the accuracy of such reports—especially important to poor relief. The perception of the parliament as full of religious radicals previously unqualified for political office due to occupation or social standing grew thanks to men like Praise-God Barebone.[48] This parliament's critics drew its name from Barebone, as a symbol of the humble origins and religious opinions of the members. However, the majority of members were similar to many who served before and after. They were drawn from moderate gentry families who had lost interest in supporting a minority of sectarian radicals. It was MPs such as these who ushered in the next attempt to govern the republic.

---

47 Gardiner, 405. Summons to a Member of the so-called Barebones Parliament, June 6, 1653.

48 Toby Barnard, *The English Republic, 1649-1660*, 2nd ed. (London: Longman, 1997), 29.

The Barebones Parliament was in trouble almost from its inception. Led by a radicalized minority, it managed to offend the army, lawyers, and its moderate members. The moderate members voted on December 12, 1653 to surrender their power to the Lord General. Cromwell and his council of officers were ready and on December 16, Cromwell took the oaths that created him Lord Protector of the Commonwealth of England, Scotland, and Ireland. In taking these oaths, Cromwell declared, "that the supreme legislative authority ... shall be and reside in one person, and the people assembled in Parliament."[49] The problem was how the sharing of this supreme legislative power worked. Cromwell as Lord Protector had the ability to issue ordinances with the force of law. These ordinances could be overturned by a vote of the next parliament. However, Cromwell used the army to influence voting in the newly redesigned boroughs. Cromwell's first ordinances redefined treason and worked to settle religion. The redefinition of treason was controversial, but the decision to settle religion by non-parliamentary means was even more so. The system of Triers and Ejectors had the job of appointing public preachers and removing scandalous ministers. The Triers (properly the Commissioners for the Approbation of Public Preachers) set up a system of qualifications for ministers. The nominated man had to exhibit the Grace of God in his life, have holy and profane-free conversation, and have the knowledge necessary for preaching the Gospel.[50] The nominated individual had his case presented before any five of the thirty-eight commissioners who had the authority "to grant unto such person admission to such benefice or lecture."[51] The Ejectors had much the same structure as the commissioners of the Triers. Five county commissioners

---

49 Gardiner, 405. The Instrument of Government, December 16, 1653.

50 Kenyon, *The Stuart Constitution 1603-1688*, 313. An ordinance for appointing Commissioners for approbation of Publique Preachers, March 20, 1654.

51 Ibid., 314.

had the ability to call to account any individual engaged in any public preaching, parish ministry, or as a schoolmaster. Scandalous behaviors included:

> ... profane cursing or swearing, perjury, subornation of perjury, such as shall hold, teach or maintain any of those popish opinions ... or be guilty of adultery, fornication, drunkenness, common haunting of taverns or alehouses, frequent quarrelling or fighting, frequent playing at cards or dice, profaning the Sabbath day, and such as do or shall allow the same in their families, or countenance the same in their parishioners or scholars; such as have publicly and frequently read or used the Common Prayer Book since the first of January last, or shall at any time hereafter do the same ...[52]

These two bodies were somewhat successful in creating both a national Presbyterian church and in allowing independent congregations to operate in tandem. The men who served on these committees had broad opinions in religious matters, like most things dealing with the church in the 1650s.[53] Even men who were later Restoration bishops appeared before the Triers to gain a living, as was the case for Simon Patrick, Laurence Womack, William Lloyd, and George Hall.[54] The Triers connections with men of Anglican leanings presented a problem during the Restoration: what to do with the collaborating ministers, who were numerous. It was a younger generation of men who presented themselves to the committee for examination, those that came of age during the repression of the Church of England. This gen-

---

52 Ibid., 315. An Ordinance for ejecting Scandalous, Ignorant and Insufficient Ministers and Schoolmasters, August 28, 1654.

53 See Hughes, "'The Public Profession of these Nations," 93–114.

54 Spurr, *The Restoration of the Church of England*, 8. Simon Patrick became a noted writer defending the Church of England. William Lloyd was one of the original nonjuring bishops.

eration had entered the purged universities and many had limited or no access to traditional Anglican theological training, but a great number had a fondness for the Church of England, which became evident during the Restoration when they took episcopal ordination and served to defend the restored church. Many of them had stellar clerical careers and some became High Churchmen and defenders of episcopacy. Sheldon and many of his friends and associates were guilty by their loyalty to the prayer book, which Cromwell's committee considered as scandalous as sexual or moral misconduct.

Cromwell's difficulties with parliament continued and led to direct military rule, financed by an unparliamentary tax on royalists. The rule of the major generals was unpopular and added to the burden of the overtaxed royalists in England. The moral laws, which shut down the racetracks and brothels as royalist enclaves, removed another outlet of the population and cemented the unpopularity of rule by military men. In 1656, Cromwell called a parliament to sit, but used the major generals to influence the elections and continued to use them to remove "objectionable" members. Cromwell then disowned both the actions of the major generals and the republican-leaning MPs. This purged body offered Cromwell the crown and made the position of Lord Protector hereditary. Cromwell refused the crown, but agreed on making his office hereditary. Problems continued to grow between the Lord Protector and his parliament forcing him to dissolve the body much like his kingly predecessor. In fact, many of the arguments used by Cromwell's parliaments echoed those in the parliaments of Charles I. Parliament demanded a share in the rule of the kingdom and when that was not forthcoming, it became very difficult to deal with. Cromwell's death in September 1658 and succession by his eldest son Richard only increased tensions. People began to look for another option. Evelyn recorded the stress of the time: "The Nation was now in extreame Confusion & unsetled, betweene the Amies & the Sectaries: & the

Poore *Church* of *England* breathing as it were her last, so sad a face of things had over-spread us."[55]

In this tense atmosphere, General George Monck, the commander of the Scottish forces, came onto the scene. Monck served as both a royalist commander and a parliamentary one, and from his viewpoint in Scotland, he watched the crumbling of parliamentary rule with dismay. He refashioned his army into a force loyal to himself.[56] Monck marched his army south, reaching London in early February 1660. He helped the purged members of the Rump to parliament on the condition that writs for a new election went out. Monck seemed committed to constitutional government, whatever form it took.

The decade of the 1650s was wearying to man who worked to keep a remnant of the church alive. These men made personal sacrifices for what they believe to be right and honorable. Any period of war and strife has loss and these men were no exception. The loss of the king was shocking to many in the kingdom, but for men like Sheldon, the king was not just a distant figure, but also someone he knew and worked with for the good of the church. It was a more personal and poignant loss that stayed with him. Sheldon lost his comfortable life as an Oxford don and his chance to influence scholars to come. This was probably the goal of his pre-war life and he was never to return to it—other concerns consumed his time. His Bible recorded personal losses: his elder brother Ralph died in 1656, as did one of his hosts during his wandering during the decade. Sir Robert Shirley died in the Tower as a prisoner following a failed royalist plot. Shirley had kinship ties to Sheldon through his marriage to Katherine Okeover. Sheldon offered the funeral oration for his patron, who was building a private and sumptuous chapel at the time of his death.

---

55 Evelyn, vol. 3, 231.

56 Ronald Hutton, "George Monck, First Duke of Ablemarle," *ODNB*, 15.

"He loved our nation and he hath built us a synagogue."[57] Sheldon's great friend and co-worker in the cause of the church, Hammond died just before the Restoration, falling victim to the gallstones that plagued him throughout this period. Sheldon entered the new chapter of his life upon the recalling of the king-in-exile and he would go far.

---

57 M. Dorman, "Sir Robert Shirley, Fourth Baronet," *ODNB*, 1.

CHAPTER 5

MONARCHY AND CHURCH
TRIUMPHANT, 1660-1662

The triumphant return of the king in May 1660 was cause for great celebration for the faithful remnant of the Church of England after more than a decade of underground existence. After word of the king's return spread, churches across the country dusted off forbidden prayer books and used the liturgy. Ministers offered prayers for the king and maypoles went up in villages and communities across the kingdom even before Charles II landed. Pepys recorded, "Today I hear they were very merry at Deale, setting up the Kings flag upon one of their Maypooles and drinking to his health ... which the soldiers of the Castle threatened, but durst not oppose."[1] The world changed once more for the men and women of this period. "The world turned upside down" by innovations in political and religious life returned, at least to the appearance of the world right side up.

Sheldon removed to London in late April 1660 and quickly met up with his old friend Morley, who was trying to smooth the way for the king's return and the religious settlement that would follow. The clerical leaders met May 4 and Sheldon may have been present, even though his name was not on the roll. Duppa, Wren, Morley, John Barwick, and John Warner discussed the restoration of the Church of England. The actions and importance of these men in the Restoration settlement as both religious and political leaders have been interpreted differently. Dr. Robert Bosher saw all of these men as devotees of the Laudian program of the 1630s, working closely with political figures close to the king. Others

---

1 Pepys, *The Diary of Samuel Pepys*, vol. 1, 121. May 1, 1660.

wished to place the complicated settlement largely in the hands of one or two men, creating a hybrid Anglican-Royalist messiah. John Spurr takes another view and makes the Restoration Settlement a lengthy and evolutionary process over decades, including many different people. There were leaders, but many who also adapted to the changing times.[2]

The Interregnum left a legacy of political and religious questions that needed solving with the return of the monarchy and episcopacy in 1660. Radical religious groups like the Quakers, Ranters, and even the Baptists multiplied in the tolerant society of the protectorate. These dissenters opposed any move to restore a national church. Puritans, most of them in the Presbyterian fold, wanted a truly reformed comprehensive church settlement—something they had desired since the reign of James I. The return of an episcopally governed Church of England was a triumph for the Anglicans, who lost everything during the Cromwellian regime. The church settlements and practices of the Interregnum created challenges in doctrine, in practice, and for dominant figures, causing factions to form both inside and outside of the Church of England. John Gauden, a moderate Anglican divine, preached before Monck and the Mayor of London, arguing for a reduced episcopacy like that advocated by Ussher in the 1640s. In 1660, he preached that church leadership needed "the fatherly gravity, prudence and eminence of godly and reverend bishops; by the brotherly assistance, and son like subordination of sober and orderly presbyters ... and humble and diligent deacons."[3] Both Anglicans and Presbyterians saw radical dissenters as a source of instability and republican feeling.

---

2   For a breakdown of the different views, see Spurr, *The Restoration of the Church of England*, Bosher, *The Making of the Restoration Settlement*, Green, *The Re-Establishment of the Church of England*, and Fincham and Tyacke, *Altars Restored*.

3   Spurr, *The Restoration of the Church of England*. 33.

Charles offered his subjects a "liberty to tender consciences" from Breda. The clergy and MPs had the unenviable task of defining the scope of that liberty. A liberty of tender consciences was difficult to construct due to the multitude of opinions surrounding the very idea of consciences. A small minority believed in full toleration for all religious persuasions, but this position linked itself to the more radical sort of nonconformist. Another position was to establish a broad church settlement along the lines of the church endorsed by James I. This position had support from a majority of those associated with Presbyterianism and men within the Church of England who desired as broad a settlement as possible. Additionally, within the established Church, one group wanted to return to the hegemony of the Church of England with a strict adherence to the liturgy and other practices. These groups, like many in the period, were fluid, with people moving between them at different points in their lives and their experiences. Sheldon and many of his friends and associates belonged to this final group, where they remained until their deaths.

Sheldon early on had a connection to the king. Charles II landed at Dover May 25, 1660 and then went to Canterbury. At Canterbury, the son met the father's confessor and loyal servant. The connection that Charles II felt for Sheldon was probably tenuous at best. Sheldon was a loyal servant to the martyred king and his church, but the king and cleric had little in common besides a devotion to the memory of a dead man. Sheldon quickly gained the young king's goodwill, however, and reaped the rewards associated with having a powerful patron. Sheldon became Dean of the Chapel Royal just over a week after the king's triumphant return to London. Sheldon, aided and assisted by John Earle and George Morley, worked to fill vacancies within the Church of England.

The state of the Church of England at the Restoration was unsettled. There were 8600 parishes in England and around 3600 ministers suffered some sort of disturbance between 1640-1660. The aforementioned number included 1100 cathedral or university clerics, who by and large had a rougher experience during the Interregnum.[4] The vast majority of parish clergy kept their livings and survived the turbulent decades without problem. However, the men who kept their livings without problem had new questions raised about their conformity and orthodoxy. There was an additional problem: nearly twenty years without ordinations and the filling of vacant parish positions left a number of parishes without any minister, except those who preached before dissenting congregations. English cathedrals lost their valuables to provide for the king or once captured by parliament to pay for the other side. Lichfield's cathedral, for example, was purified by parliamentary troops, who destroyed the choir stalls, smashed 12,000 feet of painted glass, destroyed tombs and monuments, and burned the chapter house's library.[5] The collegiate chapels of Oxford and Cambridge were also missing plate and the parliamentary visitation and occupations had not treated those places kindly. During the Restoration, in All Souls Chapel, the altar was quickly reinstalled to its previous place of honor when Sheldon had served as Warden.[6] Overall, the church needed to fill vacancies with loyal and conformable men who agreed with prayer book orthodoxy. So the real issue was finding the right sort of men to work with the episcopal establishment, and this task fell to the Dean of the Chapel Royal and his loyal fellow workers.

In this post, Sheldon and his associates helped those deemed worthy for positions in the church by the individual's loyalty to the crown or the church. Robert Say, Provost of Oriel, petitioned the king for the Rectory of Orpinton, Kent, which was void by

---

4 Ibid., 6–7.

5 Stanford Lehmberg, *English Cathedrals* (London: Hambledon and London, 2005), 196.

6 Fincham and Tyacke, 316.

death of the previous rector. Sheldon attached a note in Say's favor when the petition went before the king, as he did for numerous others.[7] An additional case was that of Edward Cotton, whom Sheldon and Morley recommended for the Archdeaconry of Cornwall and a canon's position in Exeter. The two were careful to note that the elder Cotton had lost a great deal of money for his loyalty.[8] Sheldon also received letters detailing the suffering of the clergy that remained in England.

> So far as I can learn, there is not a clergyman living who hath done or suffered (put them both together) more for the king, the Church, & the poor clergy than I have; neither can be any more ready or willing to du & suffer the like again—when justly called. Rev'd Sir, If you ask me why I write all this; and why to you? Know I pray, that you may be pleased to witness for me; that tho I am utterly forgotten in all yet that I have not forgot in any kind to discharge the part of a true & loyal subject to my Sovereign Lord, nor of an dutifull son to my Holy Mother the Church.[9]

The chronicles of the suffering clergy during the Interregnum became a useful tool to use in the ever-present propaganda battles between those of differing religious opinions. Sheldon and his compatriots also dealt with requests concerning the proper ordering or re-ordering of places where a bishop had installed a minister, but that individual minister could not take the living due to a prior ejection or another assuming the living. Francis Davis belonged to the former category, and for his sufferings, he

---

7   *CSPD*, C2, vol. 4, 63. June 22, 1660.

8   Ibid., vol. 6, 83. Cotton received both livings at the end of August 1660. One assumes the loyalty and loss of money was both for religious and royalist leanings. This was a directive sent from the dean of the Chapel Royal to his religious brethren in Exeter and Cornwall, who did as he requested.

9   MS Tanner 49, f. 23a. Jo: Rottens to Sheldon, September 12, 1660.

became Archdeacon of Llandaff with Sheldon's favor and recommendation.[10]

Sheldon also had to serve as mediator of the even more contentious religious settlement in Scotland. The Scots had recognized Charles II as king nearly a decade before their southern neighbors, but episcopacy was at best problematic in the northern kingdom. In March 1661, Charles sent instructions to his Scottish Privy Council of his intention to restore the episcopacy. Charles rationalized that doing so would "promote its better harmony with the government of the churches of England and Ireland."[11] James Sharp, former Presbyterian and future Archbishop of St. Andrews, met Sheldon and Morley in April 1661 and began his turn toward episcopacy. Sharp wrote before the meeting to Patrick Drummond in March 1661, "... I lookt upon Dr. Sheldon as a judicious person, his text of pacifica°n is fitted to ther purpose; they are going on with ther work we hear."[12] Sharp was nominated to the see of St. Andrews on November 14 and was consecrated December 15, using the prayer book by Sheldon and Morley.[13]

The restructuring of the church depended upon the selection of the right men for the job. Sheldon was a key player in returning the right sorts of men to important positions in the church and universities. One such man was William Sancroft, who became Sheldon's eventual successor at Canterbury. He wrote to the younger man, "I am sorry there are such barrs against your Enter-

---

10 *CSPD*, C2, vol. 12, 219. Davis was appointed October 16, 1660 to Llandaff.

11 Harris, *Restoration*, 113.

12 Osmund Airy, Ed., *The Lauderdale Papers*, vol. 1 (London: The Camden Society, 1884), 81. The text pacifica°n referred to by Sharp is unknown. It may have been a manuscript that circulated among Sheldon's circle in the 1650s.

13 David George Mullen, "James Sharp," *ODNB*, 3. See also Alasdair Raffe, "Presbyterians and Episcopalians: The Formation of Confessional Cultures in Scotland, 1660-1715," *The English Historical Review* 125, no. 514 (2010): 570–598.

ing into Emmanuel Colledge; we must remove them for you the best way we can, and you ought not to decline this opportunity of doing the coll: and university service; I will set about it as soone as I can and you shall receive an account of what is done."[14] Sheldon worked with the king to have Sancroft incorporated at Cambridge. Sancroft was unsure if he desired to return to university life, but Sheldon pressed the issue and the need for the right sort of able men in those places. Men who wanted to protect and to ensure the survival of the Church of England were on Sheldon's mind and Sancroft fit the bill admirably.

> The church and university want your service in these parts and you must not prefer your personal content before your duty to them; both your cantedentecy and advantage shall be considered and pleaded for as soone as may be. This enclosed wch the king will send to be there before you, will let you into the colledg without scruple, and I hope you will do much good there…for the king hath promised you a liberty (not withstanding any letters he shall send) to do what you think best for the promoting of piety and learning there, and if you need any assistance from him you shall have it. The moulding of new statutes for Cathedralls and some Colledges (when we have leasure for it) is like to be a part of your burden when you come among us; my declining age stands in need of fresh assistants, and when I shall be able to put those that are best able to serve the church in the readyest way to do it.[15]

Sheldon also helped pick candidates for promotion in the church. John Earles wrote, "I give you my most humble [and] hart[y] thanks for the great favour you intended mee, an likewise for the

---

14 MS Harleian 3784, f. 71. Sheldon to Sancroft, September 20, 1662.

15 MS Harleian 3784, f. 77. Sheldon to Sancroft, October 2, 1662.

good opinion of me (as well as great affection) that you thinke me capable of such a position in the Church."[16] Earles wished to decline the promotion due to his age, but less than two months later, he was sitting on his own see, Worcester, and was later translated to Salisbury.[17]

Sheldon as Dean of the Chapel Royal gave the official thanksgiving sermon for the king's restoration on June 28, 1660. Sheldon selected as the text for the sermon Psalm 18: 46-49.

> [46] The Lord liveth; and blessed be my rock; and let the God of my salvation be exalted.
>
> [47] It is God that avengeth me, and subdueth the people under me.
>
> [48] He delivereth me from mine enemies: yea, thou liftest me up above those that rise up against me: thou hast delivered me from the violent man.
>
> [49] Therefore will I give thanks unto thee, O Lord, among the heathen, and sing praises unto thy name.[18]

The sermon drew the analogy between King David's turbulent relationship and war with Saul to the experiences of Charles I and Charles II. Sheldon preached that the best and godliest of men or kings have had enemies and therefore needed God's aid in delivering them from their enemies. Thus, the godly man or king offered thanksgiving for divine deliverance. Sheldon warned of the danger of constant observation that a king endured: "for they stand high, and all eyes are upon them, nothing they say or do escapes observation and censure; if anything be amiss they are sure to hear of them to their greatest disadvantage."[19] Shel-

---

16 MS Tanner 48, f. 46. John Earles to Sheldon, September 25, 1662.

17 John Spurr, "John Earles," *ODNB*, 2.

18 *Holy Bible*, King James Version (Grand Rapids, MI: Zondervan, n.d.).

19 Gilbert Sheldon, *David's Deliverance* (London: Timothy Garthwait, 1660), 5.

don's sermon was conservative and he used non-inflammatory language as the future of the church was far from settled at this early point. Sheldon alluded to his former master, however: "... if they cannot be justly charged with any miscarriage, yet that helps not: Innocency is no protection for them; their place and power is crime enough to pull them down, others would be where they are."[20] Sheldon reminded his audience that no great biblical king or modern ruler was immune from the grumbling of his subjects and that furthermore no virtue, religion, or government existed without some belief in a higher and judging Divine Power that called governments and individuals to account. God allowed the collected sins of the nation to bring about destruction and disorder to the land.

> ... thus it would have been till we had been utterly consumed, had not he had mercy on us, had he not raised up a *Deliverer,* never to be mentioned without Honour, nor to be forgotten in the *Prayers* of all good People, that God would multiply his favours and blessings, both temporal and spiritual, upon his *Person* and *Posterity* for many Generations.[21]

Just as Israel saw deliverance from the threat of war and disarray through David and Solomon, so England would see it through Charles II and his heirs. Furthermore, Sheldon offered the timely advice that if the king had a reason to give thanks to God, so did all his subjects, regardless of condition. He reminded his audience what they owed thankfulness, using careful language so as not to inflame those of differing religious opinions:

> So that if we consider what we have escaped, the *miseries of War,* and of a *Civil War,* the worst of all wars; and what we have gained, the *blessings of Peace,* and *Kingly Govern-*

---

20 Ibid., 6.

21 Ibid., 17–18.

ment the best preserver of them; a gracious PRINCE, and together with him our *Laws, Liberties, Properties;* the *free exercise of Religious Duties,* indeed all that is or ought to be dear to a Christian Common-wealth in this world.[22]

The free exercise of religious duties was a sticky issue for many interested in the settlement of the church, but early into Charles II's return, vague words soothed fears and kept the fragile peace between the two largest religious groups: the Church of England men and the Presbyterians.

Whatever the real relationship between Sheldon and the king, many believed that Sheldon was the closest cleric to Charles II and a source of influence on the younger man's decisions; this relationship developed from the loyalism Sheldon offered to his former royal master. Many of Charles I's former confidants and allies found themselves in positions of influence around the young king, despite differences in attitudes and experiences during the Interregnum. Charles II needed trustworthy men around him and those who had served his father and the monarchy even when it was in abeyance had trustworthy political and religious pedigrees.

Duppa wrote to the Dean of the Chapel Royal, complaining about the lengthy passage of time without a decisive settlement of the church. Duppa moved from Salisbury to Richmond by the king's request, to serve Charles II. He noted his concern for the little being done for the church: "What may be done now the Bp of London is arrived (whose absence was the only honest Apology we could have that nothing was done in behalf of the Church) I know not, but if nothing be, we have lost our Excuse."[23] With the

---

22 Ibid., 32.

23 MS Tanner 49, f. 17. Brian Duppa to Sheldon, August 11, 1660. The ailing William Juxon, Bishop of London, returned to the capital as the most senior remaining bishop.

remaining bishops of the church returned to the king's proximity, Duppa and others believed the affairs of the church deserved, nay demanded, the king's attention. Duppa wrote:

> You are the only person about his Majesty, that I have confidence in and I persuade myself that as none has ease more, so none is likely to prevail on his Heart more, and where was never more need of it, for all the profess'd enemies of our Church, look upon this as the critical time to use their dernier resort to shake his Majesties constancy. But I hope by this time you have recover'd those buried papers, wch can't but have a powerfull influence upon so dutifull a soul as his. I shall wait upon you as soon as I hear, that my coming may be anyway usefull. In the mean time I am the more at ease, because I know you stand and are diligently upon your Watch.[24]

The vow Sheldon preserved underground for thirteen years was the powerful promise of Charles I to restore the church to a state of power and prestige, and it guided his policies during the Restoration.

> I do here promise and solemnly Vow, in the Presence and for the Service of Almighty God, That if it please the Divine Majesty, of his Infinite Goodness, to restore to me my Just Kingly Rights, and to re-establish me in my Throne, I will wholly give back to his Church all those Impropiations, which are now held by the Crown; and what Lands soever, I do now enjoy, or shou'd enjoy, which have been taken away, either from any Episcopal See, or any Cathedral or Collegiate Church, from any Abby, or other Religious House. I likewise promise for hereafter to hold them from the Church, under such reasonable Fines and Rents as shall be set down by some

---

24 MS Tanner 49, f. 17.

conscientious Persons, whom I propose to chuse with all Uprightness of Heart, to direct me in this Particular. And I must humbly beseech God to accept this my Vow, and to bless me in the Design I have now in hand, through Jesus Christ our Lord. Amen.[25]

The king vowed these things in April 1646 while living in Oxford. Whether the vow was true or a clever piece of propaganda, more people than Sheldon knew of its existence. Echard recorded that Sheldon revealed the "King's Vow" August 21, 1660, only ten days after the aforementioned letter from Duppa, and it lined up with the opinions many held about their martyred royal master. The men who fought to preserve a remnant during the Interregnum received positions of prominence; their devotion to restore the Church of England and protect it from its enemies did not waver in the new political climate. In their view, restoring the church was preordained and something desired by both God above and the king below.

One early indication that the religious settlement was not going to please everyone was the return of the bishops. Sheldon took the oath of Supremacy and Allegiance October 23, 1660, after being elected bishop of London upon Juxon's elevation to Canterbury.[26] Sheldon, Humphrey Henchman (Salisbury), George Morley (Worcester), Robert Sanderson (Lincoln), and George Griffiths (St. Asaph) were consecrated as bishops on October 28, 1660 at Henry VII's chapel at Westminster Abbey. Surviving bishops Brian Duppa (Winchester), Matthew Wren (Ely), John Warner (Rochester), Henry King (Chichester), and the new

---

25 L. Echard, *An Appendix to the Three Volumes of Mr. Archdeacon Echard's History of England Consisting of Several Explanations and Amendments as well as New and Curious Additions to that History* (London: Jacob Tonson, 1720), 551. This item found in Miscellaneous Tracts 1720-1661, Bodleian, Oxford.

26 *CSPD*, C2, vol. 19, 320.

Archbishop of York, Accepted Frewen consecrated the five men nominated to join them as leaders of the church.[27]

The consecration included a sermon preached by John Sudbury, a prebend of the Abbey. Sudbury's sermon used the text 1 Timothy 3:1: "This is a true saying, If a man desire the office of a bishop he desireth a good work."[28] From the outset, the sermon unabashedly praised the office and duties of a bishop in the church. The dedicatory addressed to Lord Clarendon stated:

> ... I will say no more to them here, than that the peace of the *Kingdome* is so bound up with that of the *Church*, that he that is a friend to the one, cannot be an *enemy* to the other: And the Office and Dignity of a Bishop is so *necessary* to the peace and safety of the Church, that the opposing of the *one* must needs beget disorder and confusion in the *other*.[29]

Sudbury argued that the office of a bishop was necessary and needful for many reasons, primarily to keep the peace and unity in the church and the state. He used the reasoning that religion was the best way to control the multitude. An individual minister had great influence over his congregation and it followed "... that there is scarce any *Errour* so *grosse* which some of them will not believe, or any *Wickedness* so *great* which some of them will not practice, and think thereby to do God service, if it be preach'd to them as a matter and duty of *Religion*."[30] This was in Sudbury's mind a large part of what led the nation into rebellion and war.

---

27 Spurr, "Gilbert Sheldon," 6. See also *Fasti Ecclesiae Anglicanae*, vols. 2, 3, 4, 7 for a listing of clerical personnel relating to the consecrating bishops.

28 KJV, Zondervan.

29 John Sudbury, *A Sermon Preached at the Consecration of the Right Reverend Fathers in God, Gilbert Lord Bishop of London, Humphry Lord Bishop of Sarum, George Lord Bishop of Worcester, Robert Lord Bishop of Lincolne, George Lord Bishop of St. Asasph* (London: R. Royston, 1660), Dedicatory.

30 Ibid., 6.

The largest duty of the bishop, according to Sudbury, was to over-see the congregations and their respective ministers in his diocese to prevent the teaching of religious errors and to remove those unfit for positions in the church. Sudbury answered the common complaint that the bishops were not preaching with "The work of the Bishops ... was not so much to convert Infidels, as to con-fute Hereticks and Schismaticks, not so much to gather the sheep in the fold, as to keep them from going astray, and to keep the Wolves from entering among them."[31] Bishops preached, but not in regular rotation, because it was one part of a multitude of their duties, unlike parish priests, who had preaching and teaching as a primary function of their living.

Before the consecrations and filling of vacant bishoprics, in June 1660, Charles II issued a proclamation forbidding the ejection of any minister until Parliament resolved the issue. William Prynne orchestrated the Act for Settling Ministers in September 1660. Prynne argued that any man with ordination by any ecclesias-tic person from January 1, 1642 was the lawful minister unless a previous minister lived.[32] The act confirmed all ministers except those who denied infant baptism (like Baptists and Quakers), petitioned for regicide, or held a living while the previous min-ister still lived. This act was the first in a series of actions taken by the government to reorder religious life in England. However, this action also caused a number of complaints and lawsuits that the overextended and not yet full strength episcopacy had to deal with. Sheldon received several complaints about Interregnum ministers refusing to vacate their livings to previous incumbents. A typical case was that of John Barwick, a friend and fellow work-er in the struggle to preserve the church:

> For presentation to the Rectory of Houghton-le-Spring, diocese of Durham, to which he was appointed by the

---

31 Ibid., 18.

32 N.H. Keeble, *The Restoration* (Oxford: Blackwell Publishing, 2002), 80.

Bishop, the lawful patron, on May 1, 1653, on decease of Dr. Hamlet Marshal; but the right to which Mr. Battersby, put in by Cromwell, when he was ejected for his loyalty, contends with him, having obtained, on false suggestions, His Majesty's presentation thereto.[33]

Over 700 parishes experienced a change in ministers, 300 due to the survival of the original incumbent. Richard Baxter was one example of a man who lost his living at Kidderminster due to the survival of his predecessor.[34]

Charles II followed his promise at Breda with the Worcester House Declaration, in October 1660. This declaration reconfirmed Charles II's ideas of tolerance and moderate episcopacy. The Presbyterians in London reassured their king that they were loyal and wanted little more than to aid in the restructuring of the church. However, the Presbyterians and Puritans faced an uphill battle, as they had to live with the legacy of their decisions two decades before. The minsters ejected and barred from universities never forgot who caused their suffering, despite new claims of loyalty.

Wee your Majesties most loyall Subjects, cannot but acknowledge it is a very great mercy of God, that immediately after your so wonderfull and peaceable restauraton unto your Throne and Government for which wee bless his name, hee hath stirred up your Royall tears to a zealous Testimonie against all prophaness in the people; so to endeavour a happy Composing of the differences, and healing of the sad breaches which are in the Church ... In humble Conformity to this your Majesties Christian designe, wee takeing it for granted that there is a frind agreement betweene our brethren and us in doctrin-

33 *CSPD*, C2, vol. 6, 87. June 1660.

34 Spurr, *The Restoration of the Church of England*, 34.

all truths of the Reformed Religion, and in substantiall parts of Divine worship; and that the differences are only in some various Conceptions about the antient forme of Church Government, and in some particulars about Liturgy and Ceremonies: doe in all humble obedience to your Majestie represent.[35]

Charles II's opinions regarding church governance looked for accommodation from both Church of England men and Presbyterians. Thus in the restored Church of England, the king and some of his ministers desired "no bishop shall ordain, or exercise any part of jurisdiction which appertains to the Censures of the Church, without the advice and assistance of the presbyters."[36] Charles praised the existing bishops as "men of great and exemplary piety in their lives, which they have manifested in their notorious and unexampled suffering during these late distempers."[37] Perhaps the most significant matter addressed lay in the promise to appoint a commission to review the *Book of Common Prayer*.

... though we do esteem the liturgy of the church of England, contained in the Book of Common Prayer and by law established to be the best we have seen, yet, since we find some exceptions made against several things therein, we will appoint an equal number of learned divines of both persuasions to review the same and to make such alterations as shall be thought most necessary.[38]

In September, Charles II appointed a number of moderate bishops who agreed with the principles of the Declaration. John Gauden was one of the men elevated to the episcopacy, as Bishop of Ex-

---

35 MS Tanner 49, f. 7. Presbyterian Proposal to Charles II, 1660.

36 Browning, 367. Worcester House Declaration, October 25, 1660.

37 Ibid., 367.

38 Ibid., 369.

eter.[39] Sheldon was not impressed with those who espoused views on moderate episcopacy or a willingness to make conciliatory gestures to those outside the church, especially the Presbyterians.

The Church of England had numerous defenders during the Interregnum and these defenses re-emerged as the first arguments in the settlement of the church. The defenders of episcopacy and liturgical services wrote against the tyranny of Presbyterian Directories of worship. One such defender was John Bramhall. Bramhall succeeded Ussher to the archbishopric of Armagh in 1660 and was a notable defender of the Church from the dual threat of Papists and Puritans. For Bramhall and others, Presbyterians were simply older Puritans writ large. Constitutional scholar and jurist, John Selden, wrote, "To know what was generally believed in all ages, the way is to consult the Liturgies, not any man's private writing. As if you would know how the Church of England serves God, go to the Common Prayer Book, consult not this or that man."[40] Opinions about how the church would look once the dust cleared revolved around the major issues of the prayer book and liturgy. The issue of episcopacy was moot, thanks to the restoration of the bishops to vacant sees around the kingdom. The bishops would also return to the Lords and take an active part in the Cavalier Parliament's agenda upon the July 30, 1660 revocation of the act that banned the bishops from sitting in the House of Lords.[41] The bishops returned in November 1661, when parliament reconvened. The House of Lords was strengthened in its pro-Anglican stance when two archbishops and twenty-four bishops resumed the seats taken from them in 1642.[42]

---

39 Spurr, *The Restoration of the Church of England*, 35. Davies, vol. 2, 368.

40 More and Cross, 178, John Selden *Table Talk*, section LXXXI.

41 Keeble, *The Restoration*, 91. The act banning bishops from any secular jurisdiction was called the "Clerical Disabilities Act," which passed February 13, 1642.

42 Seaward, *The Cavalier Parliament*, 56–57.

The Savoy Conference had the duty of revising the prayer book and liturgy. The Savoy Conference received royal authorization on March 25, 1661 and convened April 15 through July 21 of the same year.[43] Two distinct groups emerged within the debates of the conference. Presbyterians, who hoped for a broad church settlement, faced the Anglicans, who varied in the interpretations of what instituted conformity to the liturgy. Among Anglicans, some wanted the church to return to the moderate episcopacy evident during the time of James I, some wanted to continue in some fashion with the Laudian programs, and others wanted prayer book orthodoxy. Sheldon was among those who favored orthodoxy and cohesion amongst the Anglican position at large. Even among Presbyterians, there were divisions over what was absolutely necessary to remain in the established church and what practices made it necessary to leave the church. Consensus was hard to find between the two groups and their accompanying sub-groups. However, the bishops found common ground first. Orthodoxy meant conformity to the rubrics and liturgy of the *Book of Common Prayer.* Outward conformity was all that was necessary; gone were the bitter theological debates of previous decades. What mattered now was the practical expression of religious belief under the umbrella of prayer book orthodoxy.

Outside the conference, the Cavalier Parliament wanted a return to the 1604 *Book of Common Prayer,* convinced that the monarchy, the church, and the liturgy supported one another. The Commons decided on June 25, 1661 "to view the several laws for confirming the Liturgy of the Church of England ... and to bring in a compendious Bill to supply any defect in the former laws, and to provide for an effectual conformity to the Liturgy of the Church for the time to come."[44] This action was taken with the knowledge that the Savoy Conference was working on liturgi-

---

43 Davies, vol. 2, 368.

44 Bosher, 223.

cal revisions. The cavaliers and some of the restored bishops and clergy viewed the prayer book as persecuted and paid for with the martyrdoms of Charles I and William Laud.[45] Sheldon was busy with his duties as a Privy Counselor, Dean of the Chapel Royal, and Master of the Savoy, but he was working with MPs in the Cavalier Parliament before he took his own seat in the Lords in November.

The conference was as much a political tool as a liturgical one. The men of the Great Tew Circle arrived in positions of power politically and spiritually and affected the outcome of the restoration settlements. It was a period for Sheldon, like many others, to renew old friendships face-to-face after a decade of letter writing and praying for the return of the monarchy and the church. Gilbert Sheldon, Bishop of London, and Chancellor Edward Hyde, Earl of Clarendon, met at Lord Falkland's Great Tew Estate, forming a connection that survived civil war, exile, and public office. However, new tensions and changed opinions caused many of this circle to diverge in matters religious or political. The bishop's party had Accepted Frewen, Archbishop of York, as its nominal leader. The actual mantle of leadership fell to Sheldon. His fellow workers were Robert Sanderson, Bishop of Lincoln, John Gauden, Bishop of Exeter, George Morley, Bishop of Worcester, and John Cosin, Bishop of Durham. The Presbyterian leader was Edward Reynolds, newly appointed Bishop of Norwich. He selected two London ministers, Edward Calamy and Mathew Newcomen, Professor John Wallis of Oxford, and the eminent Richard Baxter, who declined a bishopric.[46]

Liturgists Wren and Cosin agreed that the prayer book could be improved; Cosin wished to adapt it along the lines of the Scottish prayer book of 1637. Robert Sanderson, among others, used a slightly modified prayer book during the Interregnum. Sheldon

---

45 Davies, vol. 2, 363–364.

46 Ibid., 368.

encouraged his brethren not to modify the liturgy in the Interregnum, but to continue to use it whenever possible. Baxter wanted a liturgy acceptable to both Presbyterians and Anglicans that would adapt the wording and make certain ceremonies and behaviors optional. Sheldon, however, opened the Savoy Conference saying the bishops were happy with the prayer book as it was. The Presbyterians wanted revisions; therefore, they had the responsibility to present both their exceptions and alternatives. The Presbyterians produced a long list of exceptions from conformity to the prayer book—eighteen general in character and seventy-eight particular.[47] The Presbyterian criticisms of the liturgy were in large part historic objections to the liturgy advanced from the days of Elizabeth and the Millenary Petition. For example, extemporaneous prayer should be allowed to supplement the liturgy, apocryphal readings should be banned, and the practice of naming godparents should not be resumed, among many others.

Baxter produced his own set of exceptions, which outlined his moderate viewpoint, echoing complaints from the past years of church disagreements. He differed from some of his other brethren by not standing completely against the prayer book.

> From the beginning I told them I was not of their mind, who charged the Common Prayer with false doctrine, or idolatry, or false worship in the matter of substance, nor that I took it to be a worship which a Christian might not lawfully join in, when he had not liberty and ability for better; and that I always took the faults of the Common Prayer to be, chiefly, DISORDER and DEFECTIVENESS; and so, that it was a TRUE WORSHIP THOUGH IMPERFECT.[48]

---

47 Ibid., 369.

48 A. Harold Wood, *Church Unity without Uniformity* (London: The Epworth Press, 1963), 185. See also Michael P. Winship, "Defining Puritanism in Restoration England: Richard Baxter and Others Respond to 'A Friendly De-

His main objections lay in the sequences of the prayer book and the wording of many of the prayers, especially the repetition of petitions already stated elsewhere. He also disagreed with the practice that all persons, regardless of worthiness, should partake in communion three times a year. He believed that ministers should not baptize the children of the ungodly if it went against the conscience of the minister. Baxter also presented an alternative liturgy written in a two-week span.

The main basis of the Presbyterian reforms was Ussher's model of limited episcopacy. Ussher's idea returned to the use of bishops and presbyters in the primitive church. The bishop's work was in tandem with the work of the lower clergy, removing the distance between the offices. Ussher never dismissed episcopacy because of the historicity of the office. The basic requests of the Presbyterians can be simplified into four statements:

1. Freedom to use an alternative liturgy.

2. The right of pastors to exercise discipline in their own churches.

3. Freedom of ministers from subscribing to use the whole of the Prayer Book and particular ceremonies to which some objected.

4. Freedom from swearing canonical obedience to diocesan bishops.[49]

The bishops only answered seventeen of the ninety-six exceptions—three in general and fourteen of a particular nature. The most important was the requirement for the use of the Authorized Version for all scriptural readings.[50] The bishops believed that upholding the prayer book offered the best route for peace

---

bate,'" *The Historical Journal* 54, no. 3 (2011): 689–715.

49 A.H. Wood, 193.

50 Davies, vol. 2, 370.

and stability within the church. They believed that no one could write public prayers to satisfy everyone, but that the liturgy used scripture and had the weight of tradition and long use. The bishops considered "devotion apt to freeze or sleep, or flat in a long continued prayer" and that short prayers were preferable as worshippers were "therein often called upon and awakened by frequent 'Amens' and responses."[51] Extemporaneous prayer was to the bishops a tool of the mischievous and radical sectaries and had no place in proper worship.

The Savoy Conference was a complete failure in reaching any type of comprehensive church settlement. Despite the failure of the divines within the conference to come to any agreement, the political atmosphere made any Puritan or overtly Laudian Prayer Book doubtful. The loyalist Churchmen of the Interregnum found that working within the government was the easiest way to implement their desires and designs. The Cavalier Parliament consisted of many individuals who lost lands and faced persecution under the Cromwellian regime. These men were not tolerant of even the most moderate Presbyterians. This parliament acted in hopes of passing a new Act of Uniformity and the 1604 Prayer Book while the Savoy Conference was still in session.[52] The Convocation of Canterbury overlapped with the meetings at Savoy, but Charles pressed for a hurried settlement of the church. He authorized the convocation to work on the settlement of the Church within the rubric of already established ceremonies and the Thirty Nine Articles.[53] The Savoy Conference ended midsummer 1661, with little success. Both parliament and the Convocation reconvened in November 1661. The bishops were to sit in the House of Lords and Sheldon wrote to Cosin reminding him of their duty, "... for the King expects it from all of our or-

---

51 A.H. Wood, 196.

52 Davies, vol. 2, 372.

53 Bosher, 230.

der, and when his great business for his revenue and that of the Church is over, any may have liberty to return to his diocese."[54] Twenty-three of the twenty-seven bishops took their seats when parliament reconvened to vote on the settlement of the church.[55]

The Prayer Book of 1662 was conservative and completed in record time. The Convocation of Canterbury met from May 8 to July 31, 1661, reconvened November 21 to December 18, 1661, and sent the amended prayer book to the king on December 20.[56] Bishop Sanderson wrote the preface of the new *Book of Common Prayer*. In the preface, he repeated the arguments for its return and the illegality of those who spoke and wrote against it in times past.

> But when, upon His Majesty's happy Restoration, it seemed probable that, amongst other things, the use of the Liturgy also would return (the same having never been legally abolished) unless some timely means were used to prevent it, those men who under the late usurped powers had made it a great part of their business to render the people disaffected thereunto, saw themselves in a point of reputation and interest concerned (unless they would freely acknowledge themselves to have erred, which such men are very hardly brought to do) with their utmost endeavours to hinder the restitution thereof. In order whereunto divers pamphlets were published against the *Book of Common Prayer,* the old objections mustered up, with the addition of some new ones, more than formerly were used to make the number swell. In fine, great importunities were used to His Sacred Majesty that the said Book might be revised, and such alterations therein and additions thereunto made, as should

---

54 Ibid., 237.

55 Ibid.

56 Davies, vol. 2, 379.

be thought requisite for the ease of tender consciences. Whereuto His Majesty, out of his pious inclination to give satisfaction (so far as could be reasonably be expected) to all his subjects of what persuasion, did graciously condescend.[57]

Sanderson listed three reasons for the alterations: clearer direction for ministers of the divine service, removal of archaic terminology for current use, and inserting scripture of the Authorized Version.[58] The few additions were necessities. They inserted an Office for Adult Baptism useful to combat Baptist practices and for the use on natives converted on plantations. The prayers added included one for burial at sea. Prayers were added for the death of Charles I, commemorated on January 29, and the restoration and birth date of Charles II, celebrated on May 29. The major changes clarified ordination to the priesthood. The ordination formula changed for a priest from "receive the holy ghost" to "Receive the Holy Ghost, for the Office and work of a Priest, in the Church of God, now committed by the imposition of our hands."[59] Bishops ordained priests and the archbishop ordained bishops, using the formula "by the imposition of our hands." The bishops were no doubt attempting to insure the indispensability of the office and acting upon their shared beliefs about the proper ordering of the church. The Prayer Book received the final royal approval on May 19, 1662 and was to come into use by St. Bartholomew's Day, August 24, 1662, as a provision of the Act of Uniformity.[60]

The passage of the Prayer Book was one step towards the settlement of the church. The bishops had other concerns in their dioceses, as Robert Skinner of Oxford wrote:

---

57 More and Cross, 167–168, Preface, *Book of Common Prayer,* 1661.

58 Davies, vol. 2, 378.

59 Ibid., 382.

60 Ibid.

> I well hope to have seen that Uniform book of Articles
> [viz. for Visitation] before this day, resting assured
> that no pretences could take of your Ldsps resolutions
> from what so much concerns the herer & peace of
> the Church. If with that book of Articles, an Uniform
> Order of Consecrating Churches and Chapels came
> along with it; it would all to the gent satisfaction and
> pleasure me much ...[61]

The political atmosphere changed in 1660, with the November vote for the Cavalier Parliament. The Presbyterian faction in the new parliament, which began May 8, 1661, declined to fifty members.[62] The largely royalist and prayer book men of the Cavalier Parliament included many who fought for the martyred king or whose family members fought on the king's side against parliament. These men wanted nothing more than to turn back the clock to 1640, sweeping away twenty years of religious and political experimentation. Those with Puritan tendencies were discredited further by the January 1661 uprising of Fifth Monarchists. Venner's rebellion was never dangerous to the city of London or the newly constituted government, but it was evidence to many that religious nonconformity was the greatest danger to the church and the state. Baptists and Quakers tried to distance themselves from the small rebellion of fifty in London, but a royal proclamation on January 10 forbade any meetings of Quakers, Baptists, or Fifth Monarchists.[63] Secretary of State Sir Edward Nicholas and others believed that "under the specious pretense of Religion and piety" sectaries "hid their horrid designes."[64] Religious dissent in any form was a cloak for political rebellion and seditious activities.

---

61 MS Tanner 48, f. 14. Robert Skinner to Sheldon, June 26, 1662.

62 Keeble, 115.

63 Ibid., 116.

64 Ibid.

This was a dominant attitude among the members of the Cavalier Parliament strengthened by the coronation of Charles II in full episcopal regalia and ceremony the preceding April. Evelyn wrote of the occasion:

> ... his Majestie was placed in a Throne elevate before the Altar: Then the Bish: of Lond (the A Bishop of Canterbury being sick) went to every side of the Throne to present the King to the People ... attended by 3 Bishops went up to the Altar ... the sermon, which was preached by Dr. Morley then B: of Worcester.[65]

Evelyn was not present and drew his recollection from the news-sheets. Pepys attended the coronation and watched the magnificent spectacle. He recorded the king "taking the oath and having things read to him by the Bishopp, and his lord (who put on their capps as soon as the King put on his Crowne) and Bishopps came and kneeled before him."[66] The pageantry of the bishops in copes and episcopal dress serving and ministering to the king was an illustration of the deep connection between the church and the state, to the exclusion of other forms of religious life.

The Act of Uniformity drew from the existing Elizabethan Act of Uniformity, passed in 1559.[67] Religious conformity provided political peace and stability in the minds of many by reinforcing the order of society. Richard Allestree preached a sermon on the second anniversary of the restoration:

---

65 Evelyn, vol. 3, 281–282. April 23, 1661.

66 Pepys, vol. 2, 84. April 23, 1661. Both Pepys and Evelyn mention that Juxon was ill and that Sheldon took the lead in addressing the king during the coronation ceremony. Juxon performed the ceremonial anointing of the king with oil. The following April, Sheldon stood in for Juxon in performing the marriage service for the king and Princess Catherine of Braganza. Sheldon noted the significant date in his own Bible. Eng bib 1648 d 3.

67 Keeble, 117.

... when men once depart from Uniformity ... why may not divisions be as infinite as mens phansies? ... It is *one God, one Faith, one Worship* makes *hearts one*. Hands lifted up together in the Temple they will joyn and clasp: and so *Religion* does fulfill its name as a *religando*, binds Prince and subjects all together; and they who thus do seek the *Lord their God*, will also seek *David their King*.[68]

The 1662 Act of Uniformity was far stricter than its Elizabethan predecessor. The opening paragraphs of the act reminded the nation "that nothing conduceth more to the settling of the peace of this nation ... than an universal agreement in worship of Almighty God."[69] The Act of Uniformity targeted and ejected men who failed to conform, unlike the Act for Settling Ministers, which ejected men only if the incumbent still lived. The act required those receiving a clerical living to consent to everything in the *Book of Common Prayer,* follow the Thirty Nine Articles, renounce the Solemn League and Covenant, and receive ordination from a bishop. Each minister was to declare publicly:

I, A.B., do declare my unfeigned assent and consent to all and everything contained and prescribed in and by the book entituled, *The Book of Common Prayer and administration of the sacraments and other rites and ceremonies of the church according to the use of the Church of England, together with the psalter or psalms of David, pointed as they are to be sung or said in churches, and the form or manner of making, ordaining and consecrating bishops, priests and deacons.*[70]

The act reinforced the authority of the civil magistrates and denounced those who "take arms against the king ... or against those

---

68 Ibid., 118.

69 Browning, 378. Act of Uniformity, 1662.

70 Ibid. Act of Uniformity.

that are commissionated by him."[71] In particular, Article 37 of the Thirty Nine Articles reinforced the power of the king over matters civil and ecclesiastical. The provisions went into effect August 24, 1662 and ejected 936 ministers.[72] Most of the ejected ministers hoped for a church along the model of the Worcester House Declaration. They disliked the inflexibility of the language and the ceremonial requirements in the communion service. Some refused reordination at the hands of a bishop, because that action seemingly invalidated an earlier ordination by presbyters. Some lacked the time to review the new prayer book before the required date, like Richard Kidder.

> I had a good title to my living, I never took the Covenant or Engagement; I was entirely satisfied with episcopacy, and with a liturgy; I had no hand in the late confusions and was so far from it that I lamented them; I had orders from a bishop when it was dangerous to receive them that way. The truth is I had not due time given to me to consider, and was deprived of my living for not subscribing to a book that was not (as it ought to have been) laid before me.[73]

Kidder later conformed, following the lead of the majority of parish clergy, and accepted the rule of uniformity. The Act of Uniformity tarred moderate nonconformists and radical sectaries with the same brush, as a danger to order and stability. Sheldon believed that the only solution to the religious question was submission to the law.

> 'Tis only a resolute execution of the law that must cure this disease, all other remedies serve and will increase it; and it's necessary that they who will be governed as men

---

71 Ibid., 379. Act of Uniformity.

72 Spurr, *The Restoration of the Church of England*, 43.

73 Ibid., 44.

by reason and persuasions should be governed as beasts by power and force, all other courses will be ineffectual, ever have been so, ever will be so.[74]

There was no such thing as a loyal or moderate dissenter. The moderation and toleration espoused by Sheldon when a young man altered in the face of political and spiritual necessity and no doubt shifted due to his own experiences during the Interregnum. Sheldon believed firmly that the church's survival and the survival of the monarchy depended on conformity in law and in religious practice. He began the official process of linking membership in the Church of England with full rights of an Englishman in the state.

Sheldon worked tirelessly in the House of Lords and with his allies in the Commons to pass legislation he viewed as vital to the survival of the church. Sheldon wrote numerous letters to his subordinate bishops during the parliamentary sessions and encouraged attendance, especially when matters relating to the church were under discussion. During the discussion of the Act of Uniformity, the average clerical attendance was seventeen, or 70 percent.[75] Sir Henry Yelverton was one of his staunchest supporters and worked to get the Act of Uniformity through the Commons. Yelverton wrote to another supporter, Mr. Palmer:

> I am now returned from Whitehall, where I used my utmost endeavours to speak with my L London ... but I heard him locked up with severall Drs that ... I could not press to see him. I waited until it was very late, but then he was gone to bed, being much tired with business ... Tis true the Convocation do intend to frame a prayer for all to use before their sermons & truly did you live in

---

74 Keeble, 120. MS Carte 45, f. 151. September 15, 1663. Sheldon to Ormond.

75 Andrew Swatland, *The House of Lords in the reign of Charles II* (Cambridge: Cambridge University Press, 1996), 35.

this towne, and heare the extravagant passages are used by some, you would judge it an absolutely necessary for the service of the Church and the peace of the Nation. The bill of Uniformity wil quickly be don those additions only added, wch the Convocation hath made in the Liturgy being to be inserted by the Bps. There are some offices added as for the sea ... some words are added, some phrases altered, but as yet I have not seen it.[76]

The activities in the capital were of great interest to everyone and the sharing of news with those out of the metropolitan loop for however brief was vital. Yelverton wrote once again to Palmer, "But because I suppose, news wil be welcome I can only assure you that the resolute Councills are taken as to the Act of Uniformity, and that through the prudence and wisdom of my L London the Presbyterians were totally foiled last Thursday at the Privy Council."[77] The infighting among the political elites of England was not always so smooth, for neither Sheldon nor anyone else always received the outcome they desired. Longstanding friendships forged before the start of the Civil Wars often fell apart during the debates, as was the case between Sheldon and Clarendon over the issue of religious toleration. Sheldon wrote on August 30, 1662, just days after the contested Act of Uniformity went into effect:

And now My Ld not being able wayt upon you today as I intended & having this occasion to send, give me leave to complayne of your great unkindness upon Thursday, in offering to expose me to certain ruine by the parliament or the extreme hatred of the malicious party in whose jaws I must live, and never giving me the least notice of

---

76 MS Eng. let c 210, f. 69. Henry Yelverton to Palmer, June 29, 1660.

77 Ibid., f. 78. Yelverton to Palmer, July 8, 1662. Date noted in a different hand on the back of the letter.

it. You can not blame me, if it be sadly resented by, your Lordships very humble servant.[78]

Sheldon and Clarendon had a long friendship that lost its cordiality over the multitude of debates around the restoring of the church and state. Early in the debates, Clarendon wrote a pamphlet, *Second Thoughts,* arguing for the reasonableness of limited toleration in the settlement of religious matters in England. Clarendon's toleration was "... no more, than a bare Exemption from Penalties, with a Liberty of Exercising their Religion under such competent Restrictions, as shall be judged Necessary ... to Secure the Publique from a Riot, and Sedition."[79] Opinions like these offered publicly forced a division between the old friends, and Sheldon chose protecting the church above all. This small illustration was just one among many, indicating how divisive religious opinions were across the country and why the laws were unable to suppress the growing religious diversity in England.

---

78 MS Clarendon 77, f. 319. Gilbert Sheldon to Clarendon, August 30, 1662.

79 Edward Hyde, Earl of Clarendon, *Second Thoughts; or the CASE of a Limited Toleration* (London, 1660), 7.

CHAPTER 6

CHURCH IN CRISIS, EXTERNAL
1663-1677

The Cavalier Parliament, named for the viewpoint of the majority of its members, had different goals than its predecessors. The Cavaliers had several common characteristics: a landed gentry social background, service in the king's forces during the Civil War, connections with the royal court, and for some, the bitter experience of exile during the Interregnum.[1] Cavalier MPs and Anglican clerics worked in tandem to suppress sedition and rebellious heresies. As a group, they worked to protect and restore what they believed to be their rights and privileges. Cavaliers disliked religious radicals for embodying an ever-present threat of rebellion. In 1662, this body struck a blow at the independent presses used by many dissenting groups by implementing the Licensing Act. An unregulated press was a feature of a republican government and a past many were eager to avoid. The basic premise of the act called for a ban upon "... any heretical, seditious, schismatical or offensive books or pamphlets, wherein any doctrine or opinion shall be asserted or maintained which is contrary to the Christian faith or the doctrine or discipline of the Church of England."[2] Robert L'Estrange was the official given the task of discovering and disciplining unlicensed pamphleteers. L'Estrange also wrote pamphlets in support of Parliament's policies, especially those policies concerning Nonconformists. He crossed pens with Richard Baxter with *The Relapsed Apostate* (1661) and *State-Divinity* (1661).[3] Even before the Licensing

---

1 Geoffrey Smith, *The Cavaliers in Exile* (New York: Palgrave Macmillan, 2003), 51.

2 Browning, 67.

3 Harold Love, "Sir Robert L'Estrange," *ODNB*, 3. In some ways censorship

Act, John Bunyan's printer, Francis Smith, had his assets seized four times, and in both Sherborne and Exeter, pamphlets of Baptists and Presbyterians fed the fires.[4] The Licensing Act also applied to newspapers and the *London Gazette* was the only licensed newspaper.

In the heated and occasionally tense situation of the press, printed debates for toleration and comprehension were easy targets for the authorities. Those against toleration generally had the support and freedom to print against their opponents, but both sides used the power of the pen and press to spread their ideas. The debate over toleration encompassed many diverse opinions and personalities. The debaters framed the argument using secular, not spiritual, grounds. The spiritual reasons for or against toleration did not vanish, but a more rational language was developing in the realm of natural theology. Natural theologians argued that it was a natural right for man to worship God in any manner he saw fit. Additionally, their argument stressed liberty of conscience as a natural right. The Latitudinarians, those within the Church of England who favored a comprehensive church settlement, based much of their arguments for tolerance on natural theology. John Tillotson, a popular London preacher and future archbishop of Canterbury, was one such natural theologian. The Latitudinarians were one of the groups within the Church of England that emerged out of the heated religious and political climate of the period. Their ascendancy to the highest places in the church coincided with the ascension of William and Mary, but those with these ideas were in place all over the church during

---

and licensing of the press was a return to older forms. See Anthony Milton, "Licensing, Censorship, and Religious Orthodoxy in Early Stuart England," *HJ* 41: 625–651. James Sutherland, *The Restoration Newspaper and Its Development* (Cambridge: Cambridge University Press, 1986). Mark Knights, *Representation and Misrepresentation in Later Stuart Britain* (Oxford: Oxford University Press, 2005).

4 Hutton, 156. *The Restoration.*

the Restoration. The Latitudinarians needed to define themselves and find common ground with their High Church brethren to survive. They noted their orthodoxy in the traditions of the Church of England:

> In like manner they have a deep veneration of her Government, which they stedfastly believe to be in it self the best, and the same that was practiced in the times of the Apostles. They did always abhor the Usurpations of Scottish Presbytery, and the Confusion of Independent Anarchy; and do esteem it one of the methods which the Prince of darkness useth, to overthrow the Church and Religion, by bringing the Clergy into contempt, which experience tells us will necessarily follow upon the removing of several Dignities and preeminence among them; for when the Bishops are once leveled with ordinary Presbyters, the Presbyters will soon be trampled on by the meanest of the Laity: and when every Preacher would needs be a Bishop, every Rustick and Mechanick took upon him to be a Preacher.[5]

Sheldon, for his part, distrusted the Latitudinarians because of their leniency toward partial conformists.

The idea of liberty of conscience appeared in the *Declaration in Favour of Indulgence* (1662) and the *Declaration of Breda* (1660). Leading the call for complete toleration in religious matters were the Quakers and the Baptists. Both

---

5 Simon Patrick, *A Brief Account of the New Sect of Latitude-Men* (London, 1662), 8. For a discussion of rational religious trend in the Church of England and the Latitudinarians in particular, see B.J. Shapiro, "Latitudinarianism and Science in Seventeenth-Century England," *Past and Present* (40): 16–41. W.M. Spellman, *The Latitudinarians and the Church of England, 1660-1700* (Athens: University of Georgia Press, 1993). John Spurr in both "'Latitudinarianism' and the Restoration Church," *HJ* 31: 61–82 and "'Rational Religion' in Restoration England," *Journal of the History of Ideas* 49: 563–585.

of these sects advocated for some form of separation between church and state. By the end of the seventeenth century, both the Whigs and Nonconformists argued for toleration using a contract theory of government. They argued that government existed to protect property and that the greatest property of an individual was the conscience. They also argued that the government had the duty to preserve liberty by protecting all societies and organizations loyal to the state, including religious sects.[6] John Locke's (1689) *A Letter Concerning Toleration* entered the seventeenth-century debate too late to have a real impact in the late 1680s. His ideas echoed what he observed during the late seventeenth-century debates and profoundly influenced the next generation of thinkers and rebels.

The Convention Parliament tried to satisfy as many diverse parties as possible with the religious settlement and pleased few. The debate around the church raged in print, beginning before the Restoration and continuing until the Glorious Revolution. The major divisions of opinion developed into three categories: those in favor of full toleration, those opposed to any form of toleration, and those in favor of limited toleration. Those in favor of limited religious toleration believed "... nothing were more to be desired, in order to the lasting Happiness of this Nation, than a Conformity of all Minds, under the same Doctrine, and Worship in Religion."[7] However, this group of adherents believed that compromise in religion was permissible for the political well-being of the nation. Charles and Clarendon believed this. Clarendon explained:

---

6   Raymond C. Mensing Jr., *Toleration and Parliament* (Washington, DC: University Press of America, 1979), 25–27.

7   Edward Hyde, Earl of Clarendon, *Second Thoughts* (London, 1660), 2.

> ... I plead for a Toleration of Non-Conformists; thereby
> I intend no more, than an bare Exemption of Penalties,
> with a Liberty of Exercising their Religion such compe-
> tent Restrictions, as shall be judged Necessary, both to
> secure the Publique from a Riot, and Sedition, and to
> put a Difference between their Conventions, and the
> Religious Assemblies of the Church, Established by law.[8]

Charles expressed his own beliefs in a declaration that argued for
the necessity of guidelines in religion for the peace of the kingdom by the Act of Uniformity, but hoped for a day in which tender consciences had freedom in religious expressions. The church
needed its own precedent established and solidified from the tur-
moil of the Civil Wars and Interregnum before exceptions to its
orthodoxy were available. Charles hoped that once the Church
was settled by the Act of Uniformity, it might allow others freer
religious worship.

> ... we are glad ... to renew unto all our subjects concerned
> in those promises of indulgence by a true tenderness of
> conscience this assurance, that as in the first place we
> have been zealous to settle the uniformity of the Church
> of England in its discipline, ceremony and government
> ... as for what concerns the penalties upon those who
> (living peaceable) do not conform ... through scruple
> and misguided conscience.[9]

Limited toleration allowed Nonconformists to practice their
religion under a set of guidelines provided by the government.
Protected under the guise of limited toleration were those who
sought a broad Church of England and partial conformity to the
liturgy and prayer book.

---

8   Hyde, *Second Thoughts*, 7.

9   Browning, 373. Declaration in favour of toleration, December 26, 1662.

This ideology of comprehension was popular with moderate Presbyterian dissenters, like Richard Baxter. The comprehension favored by Baxter was with the moderates in the Church of England. He wrote, "... it was impossible for the Presbyterian and Independent party to associate with them that take them and their churches and all the reformed ministers and churches that have not episcopal ordination, for null."[10] The churchmen who rose to leadership in the restored episcopate were those Baxter found impossible to work with. Those who favored toleration made their assertions of religious freedom using many methods, but a common argument was to attack the liturgy using early church history.

> Again, if Liturgy, prescribed forms of prayer imposed by Authority, be so esential to the planting and preserving of the Christian Religion, I wonder why Christ (the Wisdom of the Father) and his Apostles (immediately inspired) did not digest, and prescribe, and by his Regal, and their Apostolical authority, impose a Liturgy on all Nations, and Christian Churches, and how they planted the Christian religion without it?[11]

In countering this type of argument, those against toleration stated the unassailable bond between the forces of civil government and ecclesiastical authority. The argument claimed that "take away these two pillars of Magistracy and Ministry, and you destroy both Church and State."[12] Anonymous author, G.S., wrote in *Monarchy Triumphing* (1661) about the danger of radicals in charge of the government and in the legality of the decisions questioning "Or can the Parliament of England consist without a House of Lords?"[13] Further questioning whether former parliamentarians

---

10 Richard Baxter, *The Autobiography of Richard Baxter*, ad. J. M. Lloyd Thomas and ed. N.H. Keeble (London, Dent, 1974), 137.

11 Thomas Bolde, *Rhetorick Restrained* (London, 1660). 6.

12 Thomas Hall, *The Beauty of Magistracy* (London, 1660), 3.

13 G.S., *Monarchy Triumphing over Traiterous Republicans* (London: T. R.,

and republicans, who in the view of the author trampled on the religious and civil liberties of the people, he wrote: "Are these the acts of men who are likely to secure our Religious and Civil Liberties?"[14] This author feared the answer was no. The fear of religious radicals fomenting rebellion seemed proven correct with Venner's Rebellion in January 1661. Thomas Venner's Fifth Monarchy men marched on London, proclaiming "King Jesus." The rebellion passed quickly, and with its leaders executed for treason, the Fifth Monarchists faded. However, suspicions remained for those who associated with Venner or other radicals, and in the charged political atmosphere, casual or perceived association was reason enough for the state to intervene in a person's life.

Sheldon used his position and influence to argue against toleration in the continuing religious debates in the country, even after the passage of the initial decisions of Charles I touching on religion and the Acts of Parliament governing religious life in a restored Church of England. Sheldon was like a number of the restored clerics who survived the Interregnum: he opposed toleration for any group. The Presbyterians and some independents who hoped for a tolerant or broad-church settlement along the lines of that under James I were disappointed. The restored bishops in the Lords and the Cavaliers in the Commons worked together for a settlement governing religion that was inflexible at best and intolerant at worst. Many of these men believed that the fault of the late rebellion lay with those dangerous religious fanatics who brought down the church and the state. The inflexibility of those now in power was a change for many; Sheldon

---

1661), 27. Authorship of this pamphlet remains debated, however, Gilbert Sheldon, George Searle, and George Starkey have all been mentioned as possible authors. The author gave a clue in the opening, stating that he was not a politician by training or a relative of the royal family, emphasizing his duty as a Christian to pray for peace in the land he lived in. Sheldon was capable of writing this document and shared the sentiments expressed within its pages.

14 Ibid., 32.

had espoused tolerant views as a younger man and member of the circle at Great Tew. Sheldon may have even questioned the legitimacy of the new canons promulgated in 1640, despite the wishes of Charles I and Laud, because he was only present for the first session.[15] At Tew, Sheldon, Morley, and Hammond were Oxford divines befriended by Viscount Falkland, who shared his home and his library with those interested in intellectual exercises. The circle at Tew was hostile to Catholicism, and while several of the members were of an Arminian persuasion, all of the divines espoused a view of Christianity that had some space for individual effort and works.[16] Sheldon's friendship with Morley had deep connections with Tew; both men worked as executors of Falkland's estate after his death. Sheldon and Morley's friendship remained solid in the Interregnum and during the Restoration, as they worked to protect the church. However Sheldon's friendship with Edward Hyde, now Earl of Clarendon, soured over differences in opinions regarding the religious settlement. Sheldon, like many of his closest friends and associates, stayed and served the remnant who were faithful to the prayer book during the Interregnum and who shared suffering, allowing bonds of trust and association to form between them. Sheldon was simply one in a long line of men that lost livings and positions for their loyalties, watching their extended families risk punishment and penalties for offering aid. These men focused their skills and talents on preventing wild-eyed republicans and religious fanatics from turning the world upside down once again.

The Cavalier Parliament passed in succession a series of acts governing religion. These acts formed the Clarendon Code, named

---

15 Davies, 321–322. Sheldon served as procurator for the Chapter of Gloucester during the April 1640 meeting of the convocation. Sheldon was replaced by George Palmer before the vote in November 1640. His friend John Hackett served as Archdeacon of Bedford.

16 Mortimer, "Great Tew Circle," 2. For more on the Great Tew Circle, see Hugh Trevor-Roper, *Catholics, Anglicans, and Puritans*, Chapter 4.

for the comprehension-minded Lord Chancellor of England. The four acts of the code were the Corporation Act (1661), the Act of Uniformity (1662), the Five Mile Act (1665), and the Conventicle Act (1670). Each of these acts caused a specific group of dissenters to feel the pressure of the law. The Corporation Act was the first of the series and it went into effect December 24, 1661, to expire March 25, 1663. This act went after those in secular positions of power serving as bailiffs, town clerks, mayors, council members, or any other magistrate requiring new oaths that disavowed the Solemn League and Covenant. These men were required to declare "... that it is not lawful upon any pretence whatsoever to take arms against the king, and that I do abhor that traitorous position of taking arms by his authority against his person, or against those that are commissioned by him."[17] The bill that went into effect was much gentler than the versions of it prepared by the Cavaliers, which required the surrender of municipal charters within a year and the king's nomination of a set of aldermen and other officials. The county Justices of the Peace (JPs) would be able to enforce their authority within the limits of the town. This bill would have drastically reduced municipal independence, but it horrified the Commons. In brief, the Commons bill allowed commissioners to remove those who refused the oaths and the declaration against taking arms against the king. The commissioners also had the authority to restore those ejected from their places during the Interregnum. The bill that passed offered oaths and religious qualifications for public office that went into effect without the drama associated with its introduction between the Lords and Commons. The men who wished to serve had to take the Oath of Allegiance, a Declaration against the Solemn League and Covenant, and an Oath against taking arms against the king and partake of the sacrament in the Church of England.[18]

---

17 Browning, 375–376. The Corporation Act, 1661.

18 See Miller, *After the Civil Wars*, 171–174 and Seaward, 152–155 for greater

The next piece of legislation was the Act of Uniformity, which was discussed in Chapter 5. Briefly, the Act of Uniformity made all worship outside the Church of England illegal and open to prosecution under the law. These two acts first impacted men involved in leadership (local or national) by mandating that all men in positions of authority (political or spiritual) follow the rubrics of worship established by the Book of Common Prayer, including the taking of the sacrament. The taking of the sacrament forced partial conformists out of power, because certain dissenting members would attend the service but absent themselves from the sacrament.

The remainder of the legislation passed as part of the Clarendon Code focused on ordinary individuals who argued for religious worship and expression outside the framework of the established church. The Five Mile Act passed in 1665 limited the population's exposure to unlicensed ministers and their ideas by forbidding the presence of any nonconforming minister within five miles of any corporation, town, or borough that sent representatives to Parliament. This reinforced the opinions stated by Edward Turner, Speaker of the Commons, that letters "... representing the unsettled Condition of some Countries, by reason of Fanatics, Sectaries, and Non-conformists. They differ in their Shapes and Species, and accordingly are more or less dangerous: But in this they all agree; they are no Friends to the established Government either Church or State."[19] The only exception to this act allowed dissenting ministers to pass through the town on the road. MPs and their clerical allies believed that nonconforming ministers would take the "... opportunity to distil the poisonous principles of schism and rebellion in the hearts of his Majesty's subjects, to the great danger of the Church and

---

detail on the events surrounding the passage of the Corporation Act.

19 *Journal of the House of Lords*, vol. 11 (London, 1802), 619–621. Afterwards JHL.

kingdom."[20] The ejected ministers were forbidden to take in boarders or to earn a living as a public or private teacher. Those prosecuted under the terms of this act faced a fine of £40 for each offense. The monies collected divided neatly into three parts, with a third to the king, a third for poor relief in the parish of the offense, and a third to those bringing the suit against the non-conformist, the local informant. Additionally, any two JPs of the county had the power to hold the offender for up to six months without bail, unless the offender took the oaths of allegiance in the interim. During this period, ministers who refused to conform in 1662 began to conform in small numbers to the Church of England, but still many refused to rejoin the church. Baxter wrote of those who refused to obey the law, "By this Act the case of the ministers was made so hard that many thought them necessitated to break it, not only by the necessity of their office, but by a natural impossibility of keeping it unless they should murder themselves and their families."[21] The partial conformist minister Ralph Josselin reported in November 1665, "... sharper penalties in the act against non-conformity, yett I hope. One suspended is restored on promise once a year to wear the surplice."[22]

The Conventicle Act of 1670 was particularly useful in rounding up dissenters, due to the looseness of its definition of a conventicle and the broad powers given to the local JPs. It replaced the Conventicle Act of 1664, which was a temporary act aimed at forcing Presbyterians to conform. The 1664 bill advocated strict penalties for leaders, but leniency toward others, to help persuade them back to the Church of England. The 1670 bill included severe penalties for those convicted: stiff fines, up to £10 per person per infraction. Property owners where the meeting occurred faced a penalty of £20. Those who dared to preach or

---

20 Browning, 383. The Five Mile Act, March 24, 1665.

21 Baxter, *The Autobiography of Richard Baxter*, 196–197.

22 Josselin, 522. November 19, 1665.

teach also faced fines of £20 and if that individual were too poor to pay, the fines were spread among those who attended. The act effected any individual "... of the age of sixteen or upwards ... present at any assembly, conventicle, or meeting under any colour or pretence of any exercise of religion in other manner than according to the liturgy and practice of the Church of England."[23] Five unrelated persons meeting together in a private home, field, or uninhabited dwelling were open to charge as a conventicle.

The first conventicle act was unpopular and caused some odd behavior by some opposed to it, strengthening the churchmen's opinion that dissenters were revolutionaries. Josias Warne allegedly said in August 1670 in response to the rumored rebellions against the Conventicle Act, "You Cavaleers say this King is the head of the Church ... And wee never had good dayes since the King came in ... And if I had but sixpence in all the world I would give it to fight for the good Ole Cause."[24] Warne was but one example of the type of anger the act caused among those persecuted under its wide parameters. While no actual large-scale rebellions took place because of the act, the rumors were enough to reinforce the church's cry that it existed in an age of danger.

Sheldon entered the discussion over the Conventicle Act by sending a circular letter to his bishops. Sheldon stressed conformity to the prayer book and uncontroversial ministers who lived soberly to offer themselves as guides to the people under their charge. Even so, Sheldon believed the success or failure of the act rested with God.

> ... what the success will be we must leave to God Almighty; yet (my Lord) I have this confidence under God, That if we do our parts now at first seriously, by God's

---

23 Browning, 384. The Conventicle Act, May 10, 1670.

24 Tim Harris, *London Crowds in the Reign of Charles II* (Cambridge: Cambridge University Press, 1987), 75.

help, and the assistance of the Civil Power, [...] We shall have within a few months see so great an alteration in the destractions of these times, as that seduced People returning from their seditious and self-seeking Teachers, to the Unity of the Church, and the Uniformity of God's Worship, it will be to the Glory of God, the welfare of the Church, the praise of his Majesty and Government, the happiness of the whole Kingdom.[25]

Sheldon spent much time and energy after the bishops returned to the Lords working on various committees that produced the Lords versions of the bills that became the Clarendon Code. Sheldon, as Bishop of London, was on the committee that oversaw drafting of the Act of Uniformity in 1662. Juxon (Canterbury) was also named, but his attendance at this point was sporadic, due to his increasingly ill health. Sheldon's fellow clerical workers on this committee were John Cosin (Durham), Humphrey Henchman (Salisbury), George Morley (Worcester), Robert Sanderson (Lincoln), John Gauden (Exeter), and Edward Reynolds (Norwich).[26] Sheldon shared friendships with Sanderson and Morley due to their work together during the Interregnum and one can easily assume that they worked as a unit on this committee and rallied the other bishops behind them, even the comprehension-minded Cosin and the former Presbyterian Reynolds. Sheldon was also on the committee that worked on the bill to repeal all the acts of the Long Parliament. Here he worked with John Hacket (Lichfield and Coventry), Mathew Wren (Ely), John Earles (Worcester), Morley, Cosin, and Henchman.[27] In the same year, Sheldon was on the committee to prepare a petition con-

---

25 *The Act of Parliament Against Religious Meetings, Proved to be the Bishop's Act* (1670), 4. This print document also contains an attack on Sheldon both as a man and primate. One can safely assume that the anonymous attacker did not share Sheldon's desires and might have been an ejected minister.

26 *JHL*, vol. 11, 366. January 11, 1662.

27 Ibid., 494–495. March 19, 1663.

cerning Jesuits and Catholics for the king and both house of parliament. Sheldon considered papists and dissenters to be a threat to the newly restored church. The final petition presented to the king requested that he, "... issue out Your Proclamation, to command all Jesuits, and all English, Irish, and Scotish Popish Priests, and all others such other Priests as have taken Orders from the See of Rome ... to depart this Kingdom by a Day, under pain of having the Penalties of the Laws inflicted upon them."[28] Of the thirty members that made up the committee for what became the Five Mile Act, a third of the members were bishops. The bishops led by Sheldon, now Archbishop, included Henchman, Earles, Morley, Hacket, Seth Ward (Exeter), Joseph Henshaw (Peterborough), Herbert Croft (Hereford), George Hall (Chester), and Benjamin Lany (Lincoln).[29] Both Conventicle Acts went before the whole house for debate, and Sheldon attended regularly for both times the act was under discussion, encouraging the attendance of his subordinate bishops.[30] Seventeen members of the Lords entered their disagreement with the bill.[31]

The Church of England, as an entity, supported this legislation, but individual priests and parishioners disagreed. The Clarendon Code failed in its attempt to compel uniform religious practice on the people of England and Wales. The punitive legislation could not be uniformly enforced, leading to sporadic persecutions of dissenters. Some of the legislation required juries to hear the trials of the accused Nonconformists, and jurors sometimes refused to punish their neighbors. The laxity or severity of the enforcement also related to external foreign affairs, such as the war

---

28 Ibid., 496–497 for the committee and 499–501 for the petition. March 23 and 28, 1663, respectively.

29 Ibid., 695–686. October 27, 1665.

30 *JHL*, vol. 12, March 11-April 12, 1670, discusses the activities concerning the renewal of the Conventicle Act.

31 Ibid., March 26, 1670. Some notable names among the dissenters include the Earl of Manchester and Viscounts Say and Sele.

with the Dutch and interactions with France. The Indulgence of 1672 was to unify the kingdom behind the war effort during the third Anglo-Dutch War. The difficulties of enacting religious legislation were numerous. Sheldon depended on the support of the bishops and the largely loyal-to-the-church peers in the Lords. The bishops and peers were natural allies because both groups had their traditional privileges revoked or suspended during the Interregnum. John Hacket, Bishop of Lichfield and Coventry, praised Sheldon's management of the situation:

> Most reverend, and my most gracious Lord, your Grace is pleased, beyond all desert of mine, to impart unto mee the constancy of the votes of the house of Commons, for the suppressing of Conventicles, and non conformists, wch gives to my old age a new vigour & reparation of health. The Lord be praised, who hath entered into the harts of those prudent, & religious patriots.[32]

In the Commons, Sheldon had a group of influential MPs on his side that served on pivotal committees during the time the Clarendon Code was under discussion in both houses. Men like Sir Job Charleton, Sir Heneage Finch, Sir John Berkenhead, and John Vaughn worked in the Commons, either introducing or supporting legislation that protected the Church of England. Finch introduced the bill in the Commons that repealed the bar on the bishops entering the Lords.[33] Another MP, Sir John Bramston, may have aided Sheldon in providing information about the sees in the gift of the Bishop of London.[34] The introduction and passage of the ecclesiastical laws were due in large part to these

---

32 MS Tanner 45, f. 295. Hacket to Sheldon, March 16, 1667.

33 Maxwell P. Schoenfeld, *The Restored House of Lords* (The Hague: Mouton & Co, 1967), 217.

34 Seaward, 97. See also the *ODNB* articles on "Heneage Finch" by D.E.C Yale and "Job Charleton" by Newton E. Key for further details on their parliamentary careers.

diverse groups of men working together for the restoration and continued preservation of the Church of England. These MPs spent much of their careers attempting to protect the church from opposition from dissenters or the king and his councilors. The provincial officials in the posts of lord lieutenants and their deputies were men loyal to both the monarchy and the church.[35] However loyal these men were, many of their underlings at the county level were less likely to enforce religious laws against their neighbors and friends. Some might argue that the Clarendon Code was a lost cause before the first laws ever took effect. Sheldon believed in the necessity of the laws to govern religion and in the occasionally harsh enforcement of those laws. In his mind, like in many of his colleagues' minds, the alternative was more than they could bear. They refused to live through the call that "the '41 has come again." The rules were in place by the actions of the Cavalier Parliament, but having them enforced across the length and breadth of the country was much more difficult.

One of the many difficulties of creating uniformity in religion was the wealth of religious expression and diversity of opinions on the subject. Many individuals had different opinions on the subject and very few advocated complete religious toleration. What would have made the largest group content was allowing a Presbyterian-style minister serve in the Church of England. This service needed the provision of choosing to ignore the parts of the liturgy the old Puritan faction found objectionable; however reasonable this sounded, the staunch Cavaliers and Clerics in the parliaments of the 1660s wanted no part of such a settlement. What these men wanted was to recover those close to the Church of England and return them to the fold. The printed pleas questioned those that chose to separate but who remained theologically closer to the Anglican modes than nonconformists, who

---

35 See Victor Stater, *Noble Government*, especially Chapter 3, for more detail on the Restoration lord lieutenants.

were more radical. One effective point of questioning and attack was over the question of conscience.

> A Scrupulous Conscience therefore starts and boggles, where there is no real Evil or Mischief; is afraid of omitting or doing what may be omitted or done without Sin. Which I know not how better to illustrate, than by those unaccountable Antipathies or Prejudices that some Men have against some Sort of Meats, or living Creatures, which have not the least Harm or Hurt in them; yet are so offensive and dreadful to such Persons, that they fly from them as they would from a Tyger or Bear, and avoid them as they would do Plague or Poyson. Just so do some Men run out of Church at the Sight of a Surplice, as if they had been scared by the Apparition of a Ghost.[36]

The wearing of the surplice was an oft-addressed point of contention, as one of the primary evils the Church of England inflicted upon pious Christian ministers. "As to the *Surplice*; our Church requires not the wearing of *this* Garment as an Holy Vestment, like the Priestly Garments under the Old Law, but meerly for the Sake or Order and Uniformity."[37] The desire for orderly and regulated religious worship was a common theme from the accession of Laud to Canterbury. One additional argument for remaining within the church or returning to it dealt with the question of the sin of schism.

> Since to preserve the Unity of Christians, and one Communion, is the necessary Duty of every Member of the Church; and it can never be thought a justifiable Thing to cut off our selves from the Communion of the Church,

---

36 *A Collection of Cases, Lately Written to Recover Dissenters to the Church of England*, vol. 2, 3rd ed. (London, 1718), 4. *A Discourse about a Scrupulous Conscience.*

37 *Cases*, 306. *The Resolution of this Case of Conscience.*

or the Body of Christ, out of compliance with any erring or ignorant Brethren ... I only conclude thus much, That there is far more of the Sin of Uncharitableness in such Separation and Division, than there can be in all the *Offence* that is imagined to be given by our Conformity.[38]

Sheldon and other leaders within the Church of England viewed the act of separation to be the real issue and problem. Private thoughts and prayers that varied or strayed (within limits) from the liturgy were allowable in private devotions, as long as the thoughts followed public conformity.

Sheldon's own religious views and expression seemed to support this idea. He read and studied a variety of religious writings, including many of the patristic fathers. He was a believer in the classic settlement of the church represented by the *via media*. As a student and younger man, he leaned into the Arminian camp, but by the time of the Restoration, he was willing to put aside his earlier disdain for Calvinists in effort to restore and to unify the church.

The settlement of the church by the Act of Uniformity allowed many men who served happily under the Directory to continue their ministries upon taking the new oaths and using the Book of Common Prayer. The devotion of some of these ministers to the liturgy and rules of the restored Church of England was not deep and abiding, which caused conflict between church members and their clergy. Complaints about the inadequate devotion to the prayer book standard crossed Sheldon's desk from many places under his jurisdiction, including two remote factories of the East India Company. Some believed distance from the center of religious and political life meant that less conformable persons could circumvent the laws. However many times such a plan worked, it was not a guarantee, as those far-flung Englishmen

---

38 *Cases,* 84. *Some Consideration about the Case of Scandal, or, Giving Offence to Weak Brethren.*

had their own ideas about what was proper in worship. The complaints from the company men stationed at Fort St. George and
Machilipatnam included a charge that that company sent two lay-
men instead of ordained ministers and a charge that the minister
in Fort St. George refused to pray for the king and argued against
parliament's ability to decide rules governing religion.[39] These
men requested from Sheldon that

> ... they may have these recalled, & such other sent to them,
> with whom they pray according to the Liturgy, And from
> whom they may heare true Gospell and receive the Sac-
> raments of Baptism & the Lords Supper ... The summe
> of the letter to your Grace is. That none may be sent as
> Ministers, to the Factories of the East India Company,
> But such as shall be approved by your Grace, or the Bps.[40]

These men complained, as did many in England, that unortho-
dox ministers "were the Trumpets to the late Rebellion,"[41] echoing the oft-argued position that the church was in danger.

The case of the East India Company's complaints against Ministers Hooke and Thompson went before the Privy Council October 13, 1669. Sheldon presented the letter of complaints before
the board of governors on the eighth of the same month.

> It was thereupon ordered that the Governor & Company
> of Merchants London Trading to the East Indies should

---

39 MS Tanner 44, f. 100. Notes out of the Letters of the East India Company, undated. Author's paraphrase of the complaints. Privy Council meeting
about this business occurred in 1669. For more about this time in the larger
imperial frame, see Carla Gardina Pestana, *Protestant Empire: Religion and the
Making of the British Atlantic World* (Philadelphia: University of Pennsylvania Press, 2009), Chapters 4 and 5.

40 MS Tanner 44, f. 100.

41 Ibid. For more info on attitudes at a local level, see Donald Spaeth, *The
Church in an Age of Danger: Parsons and Parishioners 1660-1770* (Cambridge:
Cambridge University Press, 2005).

this day attend his Majesties Councill touching the said complaint ... And being called in & heard, it appearing that the said ministers are of ill Principles not lawfully constituted, & unfit for that Charge & Employment. His Majestie did this day order that the said Governor & Company of Merchants London, trading to the East Indies, be & they are required by the first ships to send positive order for the Revocation & speedy return of the said Hooke & Thompson. And att the same time to send in their Roomes two such Orthodox and lawfully Ordained Ministers according to the Rites of the Church of England as the Right Reverend Father in God, the Lord Bp of London shall approve ... the said Governor & Company are required to yield due Obedience as they will render his Majesties high Displeasure.[42]

This case had the king's full support in enforcing the ecclesiastical laws; however, to Sheldon's (and other's) frustration, the king was not a firm ally. His religious opinions changed depending upon who held his favor and attention. However, Charles II's public devotions remained aligned with the church in which he was bred, rather than any other Protestant alternative.[43]

The business of the church and the problem of dissent took up much of Sheldon's time and energy. He made great use of his friends as sources of information and for speaking his mind in a secure environment. Sheldon and the Duke of Ormond were of the same generation of men, both lost positions after the death of Charles I, and both returned to prominence serving a much younger and less pious king. Sheldon's rise to the archiepiscopal see can be viewed in this light—he had been the confessor and

---

42 MS Tanner 44, f. 162. October 13, 1669. Official notary copy via Miles Smyth, Sheldon's secretary.

43 Fincham and Tycake, 311–313 give an overview of the rituals and environment of the king's chapels.

spiritual advisor to a martyred king. He explained to Ormond the necessity of supporting religious legislation as the only cure for the ills of religious diversity. Sheldon targeted the "proud" leaders of the London sectaries. He wrote of the leaders of the nonconforming members of society that they

> ... have not reason enough to make them capable of conviction; and the most of the rest too much pride to acknowledge their error, especially while they have the honour and persit of being heads of so great a party. Tis only a resolute execution of the laws that must cure this disease, all other remydes have and will crush it; and tis necessary that they who will nor be governed as men by reason and persuasion, should be governed as beasts by power and force, all other courses will be ineffectiall, ever have been soe, ever will be ...[44]

Sheldon refused to mince his words and his belief that strong actions were necessary to prevent the collapse of the newly restored Church of England and restore those outside its fold into proper modes of worship. He was also aware that no man could do what was necessary to oversee the church in the three realms of the Stuart monarchy. Sheldon promised Ormond that he "... will find no obstruction here in filling up those ecclesiasticall preferments that will be yoyd by it" if the Lord Chancellor of Ireland died.[45] Ormond was a loyal son of the church and was loyal to the Stuart monarch on the throne, which made him a valuable friend and ally.

Sheldon worked with his fellow bishops to ensure that filled vacant positions had conformable men. For Sheldon, the right sort of men had university educations or connections, depending upon

---

44 MS Carte 45, f. 151. Sheldon to Ormond, September 15, 1663.

45 Ibid., f. 200. Sheldon to Ormond, October 13, 1666. The Lord Chancellor of Ireland recovered from his illness and outlived both Ormond and Sheldon.

age, and had the proper sentiments toward nonconformity. Men who toed the church's conformist line prevented the institution of the less orthodox. Preaching or publicly espousing any view that was critical of religious laws or the liturgy was a quick way to earn censure from all levels. The passage of the Act of Uniformity in 1662 was a triumph for men loyal to the church during long years of exile and underground existence. However, not all of the laity or clergy greeted the act with universal cheer and joy. Sheldon received many complaints from many communities about the irregular behavior of the parish's assigned minister. The parishioners of Wappenham, Northampton wrote, expressing concern about their rector, Mr. Theophilus Hart. The rector's parishioners reported that Hart removed furniture from the church for use at his own home, such a wainscot seat and a baptismal font, and misappropriated the wine flagon procured for use during the Eucharist.[46] The dismantling of the church's physical property usually gifted by parishioners was a quick way for a rector or vicar to get into trouble locally. Hart, according to his flock, also "hath taken in part of the churchyard to enlarge his own free hold, 40 yards in length and 3 to 4 in breadth, digging up the bones of deceased Christians, and beating them to pieces in the post holes."[47] Villages considered the church ground public spaces and infringement upon them in any manner was very bad form. The real cause of alarm might have been the desecration of the graves of the parish by the minister. While these complaints were worrisome, the authorities reacted to specific nonconforming behaviors under the law.

> [Hart] ... came into the living after it was sequester'd, and the minister turned out ... hath made his parishioners pay their Easter dues, but will not do his Easter duties ... He has forbidden Mr Bargrave and Mr Clifford answering in

---

46 Author's adaptation of MS Add c 307, f. 34. Undated, but 1666 from Sheldon's reply.

47 Ibid.

the church, and for the most part omits the Te Deum, and a great part of the prayers. He has never worn the surplice.[48]

Hart came to Wappenham during the Interregnum and kept his living due to the death of the previous incumbent by the Act for Settling Ministers. The previous minister died before the Restoration and under the act, ministers remained in their livings only if the ejected incumbent died before the Restoration. Sheldon wrote to Joseph Henshaw, Bishop of Peterborough, reminding his subordinate of the duty to police his diocese for those failing to live up to the standards of clerical behavior.

> For I have now newly received fresh complaints against him for his continued Inconformity That he reades not the Common Prayers as he is enjoyned but in parts ... Never wears the Surplice, Takes no notice of the Holy Dayes or fasting dayes, Discourages those that like & observe the Prayers & Ceremonies of the Church, & openly & frequently frees into disputes against them. I am sufficiently convinced of the naughtinesse of the man, & so may your Lordsp, if you will but make an effectuall enquiry into him To the rest of his faults I believe you will find him Rich & Stubborn, & therefore the fitter to be made an example.[49]

Sheldon had numerous complaints sent to him of every stripe of nonconformity and in some cases outright fraud. Herbert Croft, Bishop of Hereford, brought a bizarre case before Sheldon involving the charismatic Duell Pead. Croft reported that

---

48 Ibid.

49 MS Add c 308, f. 48. Sheldon to Joseph Henshaw, November 10, 1666, www. theclergydatabase.org.uk. Person Id 97073 lists a Thomas Hart as rector of Wappenham, vacated in 1686 after a violent death, so one might assume that Hart never mended his ways.

... the corporation of Boaudloy set [Pead] up for their Lecturer, without my leave or knowledge ... I sent for him, & questioned him whence, & what he was; his knowledge I found sufficient, and his profession seeming Orthodox, a very nimble port man, full of fancy & language, which, it seems, took much with the people, for they were very eager for him.[50]

Pead came into Hereford with the recommendation of Sir Edward Spragg with whom he spent several years at sea, according to the documents presented to the diocesan bishop. Pead also stated that Sheldon promised him "much favor." Croft wondered at the validity of the documents, especially the fact that Pead left a wealthier living in Kent for a poorer one in Hereford. Croft requested that Sheldon investigate the matter through his contacts at Cambridge, due to the irregularity of Pead's documents. Croft suspended Pead from his preaching duties until the matter was resolved. Pead became a deacon on May 17, 1668, under the jurisdiction of Bishop William Fuller of Lincoln. He was an ordained priest after 1672 and served as rector of St. Peters, Canterbury, Kent under Sheldon's seal.[51] Pead's recorded clerical positions continued until his resignation as rector of St. Lawrence Newland in 1712. The behavior that brought him to the attention of his diocesan bishop might have signaled the end of his clerical career, but he was episcopally ordained and that was important in this era. This was not the only instance of a petitioner claiming a living either through falsified documents or through claims of ordination by Sheldon without proof. Anthony Sparrow, Bishop of Exeter, had a similar case.[52]

---

50 MS Tanner 42, f. 108. Croft to Sheldon, undated. Probably after 1672.

51 Devel (Deullis) Pead, CCeD Person Id 73436, www.theclergydatabase.org. uk.

52 MS Tanner 42, f. 11. Sparrow to Sheldon, 1673. The claimant is unnamed, so tracing him is impossible, but it is an interesting coincidence.

Henry King, Bishop of Chichester, one of the last bishops named by Charles I, informed his primate of the problems in his diocese.

> There is one Francis Challoner who hath purchased the perpetuall patronage of a Living in Lewes within my Dioces called St John's [sub casted] He repaired to mee for Institution wch I deny'd upon a double account Insufficiency & Inconformity. Missing his aime with mee He gave out in my house that He would seek Above for that Right wch I deny'd Him at Chichester. I held it my Duty to God to the Church & to your Grace to serve notice of the Person That When he comes upp your Graces Vicar Gernerally or your Secretary might not be suprized. Lewes is a place full of Fanaticks & dis-affected people (as indeed is Chichester & diverse eminent places in Sussex) Amongst whome to better ingratiate Himself when He preached, He left out the Lords Prayer.[53]

One common complaint against suspected nonconformist ministers dealt with their prayers. Forgoing the use of the Lord's Prayer or omitting to pray for the king, queen, and the remainder of the royal family was a key indication of the presence of nonconforming ministers. The dislike of pre-formulated prayers, including the scriptural Lord's Prayer, was a complaint offered from the beginning of Stuart rule in England. Nonconformist complaints about the Lord's Prayer were surprising, since they also lamented the lack of scripture in liturgical services. These men believed that set prayers limited the worship experience. Others might stray from the rubric of the prayer book at marriages, burials, or other services, most frequently by the addition of extempore prayers, especially ones that pointed out particular sins. The church took a dim view of such activities and believed that "... those particular

---

53 MS Tanner 45, f. 64. Henry King to Sheldon, February 21, 1665. Francis Challoner, CCeD Person Id 62838, www.theclergydatabase.org.uk.

Confessions of Sin ... are not properly the matter of that Publick Service we are to offer daily unto God in *Religious Assemblies,* but that of Private Devotion which is necessary to be perform'd in our Closets."[54]

One of the provisions of the Five Mile Act was that ministers removed for nonconformity had to stay at least five miles from the site of their previous ministry. The local JPs were to work with other magistrates in enforcing the laws. They were to arrest and detain offenders, depending on the particulars of any given infraction. On occasion, blatant disregard of these duties attracted the attention of the king and Privy Council. Such was the business of the council on July 28, 1669:

> Whereas his Majestie hath receivd information that severall Conventicles and unlawfull meetings have been lately held within the Town of Syme in the house of one Ames Short an ejected non-conformist minister, And that the magistrates of that place have been negligent and remise in their duty in not discountenancing and suppressing the disenters and unlawfull meetings although they had notice thereof. Wee do therefore by his Majesties command hereby pray and require you forthwith to informe your selfe of the truth of the whole business by a strict examination and enquiry into the same, and withal speed to returne an attempt thereof to this board to the end of such course may be taken herein as shall be thought fitt.[55]

Not every conventicle had an ejected minister at its heart. A substantial number of ejected ministers, especially sober dissenters (Presbyterians or Puritans) attended occasional Church of En-

---

54 *Cases*, 225. *Certain Cases of Conscience Resolved, Concerning the Lawfulness of Joyning with Forms of Prayer in Publick Worship, Part II.*

55 MS Tanner 44, f. 137. Signed by Sheldon among others.

gland services, but absented themselves from the rituals with which they found fault.[56] This practice led to occasional conformity, which was something Sheldon and his fellows disliked, as a common ritual abstained from was communion. Occasional conformity made enforcing the laws against dissent very difficult, as some percentage of the population attended both the legal church and some sort of conventicle meeting. Even at the end of this period, communion in the Church of England once a year became enshrined with political involvement in the state, as all MPs and government officials were required to meet this annual requirement, which lasted until the nineteenth centuries. Sheldon's academic homes, Oxford and Cambridge, imposed similar rules for those seeking degrees.

Many conventicle leaders had little formal education or training and seemed an advertisement for the old saying, "When women preach and cobblers pray the fiends in hell make holiday."[57] This was the experience of Sheldon's friend and fellow bishop, John Hacket, just outside of Lichfield.

> And I have opportunitie from yesterdays worke to aquaint your Grace, that these schismatiques will never mend. For yesterday in the morning & so on till eavening a conventicle of about 80 persons, was held at Elmhurst, a mile from Lichfield in the house of one Hill, (a tenent to Sr Theo: Biddolf, who knows not of it) to wch Minors his fore-man of his shop, with the most of his family, and the wife of Jeron & most of his family resorted, with all the wanted gang and the ring-leader among them is Rixom, our cities carrier, no way fit for that trust, being a transcendent schismetick.[58]

---

56 Spurr, *The Restoration of the Church of England,* 44–45.

57 Watts, *The Dissenters,* 88. See Chapter 3 for more particulars on the experience of dissenters 1660-1689.

58 MS Tanner 44, f. 125. June 12, 1669. Hacket to Sheldon.

Sheldon's response to Hacket, which probably advised imprisonment, had the right effect. Hacket's next report stated "... I wish they [Minors and Jeron] may bee brought to better order & conformitie by their lingering restraint, wch hath struck terror into manie sectaries, yet not into all."[59] Hacket was less capable of enforcing the religious law when his own chapter house was in disarray due to a nonconforming and unrepentant dean. Hacket believed the church was in danger. Another letter of the summer of 1669 illustrated the adage that the church was in an age of danger:

> ... I do not exceed out of ill will in my information against the Presbyterians and other sectaries, that they grow so insolent & regardless of their betters that in my apprehension they are hatching some dangerous mischief, and when harvest is brought in, I feare some violent attempt from them.[60]

Sheldon expected reports on conventicles from his subordinates. It helped to keep him informed in the capital, where the debates and political moods shifted quickly. As he wrote to one of his Welsh ministers, "Your letter of the 21st of October from Brecon I rec'd, & returne you thanks for the Acct you have therein given me of the late proceedings agt Conventicles & other irregular disorders."[61]

Sheldon, as archbishop, had several capable younger men serving him as chaplains and aiding him in the continuing struggle to protect the church from external enemies. These men were the authors of a great many publications dealing with dangers to the church and/or the necessity of religious legislation enforced by the state. They used strong and sometimes volatile language to express the dangers of nonconforming opinions and especially

---

59 Ibid., f. 127. July 19, 1669. Hacket to Sheldon.

60 Ibid., f. 140. August 2, 1669. Hacket to Sheldon.

61 MS Harleian 7377, f. 9 back. Sheldon to Dr. Cruse, November 6, 1669.

the toleration of such opinions by those in power. These clerical pamphleteers defended strict uniformity to the church and
worked to thwart any movement towards comprehension or limited toleration.[62]

Samuel Parker wrote of these dangers in 1671 in *A Discourse of
Ecclesiastical Politie*. In the preface, he wrote, "In brief, whoever
is proud and conceited upon the score of Religion, naturally falls
into the most savage insolence and baseness of Nature, and is utterly uncapable of being either a good subject, or good Neigh-
bor."[63] Parker continued to play on the beliefs and fears of men
who had survived the Interregnum about the inherent instability of religious pluralism: "... That Indulgence and Toleration is
the most absolute sort of Anarchy, and that Princes may with
less hazard give Liberty to mens Vices and Debaucheries, than
to their Consciences."[64] The fear that liberty of conscience un-
dermined government had several historic examples that these
men used to argue against toleration. The specter of Munster
and the Anabaptist's revolts during the Reformation was further
reinforced by the periodic rebellions of religious radicals on the
continent and in England. The Interregnum had been awash in
religious pluralism and experienced an overthrow of established
political modes at the hands of men fomenting radically different
ideas about the state and the practice of Christian religion. For
Parker, the government had an obligation and the right to enforce
religious conformity because the alternative was unthinkable—
anarchy and rebellion.

> So that as they would expect Peace and Settlement, they
> must be sure at first to bind on their Ecclesiastical Laws

---

62 Spurr, *The Restoration of the Church of England*, 48.

63 Samuel Parker, *A Discourse of Ecclesiastical Politie: Wherein the Authority of the
Civil Magistrate over the Consciences of Subjects in Matters of External Religion
is Asserted* (London: John Martyn, 1671), vii.

64 Ibid., lxv.

with the streightest knot, and afterward to keep them in force and countenance by the severest Execution; in that wild and Fanatick Consciences are to headstrong to be curb'd with an ordinary severity; & therefore their restraints must be proportion'd to their unruliness: and they must be managed with so much a greater care and strictness, than all other principles of publick disturbance, by how much they are more dangerous & unruly.[65]

The use of the full strong arm of the law to enforce conformity was an ideal situation, but its actual application varied, to the frustration of the clergymen working to enforce conformity to the ecclesiastical laws of the Restoration settlement.

Others in Sheldon's circle employed other arguments against liberty of consciences. Thomas Thomkins wrote *The Inconveniences of Toleration* in 1667 about the fact that those who argued for toleration, like the Presbyterian-dominated Westminster Assembly, only wanted it for the people like themselves, to the exclusion of all others.

> Liberty of Conscience is a Thing which hath often made a very Great Noise in the World; and is at the first View, a thing highly plausible; but although it looks hugely pretty in the Notion: yet it was always found strangely Wild and Unmanageable when ever it came to be handled by Experience; and we shall constantly find, That those which cryed it up for the most Reasonable Thing in the world, when Themselves stood in need of it, as soon as ever They came in Power, would never endure to hear of it any longer.[66]

---

65 Ibid., 21.

66 Thomas Tomkins, *The Inconveniences of Toleration, Or an Answer to a Late Book, Entitled "A Proposition made to the King and Parliament, for the Safety and Happiness of the King and of the Kingdom"* (London: W. Garret, 1667), 1.

Tomkins further argued that the debates over tolerating tender consciences led many to the evil of spiritual hubris. As well as devaluing many who worked and prepared for the return of the king, he explained, "Surely the Church of England may say without Boasting, That Her Sons were the truest, the most constant Subjects the King had."[67] This statement was hard to refute. Many clerics went into exile with the young king or other royalist families or remained behind, working to preserve a remnant of the church and society his father died for.

> Besides to Relax a Law upon account of Conscience, or the pretences of a higher degree of Purity in the same Religion, is as much to Proclaim the Dissenters, to be the most really Conscientious: That those who do Conform, are meer Formalists, Time-Servers, compliers with that which is uppermost; but the *Non-Conformists* shall be taken for the Sincere men, who walk according to Light, and to keep the Gospel pure without the mixture of human Inventions: And this alone will be a very great Temptation to many an honest, but weak man, who hath more Zeal than knowledge, to Enrol himself among those Men, who are allowed to differ from the Religion of the State upon the pretence of higher Purity, and greater attainments.[68]

The argument that the nonconformists often used to justify their separation involved statements of this kind, infuriating many of the loyal and devout members within the clergy. Within any religious organization, the devotion of the members in charge varied over time, and accusations of time serving fell on raw wounds or infuriated younger clerics who sought episcopal ordination covertly when it was illegal.[69]

---

67 Ibid., 17.

68 Ibid., 26–27.

69 Sheldon's chaplains included Thomas Tompkins, Samuel Parker, and George

The experiment in toleration surrounding the actions leading up to the Second Dutch War was largely a desire of the king and his ministers. While at war, Charles II believed that in order to be successful, all of his subjects should support his aims; to this purpose, Charles II offered an indulgence for dissenters in March 1672, in order to unite his country before facing a military threat. The king embarked upon an ambitious religious policy that reinforced the traditional right of the monarch over all religious matters. The *Declaration of Indulgence* was issued March 15, 1672. The indulgence declared "... that the execution of all and all manner of penal laws in matters ecclesiastical, against whatsoever sort of nonconformists or recusants, be immediately suspended."[70] It also allowed dissenters to worship in approved public sites, but this was not true religious freedom. The indulgence only allowed public worship under certain conditions. The main condition was that "... our express will and pleasure is that none of our subjects do presume to meet in any such place until such place be allowed and the teacher of that congregation be approved by us."[71] The task now fell to the government to evaluate and license dissenting ministers and locations of worship. Presbyterian Oliver Heywood of Halifax received a license that gave him permission "to be a teacher of the congregation allowed by us a room or rooms in the house of John Butterworth ... to teach in any other place licensed and allowed by us according to our said declaration."[72]

Stradling. Tomkins came from All Souls in 1665 and became chancellor and prebend at Exeter. Parker became a chaplain in November 1667 after dedicating a work to Sheldon. He became Archdeacon of Canterbury after W. Sancroft and later was made a prebend of that cathedral. Parker became Bishop of Oxford in 1686. George Stradling also came from All Souls and he became Dean of Chichester in 1672. See the *ODNB* for "Samuel Parker" by Jon Parkin and "Thomas Tomkins" by E.I. Carlyle, rev. Sean Kelsey. See CCeD Person Id 3443 for George Stradling.

70 Browning, 387. The Declaration of Indulgence, March 15, 1672.

71 Ibid., 388. Declaration.

72 Ibid., 389. License of nonconformist worship to Oliver Heywood, July 25,

The indulgence was careful to exclude Roman Catholics from public worship, but suspended the penal laws pertaining to Catholics. The English feared a monarch sympathetic to Catholicism, and rumors of Charles II's secret loyalty to Rome floated about. The declaration affirmed the Church of England by naming it "the basis, rule and standard of the general and public worship of God."[73] Anglican clerics received assurance that their livings and ecclesiastical status were safe and unobtainable by anyone not entirely conforming to the doctrines of the church.

Regardless of the safeguards placed upon the Church of England by the Declaration of Indulgence, Sheldon and his associates looked with dismay on former conventicles springing up in communities under their ecclesiastical jurisdictions. A common lament was

> Wee now feel the sad effects of the Declaration. Bold Presbyterians, And Anabaptists with the Quakers are exceedingly in [?]: In so much as if there bee not a sodane stop put to their daring growth ... I have writ ... for a particular of all the Licencss they have given to the Presbyterians in my Dioceses That I may know who preach, according to that Power: And proceed against those who Teach without Licences ...[74]

The news was not all complaints about the number of nonconformists. The declaration was not universally popular, and in some instances, it made the population more inclined to the Church of England. Sparrow reported from Exeter, after his visitation, "we have found both clergy & people more affected to the Churches Govermt than ever we did. Divines who had been ex-

---

1672.

73 Ibid., 388. Declaration.

74 MS Tanner 43, f. 25. William Fuller to Sheldon, August 29, 1672.

communicated, leading men, submitting themselves & offering their service for the peace of the Ch[urch]."[75]

The indulgence to dissenters offered by Charles was dependent on a number of factors in order to remain in effect. The most pressing was victory in the war with the Dutch, which was not on the horizon in the early months of 1673. The king called parliament and in March cancelled the Declaration of Indulgence; the parliament then turned to another religious issue, the fear of popery. Some believed the indulgence gave unofficial freedoms to Roman Catholics. Many feared that the king was falling under the influence of the Roman Catholics close to him. New fears replaced old fears about dissent—fear of arbitrary government, France, and popery.[76] The licenses granted to dissenters under the indulgence lapsed in 1675 for the most part and those that continued to meet fell under the purview of the Conventicle Act. To combat the fear of popery, the parliament passed the Test Act (1673), which used similar means to ferret out Catholics in governmental positions as the Corporation Act uncovered dissenters. The act required both peers and commoners who bore any office or received any sort of wage from the king to take a series of oaths and to take the sacrament in the Church of England. This included all members of the households of the king and the Duke of York and anyone with a commission in the army or the navy. All "who inhabit, reside or be within the city of London or Westminster, or within thirty miles distant from the same"[77] were to comply with the terms of the act or face prosecution. The clergy supported this act because it targeted both nonconformists and papists.

---

75 MS Tanner 141, f. 136. Sparrow to Sheldon, November 20, 1672.

76 John Spurr, *England in the 1670s* (Oxford: Blackwell, 2000). Chapter 2 in particular deals with the political machinations that caused the revocation of the Indulgence and the passage of the Test Act.

77 Browning, 389. Test Act, 1673.

The threat from licensed dissenters was over by early 1673, with the revocation of the Indulgence and the passage of the Test Act, but the churchmen still had the fallout of this experiment in religious toleration to work through. Peter Mews, Bishop of Bath and Wells, complained about the Presbyterians in his diocese.

> Havieng proceeded to excommunication against some Leaders of the Presbyterian Faction at Chard (a place wch gives mee great trouble) they have obtayn'd Absolution and of the Arches and were absolv'd privately. They never made any formal Appeal, nor indeed could they, it being matter of Office. This has so encourages the rest of the Faction that they now plainly say they care not for the Proceeding heer, and indeed, they need noe Absolution from above bee so easily obtayn'd ... but the common discourses of the country of a Toleration and the Phanaticks are so high upon the hope of it, that they do upon the matter challenge Justice to proceed against them until they have it they shall have noe quarter from mee (I mean the Ringleaders).[78]

The Arches was an ecclesiastical court that offered both appellate and original jurisdiction for all under the rule of Canterbury. It was the court of appeals for the lower bishop's courts in each diocese. The Chancery Court did the same for those under York. The Arches is the only body allowed to deprive a person in holy orders from their office. The only appeal after leaving the Arches is the monarch.

The focus shifted from the problem of dissent to the more nebulous and phantom-like problem of Catholicism in England. The church continued to stand against both threats, but as the 1670s progressed, the elderly archbishop had to feel that the fight needed more energy and work than he had left in him. Sheldon con-

---

78 MS Tanner 42, f. 119. Mews to Sheldon, August 12, 1674.

tinued to lead, but the winds of change were on the horizon and the church was going to face one of the greatest challenges of its life in the coming years. Would the church continue its support for the monarchy regardless? What would happen between those who sought toleration and those who opposed it? Sheldon tried to keep the emerging divisions in the church from breaking out into all-out factionalism by reinforcing the idea of uniformity and conformity among the church, despite one's private convictions. Sheldon probably sympathized more with the emerging High Church than the Low Church movement. He was conscious of promoting the right sort of men from loyal colleges at Oxford and Cambridge. Sheldon's religious convictions and his loyalty to the monarchy were linked in his experiences and his overwhelming belief in the traditional Anglican position of the *via media*. Many of those closest to the elderly archbishop gravitated to the High Church position after his death including a couple of the non-juroring bishops.

Sheldon's activities within the religious atmosphere of Restoration England were vast, but not limited to just that kingdom. Sheldon from his time as Dean of the Chapel Royal had a hand in the settlement of religion in Scotland. The two archbishops of Scotland, James Sharp (St. Andrews) and Alexander Burnet (Glasgow), sent letters south with the same sort of complaints made by their southern brethren, with the added issue of having to work with the king's Scottish Privy Council led by John Maitland, Duke of Lauderdale. Sharp wrote to Lauderdale:

> ... it is most satisfying to me that my lo. Canterbury and your Lop. keep kindnes and freedom, it is my concerne to further it what I can; I wrote once to him since I came from London, and received the other day one from him, which I did communitcat to my L. Thesurer; he gets no allurums from me but such as I give your Lop., you having been pleasit to allow me the freedom of acquainting

you with what I find, hear, or fear as to the condition of this church, whose settlement in the way ordered by the lawes we have all reasons to be confident you doe and will by all effectual meanes endeavour: we promote litle, and can doe litle, without the reall assistance of the kings ministers heer.[79]

Burnet echoed the complaint that conventicles and their ministers freely flouted the laws of the land. "This weeke and last there hath beene so great a confluence of discontented and deposed ministers (as here we term them) to this place, and so many conventicles kept (both against the expresse letter of the law) that I was overwhelmed with hourely complaints from our friends both of the clergy and laity."[80] The settlement of the English church encouraged the Scottish Episcopalians. As Sharp commented, "It is well for us your affairs there proceed so hopefully, for by your stability and settlement only we can expect quiet and safety here."[81] Sheldon drafted a letter to Burnet in October 1664 from Lambeth, "My Lord I was just going to putt penne to Paper to write to your Grace ... My Lord of St Andrews hath made a very usefull journey ... for the advantage of the affairs of the church."[82] Sheldon referred to Sharp's visit from December 1663 to February 1664 when the church commission in Scotland assumed the responsibility of fighting nonconformity from the Scottish Privy Council.[83] Sharp and his allies had some successes in reforming the church in Scotland, as he dutifully reported.

The condition of this church I hope will grow better when the condition of the nation is mendit, we doe what

---

79 *LP*, vol. 1, 195. Letter CXV. Sharp to Lauderdale, April 21, 1664.

80 *LP*, vol. 2, Appendix A, i–ii. Burnet to Sheldon, Feb 27, 166³/₄.

81 Ibid., v. Sharp to Sheldon, June 19, 1664.

82 MS Add c 308, f. 14 reverse. Sheldon to Burnet, October 17, 1664.

83 David George Mullan, "James Sharp," *ODNB*, 3.

we can to ridd the church of the corrupt and perverse clergy, and have made a good progress in planting those who are orderly and obedient, but the minister who are outed doe much to poison and alienat the people from the King and authority, and the popish emissarie priests and Jesuites are no more industrious in ther way of perverting then we find these censured ministers to be in ther way; these ill disposed persons have too much matter to work upon by the poverty and discontent of many of our nobility and gentry; they resolve to forge pretexts of religion for seducing, and to be satisfied with nothing till they have overturned all and set up themselves if they can ...[84]

Despite the hope of Sheldon and his northern brethren, re-introducing episcopacy in Scotland was a difficult task. Sheldon offered encouragement, but had little real success in seeing a religious program in Scotland that mirrored the settlement of the Church of England. However, the events in Scotland and the numerous complaints within England showed one of Sheldon's strengths. He tenaciously defended episcopacy from all attackers, both within and without the Church of England. His determination to see the church prosper and recover after two decades of neglect, which it largely accomplished by the time of his death, was but one measure of his devotion and loyalty to the institution that gave him his primary identity.

---

84 *LP*, vol. 2. Appendix A, xx. Sharp to Sheldon, April 1665. Manuscript copy MS Add c 306, f. 25.

CHAPTER 7

CHURCH IN CRISIS, INTERNAL
1663-1677

The difficulties of overseeing the restored Church of England were manifold. One of the most pressing problems facing the restored episcopate was the problem of nonconformity. The debates about religious conformity have a long historical tradition, dating to the era of the first great council of the church held in Nicaea in 325. Emperor Constantine promoted a model of state and church working together to promote orthodoxy and to punish heterodox/unorthodox beliefs. The seventeenth century churchmen were heirs of this long tradition based in the teachings of Augustine and Aquinas. It was "the obligation of the church and state to use coercion to bring the heterodox back to the fold."[1] The Interregnum experience of religious diversity wed religious nonconformity to political radicalism. Roger L'Estrange wrote in 1663, "Uniformity is the Ciment of both Christian and Civil Societies: Take That away, and the Parts drop from the Body; one piece falls from Another."[2] Therefore, the use of force to return the recalcitrant to the fold was both an act of religious piety and political necessity. Battles over conformity were not always outside the established church, but often even within it. Archbishop Gilbert Sheldon and his bishops could not always depend on the support of those who ought to have been their natural allies. During the term of Sheldon's tenure as archbishop 1663-1677, there were major religious disturbances in several dioceses

---

1 Walsham, *Charitable Hatred,* 41.

2 Roger L'Estrange, *Toleration Disscus'd* (London: Henry Brome, 1663), 86. For more on the press and printing, see Jason Peacey, "Print, Publicity, and Popularity: The Projecting of Sir Balthazar Gerbier, 1642-1662," *Journal of British Studies* 51, no. 2 (2012): 284–307.

between the bishop and members of the chapter: Lichfield and Coventry, Norwich, and Bath and Wells. All of these disputes revolved around conformity to the practices of the church or, more precisely, the lack of conformity within the clerical community.

One way to enforce clerical conformity to the restored church was the use of triennial visitations in every diocese in England. During these visits, the bishops were to ensure that the modes and practices of the parish churches followed the legally established rubrics of the prayer book. They were also to discipline those breaking the laws concerning religion and to perform the lighter and more joyful tasks of ordination and confirmation. Sheldon, as primate, set an example for his fellow bishops with his visitation articles of 1667. These articles were thorough and tied to the canons that argued for this strict legal orthodoxy. Sheldon's instructions reinforced the hierarchy of both the church and the state. His first article questioned whether any resident of the parish denied the king's supremacy in ecclesiastical causes, which was contrary to the first and second canons. The second reinforced the legitimacy of the legally established Church of England as both apostolic and orthodox and reaffirmed its liturgy, rites, and episcopal structure. Those who disagreed, either moderate partial conformists or radical dissenters, were all guilty of breaking not just canon law, but also the law of the land.[3] Even more troubling were those who broke away completely from the church.

> Is there any is the Parish, that separates from the Communion of the Church of England, and the Publique Worship of God in the same by law established, Whether Baptists, Presbyterians, Anabaptists, Fanaticks, or other

---

3   MS Tanner 125, f. 33. "Concerning the Church of England," manuscript copy of Sheldon's 1667 Visitation Articles, no printed editions catalogued in the Bodleian, British Library, or EEBO. Printer listed as Timothy Garthwayt (Garthwait).

Schismaticall Sectaries; Or any that are factors & abet-
tors and [conveners] of such schismaticall persons? Or
any keepers, or maintayners of Conventicles, or favours
of the same? Or setters up of any new or other church
Discipline, governmt, or Fellowship, then what is already by Royall Authority & the Laws of this Land Established? Contrary to the 9.10.11. & 12 canons?[4]

Sheldon wanted to make certain that those serving in the churches under his most direct supervision were obeying the rules. The
lengthiest section of the visitation article was an examination
of those in clerical service. The parishes needed ministers promoting the Church of England to counter the many other voices
competing for religious patronage of different communities.

Is your minister whether Parson, Vicar, or Curate, And
your Lecturer, (if you have any) lawfully ordained according to the Canons of the Church of England, & the
manner & Forme of ordination in & by the Booke of
Common Prayer prescribed, & by law established? And
is he lawfully collated, or Instituted and Inducted, or admitted, and licensed to the charge & service of the Cure
of your Parish, or the Preaching of the said Lecture there.[5]

The need for legal ministers allowed many into the church with
just a verbal agreement to the new rubric. Personal beliefs could
differ, but only in private. Public disagreement with the liturgy, prayer book, or rites and ceremonies was the fastest way to
earn the censure of the archbishop and often the community the
minister served. Sheldon's articles outlined the standards he had
for the clergy serving in his diocese and for those serving in the
church at large. Ministers were to perform divine services and
administer the sacraments according to the Common Prayer

---

4   MS Tanner 125, f. 33.
5   MS Tanner 125, f. 34. "Concerning the Clergy."

without any form of alteration or amendment while wearing the appropriate hood and surplice. Ministers were to catechize the young and the ignorant and to present those of proper age for confirmation before their bishop. Records of marriages, burials, and christenings needed continued upkeep for each church in the diocese. Marriages needed either a license or the banns before proceeding. Sheldon also restated the need for a curate if the minister was a non-resident. Visiting preachers had to show a license and be entered into the visitors' register before being allowed to preach in any church. He was trying to ensure that all preachers, visiting or not, toed the orthodox line.

Sheldon's bishops reported on the state of things in their dioceses. These bishops followed a set of instructions most probably similar to the articles that Sheldon prepared for Canterbury. His instructions went out to his bishops and they reported back. Seth Ward of Salisbury reported, "I have now (by the blessing of Allmighty God) finish'd the Visitation of my Diocese and have every where observed such directions as formerly or lately I have had the hon'r to have rec'd from yr G[race]."[6] This was one of several reports Ward sent to Sheldon, including an earlier report in which the bishop stated:

> In pursuance of his Majesties Eccletical Lawes and of the particular directions of your Grace last yeare sent to me, requiring my particular case, in punishing such persons as should be found in my Diocese, to marry without Banes or license. One Mr Jonathan Heskins Vicar of S. Maries in Marleburgh hath been suspended in the Bishops Court of Sarum.[7]

---

6   MS Tanner 42, f. 125. Seth Ward to Sheldon, September 20, 1674.

7   MS Tanner 44, f. 129. Seth Ward to Sheldon, July 29, 1669. Jonathan Heskins, CCeD Person Id 68911. Heskins was active as a minister until 1677; he must have fallen into line, as he was at St. Mary's under Ward's supervision until his end of service.

In the diocese of Salisbury, the bishop's court followed the procedures set out in both law and tradition. Heskins could be reinstituted from his suspension if he acknowledged his wrongdoing and the local magistrates swore to uphold the ecclesiastical laws. The restoration of a suspended minister needed both the church and magistrates working together in cases where the minister was outside the authority of the cathedral personnel. John Hacket of Lichfield and Coventry reported in June 1665 that, "God gave mee strength & vigour to preach in all those eight marquet towns, in the compass of those few daies. I was meruitously resorted to everie where; & in all those eight places I confirmed 5384."[8] Hacket's visit was full of good reports and reception from the towns he visited. Hacket reported that, "I was told openly at Wem that by my sermon preached there, there were an 100 prisbyterians less then before."[9] While the claim of spontaneous conversion from Presbyterianism to Church of England Protestantism was most likely an exaggeration, the confirmation of nearly 5400 people was no doubt more genuine due to the great need to confirm people after two decades of no or limited confirmations.

Many times visitation reports brought problems to light. Anthony Sparrow of Exeter reported, "... I have discovered two counterfeit Orders. I suspected this at the visitation when these pretended orders was shewn by the persons not appearing themselves but sending the[m] in by friends."[10] Peter Mews of Bath and Wells complained in his report, "... it is my very great unhappiness to bee infested with som so grosly ignorant that they are not able to perform their Dutys with any tolerable reputation to the Ch[urch]: and more such are dayly creeping in and will certainly be the ruine of it if not timely prevented."[11] More troublesome in

---

8   MS Tanner 45, f. 13. John Hacket to Sheldon, June 17, 1665.

9   Ibid.

10   MS Tanner 42, f. 133. Anthony Sparrow to Sheldon, October 31, 1674.

11   Ibid., f. 167. Peter Mews to Sheldon, July 24, 1675.

many churches were ministers settled by the Act for Settling Ministers, because the bishop was not certain of an individual's loyalty and worried they might influence others into heterodox beliefs or outright nonconformity. William Roberts of Bangor had concerns to place before Sheldon, following his visitation of 1665.

> At present I desire your Grace to be advertised that in my Triennial Visitation held in last month, there was one Richard Rowland [?] Rector of Aberfraw in the County of Anglizey who appeared refractory & disobedient to the Authority Ecclisiasticall, peremptorily refusing the usuall & Auncient accustomed payments of Annuals, Prearations, dyes money &c affirming there were noe such things due, though he had paid the same for 4 yeares last past. He is the onely incumbent in this Diocese that holds any living without Institution & Induction being presented by the usurper Oliver & confirmed by the Act for Ministers since his Majesties most happy restitution ... I humbly begg your Graces Assistance & direction for the use of the rod of discipline, seeing he will not be reduced by the spirit of mistakenness & the rather least that others be encouraged to disobedience by his impunity ...[12]

The bishop of Bangor wanted to make an example of the disobedient minister for refusing to follow ecclesiastical laws and sought the archbishop's advice on how to best discipline one who refused to answer before the bishop's consistory court. These brief examples are but a token of the visitation reports returned to Sheldon detailing the nature of the different dioceses under Sheldon's headship. Those who were tardy in returning reports to the archbishop received a written rebuke, as Sheldon desired timely reports concerning conventicle activity.

---

12 MS Tanner 45, f. 21. William Roberts to Sheldon, August 5, 1665. Surname of the recalcitrant minister is unclear.

I doubt not but that long before this time your Lp hath received through the hands of my Ld of London, my Instructions (according to his Majesties direction) concerning Enquiries to be made by you throughout the whole Diocesse & Jurisdiction concerning Conventicles. I thought your Lp would at first sight have conceived it a businesse of that importance. That, without the least delay, you would have gone through with it, & given a speedy acct, either by returne to my Ld of London, or by an immediate address to me; But having received {none/ not a full & satisfactory one} I send this to quicken you, desiring & expecting from yr Lp, as soone as is possible after the receipt of this, as full & exact an Acct, in answere to those enquiries, as by the best of your diligence, & industry you can make.[13]

The most famous survey of the religious lay of the land in this period is the Compton Census. In early 1676, Sheldon wrote to Henry Compton of London to authorize an information gathering campaign throughout the dioceses subject to Canterbury. Compton was to receive the information about the inquiries and report his findings to the archbishop. The archdeacons and churchwardens were to report on the following inquires:

1. What number of persons are there by common account and estimation inhabiting within each parish subject to your jurisdiction

2. What number if popish recusants or persons suspected for such recusancy are there reside among the Inhabitants aforesaid

3. What number of other Dissenters are there in each parish of what sect so ever which either (obstinately?) refuse or wholly absent themselves from the Communion of the

---

13 MS Harleian 7377, f. 6. Draft of letter to unresponsive bishops, 1669.

Church of England as such times as by law they are required.[14]

Sheldon wished to know the religious composition of the dioceses under his direction so that he and his lay and episcopal allies could enforce the laws against conventicles and Roman Catholics and reinforce the traditional hierarchy of both church and state. Sheldon and his allies saw threats to the church from both those who worshipped in conventicles and those who owed allegiance to Rome. Fear of Roman influence in England both pre- and post-dates Sheldon's tenure and was a background fear in the late seventeenth century.

Canterbury modeled for the other dioceses how problems within should be resolved. The bishop played a strong role in leading the opposing sides to agree and if not, the bishop used his authority in the consistory court to bring the offenders to a peaceful and private resolution. Sheldon did not want internal squabbles broadcast to the communities to become targets for gossip and discord within the communities themselves. Sheldon desired that the church present a unified front and position to the world at large and within the particular community affected by internal squabbles. There was conflict even within Sheldon's own chapter house over the choice of the chapter's Register.

> ... we thought it our duty to return Your Grace the most humble thanks for the tender care You are pleased to expresse therein for preserving the unity of the Society wch we confesse was in some danger of being broken by reason of some warm debates among us about the choice of the Register while the common care for the good of the church made us more solicitous about the Person to be chosen. Some thinking it fitt to reward the fidelity of a Person who had served the Church under former Regis-

---

14 MS Carte 79, f. 22. Sheldon to Henry Compton, January 16, 1676.

ters; & others rather to make choice of one who might be more capable to serve us, not onely in Chapter, but in the more difficult affaires of the Church abroad.[15]

The chapter decided to select two men and to split the duties between them upon approval of their superior. They sent word to Sheldon, "we have agreed upon such an Expedient, wch with Your Graces approbation will produce that Peace & thorough reconciliation, wch you desire amongst us viz that the one might serve us in the chapter house, & the other in the soliciting the more publick busyness."[16] Canterbury's internal conflict was quickly resolved; no doubt Sheldon prayed at one time or another that all such conflicts be as easily handled. After Sheldon's death, his successor received a letter from George Thorpe a Canon of the fifth prebend in Canterbury, who referred to a minor squabble between the chapter and the archbishop over the granting of licenses to bishops not ordained at Canterbury. Thorpe wrote about Sheldon, "who upon full hearing of the matter determined for us, & as some of our company say gave Dr Thompson order that there should be noe controversy afterwards."[17] Sheldon both in his diocese and throughout the church under his jurisdiction expected obedience, which prevented conflict in Canterbury and one might assume it would have done the same elsewhere in places conflict erupted.

One of the most spectacular of the diocesan conflicts occurred between the Bishop and Dean of Lichfield, which took nearly

---

15 MS Tanner 123, f. 8. From the Dean and Chapter of Canterbury to Sheldon, August 28, 1672. Signed by Thomas Turner, Dean, John Bargrave, Vice-Dean, and canons: John Archer, John Castillion, Peter Hardres, Edward Aldey, Edward Stillingfleet, John Tillotson, Peter Du Moulin, and William Belk.

16 MS Tanner 123, f, 8.

17 Ibid., f. 7. George Thorpe to Sancroft, December 5, 1683. I am unable to determine who Dr. Thompson was, as no one of that name was part of the Chapter House during Sheldon's tenure. The Deans during the time were Thomas Turner and John Tillotson, so it could be a reference to one of these men.

two decades to resolve and involved two archbishops, the king, and the Court of Arches. These cases serve as illustrations of the deep divisions among the religious elite in Restoration England and the problem of nonconformity within the legal church. Nonconformity within the Church of England was of two sorts. The simplest was the support in any way of conventicles, including Presbyterians and the more radical sorts of religious ideas prevalent in the late seventeenth century. The more complicated idea of religious nonconformity dealt with adherence to the rules and traditions of the church, especially in matters involving discipline. John Hacket was a former royal chaplain of Charles I who spent much of the Interregnum at his living in Cheam, Surrey. He used the prayer book there, but also conformed enough to the regime of the day to stay out of serious trouble with the local authorities. He became Bishop of Lichfield and Coventry in 1661, accepting the vacated see of Accepted Frewen.[18] Thomas Wood, Dean of Lichfield Cathedral, was also a former Royal Chaplain to Charles I. He spent some of the 1650s abroad, but he did not minister to the exiles. He lived abroad and in England on family money until the Restoration.[19]

Initially, Hacket's tenure as Bishop of Lichfield and Coventry looked promising. The cathedral underwent major damage during the Civil War, at one point even being used as a stable. It needed major repairs and Hacket, having done the same at one of his first livings, was familiar with the challenges of raising funds to repair churches. Naturally, Hacket expected the restored chapter to contribute to the rebuilding and restoration of their cathedral and was not disappointed. The canons and prebends of Lichfield supported Hacket in this great task. Hacket and Wood, however, quarreled over the amount Dean Wood was to give in

---

18 Brian Quintrell, "John Hackett, Bishop of Coventry and Lichfield," *ODNB*, 3–4.

19 B.S. Benedikz, "Thomas Wood, Bishop of Lichfield and Coventry," *ODNB*, 1.

the rebuilding, but this quarrel was only a symptom of a deeper problem. Wood refused to conform to church laws and traditions despite his clerical career. Wood received aid from his family in the political wrangling associated with profitable livings, deaneries and bishoprics. Wood spent little time as a practicing priest, going abroad during the Interregnum. He only baptized one child during his earlier clerical career.

Hacket began his rule of Lichfield and Coventry intending to cooperate fully with the religious program of the restored regime and working to restore the Cathedral at Lichfield. Hacket's correspondence with Sheldon held the easy tone of old friends—and it was to this friend that Hacket brought the problems of his diocese.

> I will bring our illiterate Dean on the stage, and his lack-latin ridiculousness. First he will keep no chapter, nor suffer anie to bee call'd, among other reasons, because the Resendentians bring forth the statutes to him in Latin, & he understands not a line, till Greswold put it into English ... he told Mr Arch-bold, he had not read a booke these two years.[20]

Hacket worked quickly and efficiently in restoring the Cathedral at Lichfield. Less than ten years after his consecration, he reported to his primate that, "our Cathedrall Church being made ready to perform all holie services in it, I addressed myself to reconcile it from much bloodshed and pollution wch had defiled it and to dedicate it to the worship of the most high."[21] This was a noteworthy accomplishment in the best of times, and Hacket and the members of the chapter house were not working in the best of times. Hacket wrote plainly of his associates and subordinates, "The honest Residentiaries deserve a church thus beautified, so doth not the phrentique Dean, who sides all together with the

---

20 MS Tanner 131, f. 22. Hacket to Sheldon, February 1, 1668.

21 Ibid., f. 42. Hacket to Sheldon, January 18, 1669

Puritans, and told me to my face, I did more harm than good, in reedifying this Church. God remove him from us."[22]

The details of the conflict between the bishop and chapter and the dean have roots in the discussions around the restoration of the Lichfield cathedral. Thomas Wood was the second dean installed after the restoration of the church in 1660. Deans were in charge of cathedral chapter houses and had the duty of administering the property of the cathedral. They were also responsible for calling and holding meetings with chapter members and publishing the preaching rotation for the various ministers in the cathedral. Deans also officially presided over the elections of the bishop. His immediate predecessor, William Paule, moved to Oxford as bishop in 1663; Paule was orthodox and diligent in his canonical duties, whereas Wood was at best lax and at worst irreverent. "I heare by some reports that our Dean is married a little before Xmass. He neither comes nor writes to take order for anie thing in the Church: the yong bride, it seems, must excuse all. His peculiars are much out of frame: but I will supply all places as wel as I am able."[23] He further explained of the dean's odd behavior:

> I wonder what he does at home: for he hath not stirred out of doors since the 23 of December. Never came to publick praises, nor his wife (shee never coms to praises, but now & then before Xmass a sermon) in all the 13 festival days of Xmass wch makes the puritans mightily resort to him, whose patron he is upon all occasions; and that makes him as ridiculous as his lack-latin-ship.[24]

Hacket laid the complete case of the disaffected dean before Sheldon in a letter dated January 20, 1667.

---

22 MS Tanner 44, f. 66. Hacket to Sheldon, December 12, 1668.

23 MS Tanner 45, f. 137. Hacket to Sheldon, January 17, 1666.

24 MS Tanner 131, f. 22. Hacket to Sheldon, February 1, 1668.

> If ever anie Bishop had cause to complain of the Dean
> of his Cathedral, I am the man, as will appear ... Three of
> our Canon residentiaries, Mr Harrison, Mr Brown, Mr
> Gresold (who hath Mr Hutchinsons Proxy under hand
> & seale) appealed unto me, according to Jus Canonicum,
> and according to their local statutes against their Dean
> upon particulars following. [25]

Hacket listed the charges in a detailed letter to Sheldon. First,
Wood refused to call a lawfully required chapter meeting. This
chapter meeting was necessary for many reasons but one listed
was dealing with the vacancy of a vicarage in the chapter's possession—the vicarage in question had been vacant for six months.
Wood disobeyed the archbishop's order to call a chapter meeting
to decide what to do about the ruins of Blakewell Chancel. The
tenant of Blakewell tried to meet with Wood offering monetary
assistance for the necessary repairs, but Wood refused to meet
the tenant. Wood removed from the cathedral the chapter's register book and the records of bond debts owed to the chapter,
which included one of his own for a hundred marks for the repair
and rebuilding of the cathedral. Wood also took possession of
the *custos fabric* (records of the material possessions of the cathedral) from the canon responsible for keeping the records. Finally,
Wood refused to call a chapter to pass the schedule of preachers
for Sundays and other holy days prepared by the canons at the
request of the bishop.[26] Hacket wanted to resolve these matters
and followed established procedures in doing so after soliciting the advice of his archbishop, who preferred that this matter
with Wood go through local channels. Hacket attempted to call a
meeting between the dean and the canons of the cathedral to discuss the complaint laid against Wood. Hacket dutifully reported
the event to his superior:

---

25 Ibid., f. 18. Hacket to Sheldon, January 20, 1667.

26 Author's paraphrase. MS Tanner 131, f.18.

Because I would ... have these errors of his publiquely laid open, I summoned the Dean & 3 canons to meet at my house on Tuesday the 14ᵗʰ of this month at 8 in the morning. The canons appeared; he would not come, yet was present at the cathedral for praiers that morning. He came to mee on that Tuesday at past eight at night & would know what I had to say to him. I told him your Grace had delivered a letter of his unto mee, wherein hee had complained that the canons has put things out of order, and that I could not treat with him on upon it but in their presence.[27]

The aforementioned Thomas Brown, who served as a Canon Residentiary until deprivation as a non-juror in 1690, wrote to the archbishop about the state of the Lichfield chapter in house with similar complaints against Wood:

I hope I have not done amisse, so far as the thing concerns me & my brethren, for we did first advise, not onily with our statutes but friends therin; And that after severall councils & humble addresses to the Dean, of whom I will onily say, that he is the strangest man that evir I have had any thing to so with; And it shall bee part of my prayer, that I may never have to doe with such another.[28]

The bishop and the other members of the Chapter followed canonical procedures in trying to resolve the matter with Wood. Hacket excommunicated an unrepentant and unresponsive Wood in his diocesan court and announced the charge in early 1668. Wood then left Lichfield for his other living as a canon of Durham, while considering his response to the bishop's requests for his reunion with the church. Wood also campaigned before

---

27 Ibid., f. 18. Hacket to Sheldon, January 20, 1667.

28 MS Tanner 45, f. 255. Thomas Brown to Sheldon, January 22, 1667.

Sheldon and other bishops attempting to blacken the name and reputation of his opponent, which was not kept secret for long:

> Concerning our scandalous Dean, he plaies the hypocrite most notably, to speake wel of me before your Grace; who loaded mee with foul, and false revilings before the Bp of Durham, as his LP sent mee word. He hath not given mee one civil visit in 15 months at Lichfield, & then he reviled mee to my face in most rude & unreverent reproaches, whereof I have witness that over h[e]ard him.[29]

Wood also denied all wrongdoing in the charges laid against him by the members of the chapter of Lichfield, forcing the members to campaign on their own behalves for the daily operation of the cathedral. Hacket kept his superior well informed of the activities and trials of the quarrel between bishop and dean and between dean and chapter:

> I have received some lines from Mr. Brown the Arch-deacon of Darby, that our Dean hath with much falsehood & impudency, avouched before your Grace, that the Articles preferred against him by our Residentiaries are all false ... I know the most of them to be justly charged upon him, and the rest are reported true in all mens mouths in these quarters, and manie more might have been added, as scandalous as the former.[30]

Hacket wrote of his willingness to receive Wood back once he completed the tasks laid before him for reunion. This was the best option for all involved, but Wood remained at odds with his bishop and the chapter members. Wood left Lichfield not to return for several years, choosing exile rather than submitting to

---

29 MS Tanner 44, f. 127. Hacket to Sheldon, July 19, 1669.

30 MS Tanner 131, f. 32. Hacket to Sheldon, April 19, 1669.

the clerical authorities. Sheldon's sympathies were with Hacket. Wood's irregularity was not something he appreciated or approved. His real desire for the resolution of the matter quietly and privately evaporated quickly. Sheldon knew that the church had many enemies both within and without its boundaries that needed little excuse to use any bad press to question practices the church supported, especially the controversial policies directed at nonconformity. In Lichfield, Wood's Puritanical inclinations made the execution of the law difficult, and the problems only multiplied after he wed a known nonconformist. Lichfield had problems with conventicles, and Hacket tied Wood to their activities, "There never was a viler wretch in a place of dignitie. Puritanism hath spread excessively in our cittie, not only by his sufferance, but by his furtherance, giving countenance to none but the greatest nonconformists."[31] Sheldon wanted to use the traditional methods of the church to deal with recalcitrant ministers, but problems emerged with Wood and others that partially conforming ministers within the church were not often in agreement with the episcopacy or the attendant rules that went along with it. Disputes within the church, like the one in Lichfield, may make us question the prevailing consensus that the Restoration Church of England was without great division until the later debates over exclusion and the Revolution of 1688. It might be argued that the later divisions of the church have roots within the experiences of the Restoration churchmen. If so, the case of Lichfield represented a great weakness of the settlement, if not outright failure, and it was without wonder that diocesan conflict was such a part of the church of the 1660s and 1670s. No doubt, Sheldon wished his church was rid of Wood, although the church was desperately short of episcopally ordained clerics, and Wood was at the very least that, like Mister Pead mentioned previously.

---

31 Ibid., f. 32.

The threat of nonconformity was one constant throughout the years of Charles II's tenure. Charles and his chief ministers changed policies regarding religion and toleration depending on who was closest to the king. Charles was himself a hindrance in the eyes of some for his own quixotic nature regarding religious matters, especially through his exercise of the prerogative in freeing imprisoned dissenters and offering indulgences. The beleaguered churchmen of the 1660s and 1670s wanted to suppress nonconformity in their dioceses and parishes, but many factors prevented widespread enforcement of the laws against nonconformity. In any community, especially a diocesan center, to have a member of the legitimate clerical establishment openly resisting the rules of the church encouraged nonconformists of many stripes to press their advantage.

Wood refused to submit to Hacket's ruling and brought his case before the Court of Arches, claiming that the charges laid by his bishop were false. Through skilled backroom politicking by his family, Wood came through the court victorious, getting his excommunication overturned and even managing to get Hacket excommunicated by the Arches. Wood's older brother was a well-connected and deep-pocketed court figure and one of the members of the circle surrounding Barbara Villiers, a mistress of the king. Hacket returned to his duties after a quick reinstatement by the archbishop. Samuel Pepys recorded the quarrel in his diary. The story came to Pepys by an associate, Colonel Birch, an MP from Herefordshire. Pepys wrote of Hacket and Wood's quarrel, "the former [Hacket] of which did excommunicate the later [Wood] and caused his excommunication to be read in the church while he was there ... and so they are at law in the Arches about it—which is a very pretty story."[32]

Hacket and Wood remained at odds until the end of the bishop's life in 1670. Commonly, upon the death of a bishop, a dean

---

32 Pepys, vol. 9, 45.

assumed the see. Wood only obtained the bishopric of Lichfield and Coventry after skillful intervention of family friends and allies at court, including Barbara Villiers, duchess of Cleveland, whose daughter Mary was to wed Wood's nephew.[33] Courtly connections played a big part in ecclesiastical promotions and punishments. Sheldon fell out of favor with the king and court, as the situation with Hacket and Wood deteriorated in Lichfield and the aging archbishop was less able to sway the king to intervene while others held favor. The 1670s saw the generation of clerics loyal to Charles I and Charles II lose influence to younger men; Wood's remarkable elevation was evidence of the loss of influence of the older generation of clerics and courtiers. This, however, was not the end of the story, but just the introduction of new players. Sheldon oversaw Wood carefully and planned to excommunicate the recalcitrant cleric in 1677, but Sheldon's death in November prevented the long-awaited excommunication and suspension from ecclesiastical duties.

After Sheldon's death, William Sancroft became Archbishop and Wood was one of the problems he inherited. Sancroft also wished to excommunicate Wood, but recognized the importance of having the king's support. Lancelot Addison became Dean of Lichfield in 1683 and reported on his erstwhile bishop to the archbishop. Additionally, Sancroft had Bishop Francis Turner of Ely, a supporter of the Duke of York, reintroduce the matter at court. Charles II was no fool and knew that to keep his plans for the succession in place, he needed the support of the church.

Nearly sixteen years after the first outbreak of the quarrel, in 1684, Wood's excommunication and suspension from his ecclesiastical duties and income forced a conclusion to the feud. Both Wood and Hacket's heir, his son Andrew, had monetary fines from the drawn out legal proceedings. Wood's punishment included a monetary fee of £2565. Andrew Hacket had to pay

33 Benedikz, "Thomas Wood," 1.

£1520, of which £120 was Wood's fee in the Court of Arches.[34] Two bishops arbitrated the affair: Henry Compton of London and William Lloyd of Peterborough. More important than the monetary fines was the decision to force Wood to obey the will of the church. He had to "make a full & becoming submission to his Grace the present Lord Archbishop of Canterbury, for his absen[ces], from his Diocese & the neglect of his duty and all other Crimes alledged and proved against him in the depositions read before us & exhibited."[35] Wood finally bowed to ecclesiastical authority, ending the long, drawn-out affair.

The conflict in Lichfield was just one of several internal diocesan conflicts that Sheldon dealt with during his time as primate. Norwich was an additional diocese that had conflict over the behavior of the dean; however, unlike Lichfield, the conflict was between the dean and chapter, not the bishop. Norwich at this point was under the leadership of Edward Reynolds. Reynolds was a moderate Presbyterian with long held opinions leading toward reconciliation and unity within the church. Reynolds received his offer for a bishopric when Charles II offered sees to both Richard Baxter and Edmund Calamy, who refused Hereford and Lichfield and Coventry respectively.[36] Norwich had problems, not between the bishop and dean, but between the dean and the chapter. Reynolds worked closely with his chapter and had good relationships with the canons and prebends. These good relationships were remarkable considering these men followed different paths until the Restoration. The conflict in Norwich involved Dr. John Crofts, dean of Norwich and the members of the chapter. The complaints of the chapter against Crofts had much to do with Crofts's lifestyle. They charged that Crofts was a "striker." He fought in the church even when divine service

---

34 MS Tanner 131, f. 106.

35 Ibid., f. 106.

36 Ian Atherton, "Edward Reynolds, Bishop of Norwich," *ODNB*, 2.

was going on or when a large number of people were present. In addition to the fighting, Crofts used vulgar and foul language, even within the cathedral. While preaching around the diocese, Crofts encouraged the suspension of preaching for an unspecified time. This was contrary to the policies of the archbishop in encouraging preaching throughout the country. Crofts also disregarded canonical procedures in assuming the office of Commissary of the Peculiars. The Peculiars had the right to intervene in a given community about spiritual and moral behavior generally independent of the deanery and diocesan authorities. The Peculiars were a holdover from pre-reformation England, usually connected to former abbey lands. Crofts, like Thomas Wood, removed the chapter books and refused to allow the prebends access to their record books. Finally, the chapter house tagged Crofts as someone who sowed dissension between the members of the chapter and alienated the bishop by his unkindness.[37] One can assume that the strife in the chapter house between the dean and the prebends caused problems in the day-to-day operation of the cathedral. Croft became dean in 1660 and the complaints against him emerged after 1667; Crofts died in 1670 and left the restoration of the unity of the chapter house to others. Herbert Astley became dean and had to deal with the situation left by a non-functioning chapter house. One example would be the problem at Kings Lynn in Norfolk, which was a living in the care of the dean and chapter of Norwich. Horatio Townshend, first Viscount Townshend, went to this community twice to deal with the problems of religious nonconformity in his duties as Lord Lieutenant of Norwich.[38] The residents of Kings Lynn sent their

---

37 Author's paraphrase of MS Tanner 133, f. 50. Not dated, but after 1667. Signers William Hawkins and Hezekiah Burton came to Norwich as prebends in 1667. The other signers, Edmund Porter (1628) and Herbert Astley (1663), came to Norwich before them. *Fasti Ecclesiae Anglicanae 1541-1847*, vol. 7, 54–61. John Crofts (Croftes) CCeD Person Id 5411.

38 James M. Rosenheim, *The Townshends of Rayham* (Middleton, CT: Wesleyan University Press, 1989), 34. The first two chapters deal with the Resto-

complaint, not to the fractious chapter house to which they were beholden, but to the archbishop. They complained that the curate supplied by the vicar was not appropriate and they desired a full-time vicar for the proper ordering of worship in their community.[39] The mayor, aldermen, and town council sent in the petition and Sheldon sent his reply to the new dean, Astley.

I should be very well pleased you could find out some way to put the service of those places into such a course & method, as might give that Corporaton & Towne better satisfaction; To wch end I desire, That you & your Brethren will consult together for an Expedient; And lest you should not be able to effect it of your selves, I thinke, it will not be amisse, that you apply your selves to your Bp and take his advice into your assistance. When you have considered of this, and done what you can to apply the Remedie desired, I shall be glad to receive an Account of it from you.[40]

Any type of conflict was undesirable, but Sheldon for the most part let the local authorities resolve the matters, wanting only a report of what occurred. This served at least two functions. One, Sheldon was busy with the multitude of diverse problems that seemed to emerge on a weekly, if not daily, basis and with his own commitments in London and Canterbury. Sheldon spent most of the tenure of his primacy at Lambeth Palace, which gave him easy access to Westminster and parliament and was a good place to receive his correspondence.[41] Two, resolving problems on a lo-

---

ration era.

39 MS Tanner 134, f. 147. Undated letter from the citizens of Kings Lynn to Sheldon, enclosed with Sheldon's reply to Astley (f. 146).

40 Ibid., f, 146. Sheldon to Herbert Astley, November 14, 1671. Also, see MS Harleian 7377, f. 27b for the letter book copy of this correspondence.

41 This is my own assumption from looking at the addresses of his letters, which came to Lambeth Palace in both the Tanner and Harleian manuscripts. His

cal level using the local ecclesiastical personnel helped reinforce the legitimacy and strength of the restored church. One conflict that received Sheldon's personal touch was the conflict within the chapter house of Wells, which placed the dean and archdeacons against the prebends over the annual visitation of the cathedral church and placed the dean and archdeacons against the bishop.

The conflict in Wells stemmed from the visitation of the cathedral. In particular, the issue was the visitation rights the dean and archdeacons possessed to visit and to inquire about the service of the prebends and canons of the cathedral church. The bishop of Bath and Wells, William Piers, held the see from 1632 and supported the church programs of the 1630s with fervor. He was a former vice-chancellor of the University of Oxford, serving as such while Sheldon was probationer, then fellow at All Souls.[42] The Dean of Wells was Robert Creighton who had a distinguished royalist pedigree from his service to Charles II in exile at St. Germain, among other places. Creighton became dean in 1660 and brought a successful case against the incumbent to claim his living. Creighton and Piers had both had positions in Wells since the early 1630s.[43] The problem in Wells came about when Piers forbade Creighton from visiting the cathedral, causing a split in the chapter house of those who sided with the dean's legal right to visit the cathedral and those who obeyed their diocesan leader.

Wee the Deane & Chapter of the Cathedrall Church of Wells are become humble petitioners to your Grace, that you wil be pleased to compose[:] an unhappy difference that is fallen out betweene my Lord Bp of Bath & Wells

letters during the Interregnum also came to London in the care of his nephew, Joseph Sheldon at St. Paul's Churchyard.

42 M. Dorman, "William Piers, Bishop of Bath and Wells," *ODNB*, 1. Spurr. "Sheldon," 1.

43 John S. Macauley, "Robert Creighton [Creyghton], Bishop of Bath and Wells," *ODNB*, 1–2.

& Reverend Diocesan, and Ourselves about our power of visiting the prebendaries, wherein wee have used our utmost indeavours ... but cannot bring to passe what wee have much desired.[44]

The debate over the visitation began in June 1669, with Creighton and the archdeacons suspending the prebends and minor canons who obeyed the bishop's injunction against the visitation of the cathedral. The suspended prebends petitioned Sheldon in the Arches for aid in overturning the ruling. Sheldon wrote to Creighton, "I am much troubled to heare of the unreasonable differences, that of late have fallen out amongst your selves in the Church, and am very sorry there was none amongst you that had care enough to keepe them from breaking out into a publick flame."[45] Sheldon sent similar messages to Creighton's associates, Archdeacons John Selleck and Grindall Sheafe. Controversy within the church was one thing Sheldon desired to keep private and he was not against chiding and shaming those who allowed such things to come into the open.

> ... what thinke you can be the event of these quarrels, but to give advantage, & make sport for those who will be glad to see us ingaged on agt [one] another. Sure it will be worth your consideration to incline to a fayre & amicable composure rather than then suffer such Broyles to appeare upon the stage in an open court: And it will be much better, that betweene your selves, both parties should incline to understand & yield to reason, then to trouble me with these Controversies, wch I am unwilling to be forced to decide between you.[46]

---

44 MS Tanner 140, f. 8. June 12, 1669 to Sheldon. Signed by Robert Creighton, Dean of Wells, John Selleck, Archdeacon of Bath, and Grindall Sheafe, Archdeacon of Wells.

45 MS Harleian 7377, f. 7b. Sheldon to the Dean of Wells, October 20, 1669.

46 Ibid., f. 7b.

Despite Sheldon's claim that he was unwilling to decide between the two sides at Wells, the situation was slow to improve, forcing him to act. Sheldon's secretary, Miles Smyth, penned the next exchange between Lambeth and Wells. Smyth wrote to Creighton, "That notwithstanding any thing, either your or Dr. Sellecks Ltr say there is nothing That can seeme tolerably to excuse much lesse justify the severity wherewith you have treated your Brethren."[47]

Sheldon offered in late November his "advice" to all persons affected by the quarrelling at Wells. First, he recommended that all the protestations from either side be withdrawn and that the act of suspension made by the dean and archdeacon against the prebends and others be overturned and the affected persons returned to their rights and privileges. Second, the prebends and canons needed to acknowledge and consent to the right of the dean for an annual visitation of the cathedral at Wells. Next, the suspended canons and prebends needed to return to the performance of their duties and offices in the cathedral. In addition, the chapter acts made during the suspension were invalid unless the restored members agreed to them. Additionally, all books, registers, records, and common writing belonging to the chapter house were not to reside in any private residence.[48] Within a month, Sheldon wrote to Creighton:

> I am very glad to understand by your letter that the late differences in the Church are so well Ended amongst your selves; And although you seem to apprehend the like dissensions may break out againe, and other inconveniences may happen to you in that place, you let me assure you this, That whosoever he shall be amongst you that shall endeavour to embroyle you againe, or shall nor demeane himselfe towards you with that respect & de-

---

47 Ibid., f. 8b. Miles Smyth to Robert Creighton, November 2, 1669.

48 Author's paraphrase of MS Tanner 140, f. 27–28. Lambeth, November 28, 1669.

cency that becomes him, & is due to your dignity, as farre
as it is in my power to assist you, he shall not carry it away
with impunity.[49]

Wells continued to cause problems for Sheldon. As soon as one
complaint ended, another sprang up to take its place. Robert
Creighton succeeded William Piers in the bishopric and the former dean and new bishop had his own quarrel with one particular canon, Dr. William Piers, the son of the former bishop. Piers
was non-resident in Wells and allowed the house due to him by
being a canon fall into disrepair. Ralph Bathurst, the new dean
of Wells, wrote to Sheldon, assuring him that the difficult canon
promised

> ... that he will cause the House collated on him as Canon,
> to be forthwith altered & repaired. Secondly, that he will
> keepe and fulfill his residence in the said House, as the
> Statutes & Charter of our Church, & the Church of En-
> gland, do require. I have already signified to my Lord Bp,
> that it is your Graces pleasure that these things should be
> done: and do now again write to him, that Dr Piers hath
> faithfully promised to do them.[50]

Piers promised to obey the rules and charter of Wells; however,
a year later the troublesome canon was still causing problems for
Creighton. He complained to Sheldon that after Piers's suspension and appeal to the Arches, he continued to live in a non-ca-
nonical house and rented his canonical one. Creighton wrote,
"contrary to the custom of all well governed cathedrals & ours especially, but of this your Grace has had enough, I say no more."[51]
The problems in Wells then disappear from the correspondence,
but outside political developments might have created unity

---

49 MS Harleian 7377, f. 11b. Sheldon to Creighton, December 23, 1669.

50 MS Tanner 140, f. 14. Ralph Bathurst to Sheldon, March 16, 1671.

51 Ibid., f. 23. Robert Creighton to Sheldon, August 16, 1672.

within the chapter house and cathedral, as this correspondence was from 1672. Alternatively, Creighton and his successor might have kept their promise to not bring the matter to the archbishop again and to deal with any further conflict themselves.

The drawn out quarrel in Lichfield was one only division in the attempt to restore the Church of England after 1660. The smaller, but just as difficult, disputes for those involved in the dioceses of Canterbury, Norwich and Wells were a telling indication of the deep divisions within the established church after two decades of suppression by the authorities. The idea of the *via media*, the great hallmark of English religious life since the time of Elizabeth, was fading. The broad church of the past was incapable of dealing with the problems left by the Civil War and the religious experiences of the Interregnum. Orthodoxy to the complete liturgy and modes of clerical dress was a required component. Individuals could not define their own brand of orthodoxy. This was a marked change from the church of James I and was far from what consensus-minded individuals desired at the time of the Restoration. The problems in these dioceses often stemmed from one or more persons refusing to follow established canonical practices. This was present in Lichfield, Wells, and Norwich. The chapter houses of every cathedral were under a prescribed set of rules and regulations governing everything from the preaching and ministry of the cathedral to rules about residency and monetary obligations. Another factor in common was that the opposing parties were generally higher officers of the chapters. But as illustrated above, it is also about more prosaic and pragmatic issues, like privileges and money, rather than about theology and ideology, which marked the disputes mid-century. This conflict between clerical elites, either bishops or deans, left the chapter houses and cathedrals in states of chaos and the ministry of each cathedral and bishop's court in disarray. These arguments lent boldness to those outside the church and served as proof of the Church of England's corruption, Catholicity, and so on. Unlike during the time of Elizabeth, dissenters were ready to pounce and make the most of the opportunities presented by a fractious established church.

Complicating matters, the leadership of the church and the state worked on religious agendas, often following different modes and having different aims. Over the long term, such bitter conflicts and quarrels showed how the Civil Wars and Interregnum permanently changed the religious fabric of English society. England could not, and in some cases would not, reverse or erase the effects of twenty years of religious expansion outside the orthodoxy of the Church of England. The proliferation of new models of religious expression made uniformity unachievable, despite the beliefs and wishes of many within society, both lay and clerical. However, the Church of England had a final trump card—in the tumultuous political environment of the last years of Charles II, the church supported the king. Both the monarchs to come and the instruments of government realized the importance of having the church support their regimes. Political, legal, academic, and military careers required conformity to the established church of the realm, not a dissenting congregation. However, the Church of England that developed in the decades following the Restoration was not a monolithic institution. It split on ideological and later theological points, which would have dismayed churchmen like Sheldon and many of his contemporaries, who wanted a church with one unified expression of worship and belief.

Sheldon and his bishops faced many challenges within their dioceses and Sheldon received reports on a great many issues throughout his tenure as primate. One pressing issue that concerned places around England was the poor state of repair of many churches and cathedrals throughout the country. The quarrel between Hacket and Wood began over such an issue, but Hacket was not the only cleric to have to rebuild. Sheldon himself spent a great sum of money restoring the library at Lam-

beth Palace and contributing to the restoration and then the rebuilding of St. Paul's Cathedral and the archiepiscopal residence
at Croydon, where he was buried in 1677.[52] Sheldon requested
lists of the expenditures of the work done at different locations
throughout England. Accepted Frewen, Archbishop of York,
listed both the questions and his replies. The questions sent to
the other bishops must have been of a similar vein as those sent
to Frewen. How much money went for repairs of the cathedral
church and its ornaments for worship or of the houses owned
by the church for the bishop, dean, and prebends? What was the
amount of the money spent on the gift of the church to the king
in addition to money sent for the redemption of English captives
abroad? Sheldon also inquired about the augmentation of vicar-
ages, which was a concern of Sheldon's throughout his time in
an episcopal see. He worried that good men for the church were
hard to find if salaries were not enough to support a family. Frew-
en replied that the repairs of the cathedral and the cleric's houses
cost £3300. The chapter house of York contributed £2000 to the
king's gift with an additional £400 later. Frewen assured Sheldon
that he was augmenting the wages of the vicars so that no one had
cause to complain.[53]

Not all of the reports sent to Sheldon by his bishops were as neat
and tidy as Frewen's list of expenditures. Anthony Sparrow, the
third bishop of Exeter since the Restoration, wrote of his predecessors:

> The first Bp, who let the leases & received the most con-
> siderable sums, for ought I can learn, carried his mony
> away with him, & left his Successor to repair the Palace,
> wch he did, expending as I am told about 400*l* upo[n]

---

52 MS 244, f. 105. Sheldon's Will, February 5, 1672/3. Sheldon wished his executors to make good his subscription for £2000. In Sheldon's hand, was a side
note marked "all paid" before his death in 1677.

53 MS Tanner 150, f. 24a. Noted in Archbishop Frewen's hand.

it. But he is best able to give an account of himself. For my self, though I never had till now such revenues by the Ch. as would maintain me decently according to the (?) place I was in, without the help of mine own patrimony, yet I expensed in repair of a chancel, parsonage, house, & benevolence to the kg above 240*l* a greater sume tha[n] had ever till now received by fines.[54]

Some of the repairs necessary to make church services viable and homes livable exceeded the income of the minister. Sparrow was lucky in having family funds to fall back upon to improve his cure. His report listed a monetary sum, which was not necessarily commonplace in the answers to Sheldon's inquiries. The Dean and Chapter of Oxford gave a detailed explanation of the repairs to both the cathedral and college without disclosing the amount the chapter received or expended. Dean John Fell and his associates wrote of the disrepair of Christ Church, "we found the Stock of the House utterly exhausted, & over and above the Fabrick it selfe partly demolish't, and the timber of the whole North-side of the great Quadrangle sawed down from the Walls & Roofe, & applied to fire-wood; & the remaining Buildings wholely let goe to Ruine."[55] However, they go on to assure their primate of the care they took in repairing and rebuilding their building for the 200 of their society and augmenting the salaries of the vicars and curates beholden to the cathedral. The rebuilding efforts focused around the quadrangle and cloisters, which formed the center of the college of Christ Church.

---

54 MS Tanner 141, f. 132. Anthony Sparrow, Exeter to Sheldon, 1670. Sparrow was preceded by John Gauden and Seth Ward.

55 MS Tanner 147, f. 71. Dean and Chapter of Oxford to Sheldon, undated. Signed by John Fell, Richard Gardiner, Edward Pocock, Thomas Lockey, and George Croyden. The report had to be after 1666, by the presence of George Croyden's signature. Croyden became a prebend in that year. Gardiner and Pocock were restored to their positions in the cathedral during the Restoration.

Sheldon's concern with the physical repairs of the church began before his elevation to Canterbury while still bishop of London. Thus Francis Wilford, Dean of Ely reported to Sheldon, "According to your order I have cast up the Charges of the Church of Ely as exactly as I can, and I find (by the books) that the Benevolence mony, that for the Captives, and the expenses of the Church amount to 7726*l*—18*s*—10*p*."[56] Wilford noted that additional sums would be necessary to make the cathedral church compliant with the rules governing worship under the law. He added, "But for my owne part I am very well content if in can doe any service for the church."[57]

The bishops of the restored Church of England were not just spiritual leaders, but also very much involved in the secular governing of the realm. Sheldon spurred his bishops to this duty as well. He sent circular letters to his bishops, urging and reminding them of this duty.

> I am Commanded by His Majestie to require your Lordship to give attendance at the Parliament at the first meeting in October next; And in case your Lordship be hindered by Sicknesses, or any other unavoidable accident or necessity that you cannot be personally present, That you fayle not of sinding up your Proxie, to be given in upon the very first Day of the Sitting.[58]

The bishops were eager to resume their traditional duties and made a solid show of support for the king's programs so long as the security of the church remained unthreatened. Robert Morgan of Bangor wrote regretfully that "... I would obey with as much readiness & alacrity as any man living but that god does

---

56 MS Tanner 141, f. 45. Francis Wilford to Sheldon, 1662. Wilford was Dean of Ely from 1662-1667.

57 Ibid.

58 MS Add c 308, f. 101. Sheldon to his bishops, August 31, 1667.

not permit. For I have layn languishing all this winter & stirred not abroad at all any further then the Cathedrall ... This is a great truth. I am too old & near my grave to use false excuses."[59] The other common business of the bishops assembled for parliament was a meeting of convocation, usually at the king's request. In 1676, Sheldon wrote to his bishops of the king's desire that "there should be a full and intire convention (if it may be) att the first opening of the Parliament now approaching."[60] Those able to attend had no excuse for absence, and those ill or aged had to send in suitable proxies for their empty seats. Sheldon also organized the episcopal votes in the Lords and tied them in with MPs in the Commons, as he reminded Giles Swiet, Dean of the Arches.

> You cannot but have heard (at least somewhat) of the great Clamours that are made against the Ecclicall Courts for delay of Justice and other abuses in their proceedings, Nor can you be ignorant what a shock the Church is at this time likely to undego upon that account. If you mend not ... there are those that will undertake it for you, And if you fall under a Parlamt Regulation you many perhaps find too some instead of that amending what is amiss, you may lose all the power you have. I desire therefore, That you will call to your assistance the Judges of the Prerogative & Admiralty, the Advocates of the King & Duke ... That when it comes before the Parlamt I may have somewhat to say for you. If you doe what is right you shall have me & all my Brethren your friends, & what other friends we can make for you.[61]

---

59 MS Tanner 43, f. 68. Robert Morgan to Sheldon, January 13, 1672. Robert Morgan died 1673.

60 MS Tanner 40, f. 51. Sheldon to his bishops, January 15, 1676.

61 MS Add c 308, f. 114. Sheldon to Giles Sweit, Dean of the Arches, March, 24, 1667/8.

Sheldon was a shrewd politician, especially when it came to protecting his church from outside attacks and inward corruption. The restored church still faced many dangers both within and without, and parliamentary alliances and regulations were an effective way to protect the church. Sheldon no doubt believed the cry of "the church in an age of danger."

Sheldon's interest in parliamentary affairs and his correspondence about them went further afield than to his subordinate bishops, involving members of the king's Privy Council. Sheldon wrote to the Duke of Ormond about the meeting of the Irish Parliament, "... you will take some care that none hereafter may hold ecclesiasticall prefermt in both kingdomes, I should have done it long since here, but that I favour to move in any thing in parliamt wch concerns the church, unless of absolute necessity."[62] The Lord Lieutenant Ormond replied, "... I shall with advise of the two [Irish] Archbishops cause a bill to be prepared against one person holding preferments in both kingdomes though by it I shall provoke my own Bp of Ossory to assigne me some part in Antichrist."[63] Preferment issues, especially multiple livings throughout the three kingdoms of the British Isles, were an old complaint. Sheldon sought to eliminate those who held English and Irish livings in common.

The political and religious stresses of the restored monarchy and church were not the only issues that crossed Sheldon's desk. The mid-1660s saw a return of the plague to England. Sheldon, despite his position, elected to remain in London while the rest of the government fled. He intended to help oversee relief efforts from Lambeth. The duty of collecting relief was the job of the Bishop of London, Humphrey Henchman. Henchman was a close ally of Sheldon in parliamentary matters working together

---

62 MS Carte 45, f. 169. Sheldon to Ormond, August 22, 1663.

63 Ibid., f. 177. Ormond to Sheldon, undated, but after August 1663. Ossory was in the possession of Griffith Williams 1641-1672, per the old *ODNB*.

for the good of the church in physical repairs (post-fire) and spiritual attacks.[64] Henchman was to stay behind and organize relief for the plague-stricken areas of London and fast days for a speedy end to the plague.[65] Anyone with the means to leave wanted to flee London and its environs for safer places to spend the summer. Sheldon stayed behind, perhaps as an example to some of the clergy of London who debated leaving their parishes. John Hacket wrote to Sheldon, alluding to the former, "Our gentry begin already to fly our poor cittie, & give more discouragement, then I can see cause for I resolve to live or dy by your Graces president & not to stir unless the Parliament spoken of to bee convened at Oxford call mee hence."[66] At the plague's end in late 1665, an estimated 100,000 people in London had died—somewhere between a quarter and a third of the city's inhabitants. The final day of thanksgiving for the cessation of the plague occurred November 9, 1666, a little more than two months after another great catastrophe in the city, the Great Fire.[67]

The passage of the Act of Uniformity in 1662 and Test Acts illustrated the will of the cavaliers in parliament and Sheldon's own desire that men in positions of authority needed verification of their orthodoxy. These certificates of conformity served as letters of introduction for upwardly mobile young men. The master of Eton certified a student with such papers: "These are certify, that Mr George Roberts is a person in good life, considerable for learning, and conformable in judgemt and practice to the Doctrine and Discipline established in the Church of England."[68]

---

64 John Spurr, "Humphrey Henchman, Bishop of London," *ODNB*, 2.

65 See CM VI/1-48 Plague Relief, folios 22/CM 6/12 and 24/CM 6/13 for the Privy Council orders. Sheldon was at the first meeting on June 28, 1665, but not the second on July 5, 1665.

66 MS Tanner 45, f. 26. John Hacket to Sheldon, September 20, 1665.

67 Harris, *Restoration*, 79. See also, Keeble, 159–160.

68 MS Tanner 41, f. 100. Certificate of conformity from John Rosewell, Master of Eton. He was headmaster from 1671-1681.

Sheldon also recommended and aided in the placing of earnest and loyal men in spiritual and temporal postings. Sheldon recommended a relative of Ormond to the Dean of St. Paul's in early 1674. Sancroft received a gentle rebuke for non-attendance and a fulsome recommendation regarding one Mr. Ashton for a living in London.[69] Sheldon's gentle rebuke reminded the then Dean of St. Paul's that the archbishop expected most of his time and energy to involve working for the church in London.

Sheldon's role in the restructuring and survival of the church he loved was vast. He concerned himself with addressing puritan critiques about poorly educated clerics and the problem of pluralities. He encouraged his subordinates to augment the livings of the poorest parishes to aid in recruiting good men to the ministry. He set high standards of education and orthodox beliefs for those entering in service to his church, which was in every measurable way a positive thing. Sheldon worked with diligence and determination through many trying times inside the Church of England. He was not averse to sounding critical when someone crossed over the line of orthodox to heterodox or heretical teachings or beliefs. Sheldon was one among many who criticized Jeremy Taylor for his denial of original sin. Taylor was problematic to many within and without the Church of England, and his death in 1667 caused Sheldon to be unusually frank about a fellow clergyman.

> Though we have lost a very learned man in the Bp of Down yet I am glad he left no more trouble behind him, he was of a dangerous temper apt to branch out into extravagances, and I have had till of late yeares, much to do to keep him in order, and to find diversions for him now those feares are at an end.[70]

---

69 See MS Tanner 42, f. 61, 68. Folio 61 from Benjamin Parry later Bishop of Ossory, November 1673 and folio 68 Sheldon's response to Sancroft, January 1673/4.

70 MS Carte 45, f. 222. Sheldon to Ormond, August 27, 1667. Sheldon and

Peace in the church was one thing Sheldon wished for and worked toward until the end of his life. His church traveled stormy waters while he held the tiller, but it survived and persevered, and therefore, its survival must be one of the greatest elements of Sheldon's legacy as both a man and primate of England.

Ormond were very much of the same generation and perhaps this was the basis for their friendship.

CHAPTER 8

CONCLUSION

Sheldon died on November 9, 1677 at the age of 79. It was at Sheldon's specific directions that he was buried outside of London or Canterbury. As he stated, "My body I desire may be decently buried but very privately and speedily that my funeral many not wast much of what I leave behind mee for better uses."[1] Sheldon was buried at Croydon, where his nephew, Joseph Sheldon, erected a monument to his memory, bearing a Latin inscription prepared by his nephew by marriage, John Dolben. Sheldon prepared his will at Lambeth February 5, 1673. Within it, Sheldon affirmed his belief in standard Protestant language reminiscent of an earlier age.

> First I commend my soule in the mercifull hands of my gracious Redeemer my only Lord Savior and Master Jesus Christ relying wholly upon his goodness and mercy for my salvation giving him most humble thanks, for calling mee by his Gospell and Grace, to his knowledge and obedience; Abhorring all Sects, Sidings, & Tyranny in Religion, holding fast the true Orthodox profession of the Catholique faith of Christ, foretold by the Prophets, and Preached to the World by Christ himselfe, his blessed Apostles, and their successors; being a true Member of his Catholique church within the Communion of a living part thereof of the present Church of England, desiring God to confirme mee in this faith and in all Christian Charity and his holy feare to my lives end.[2]

---

1   MS 244, f. 105. Sheldon's will is held by the Coddrington Library at All Souls, Oxford. This document is three pages long, but in the collection it is numbered 105 for all following pages.

2   Ibid., f. 105.

Sheldon named his nephews, Joseph and Daniel Sheldon, as executors of his will. He gave generous sums to his nieces and nephews, ranging from a hundred to upward of one thousand pounds. He granted Catherine Dolben, his niece and the wife of John Dolben, future Archbishop of York, the leases from the land held in trust from the Dean of Westminster. He gave his niece Ellen Mohun 500 pounds. Sheldon also earmarked 1500 pounds for "good, pious and charitable uses ... to be disposed of as I shall direct either by writing or by word of mouth or for want of such directions as my Executors and Overseerers shall thinke fitt."[3] Sheldon directed that, out of the 1500 pounds, All Souls was to receive 300, Trinity was to receive 100, and the dean and prebends of Canterbury Cathedral were to receive 100. The money was for these institutions use as they thought fit. Sheldon directed that the poor of the parishes of Lambeth and Croydon were each to receive fifty and forty pounds respectively. Additionally, he granted 200 pounds for the two hospitals in and around Canterbury. These requests were easy and conflict free; however, that was not true for the state of the library Sheldon restored at Lambeth.

Sheldon granted his successors at Canterbury the plate, furniture, and books used at the chapel in Lambeth, with the caveat that they were not to sell them. Lambeth's library was in shambles after the Interregnum and Sheldon worked to restore the library's collection during his time as primate. He bequeathed,

> ... to my Successors the ArchBps of Canterbury for ever the severall bookes or volumes mentioned in the Catalogue or Schedule annexed (or hereafter to be annexed to this will) towards the increase and improvement of the publique library at the See of Canterbury now setted at Lambeth house.[4]

---

3   MS 244, f. 105.

4   Ibid., f. 105.

However, Sheldon never annexed a list of the books for the library from his personal collection. He added a note on February 9, 1673 that the rest of the books not listed in the catalogue were for his nephew and godson, Gilbert Dolben. Sheldon's executors entered into a disagreement with Sheldon's successor, William Sancroft, over the distribution of the books. The crux of the matter was over what was for the library and what was for the godson, Gilbert Dolben. Both sides argued for possession of the volumes of Sheldon's library (the contents of which continue to be a mystery). Joseph and Daniel Sheldon argued that their uncle intended to make a catalogue of how the books were partitioned and that therefore the books belonged to the other designee, Gilbert Dolben, who was at the Inner Temple at this point in his life.[5] The argument between the two sides showed no settlement in the manuscript sources. However, one may assume that it was an amicable arrangement. A large portion of Sheldon's books (including his personal Bible) went to Dolben and later came into the possession of the Bodleian Library. Additionally, Gilbert Dolben worked with Sancroft as an MP for Ripon, which worked for the archiepiscopal interests. Dolben was a High Churchman and lost his place on the Commission for Peace in 1688 for refusing to agree to repeal the Test Act[6]—something his great uncle would have heartily approved.

Sheldon's death prompted at least two memorials before his successor, Sancroft, took the see in January 1678. One offered a eulogy in verse:

> A Prelate, such as stem'd the Heathen Flood,
> And water'd first the Gospel with their Bllog,
> E're haughty Rome or pert Geneva tri'd

---

5   D.W. Dayton and J.M. Rigg, rev., "Gilbert Dolben," *ODNB*, 1. Dolben was called to the bar in 1681.

6   Ibid., 1.

The Churches seamless Garment to divide,
And make Truth bow to th'interests of a side.
Learned, devout, discreet, ev'ry way fir
To feed the Flock, and also govern it.
With judgement he the awful [?] sway'd;
Mildly he Rul'd, and Christianly Obey'd:
An humble gracious Grandeur, as free
From Beckets Pridem as Bonners Crueltie;
Still labour'd to exclude whatever sin
By Time of Carelessness had entered in.[7]

The other elegy offered additional and more dramatic praises for Sheldon. "Sheldon is dead! that fatal whisper sounds/Dreadful to'th Ears, as to the Heart are wounds:/And to the wise more ceasless Terrour brings,/Then Whales or Comets do to sickly Kings./Under Great Charles he was the Christians hope,/He baffled Sectaries, and still'd the Pope."[8] These two elegies offered views of how Sheldon might be remembered for his religious work. Sheldon's work as the head of the Church of England helped the church regain its former position and return to religious prominence after a period of religious experimentation.

How should Sheldon be remembered? What was his real legacy? A logical argument could consider his charitable works, as his will illustrated. Sheldon was a great patron and benefactor to many distinct causes. Despite those who disliked him, his charitable giving was immense and was not a subject he was criticized for. He contributed to the refurnishing of St. Paul's twice, pre- and

---

7   *An Elegiacal Poem, Humbly Suffered to the Memory of the most Reverend Father in god, Gilbert Late Arch-Bishop of Canterbury* (London: D. M., 1677), Broadside. Marked with allowance by Roger L'Estrange.

8   *An Elegi On the Death of the Most Reverend Father in God, Gilbert Late Arch-Bishop of Canterbury* (London: John Smith, 1677), Broadside.

post-fire. He subscribed 2,000 pounds for the repair of the cathedral after the fire and he paid this obligation before his death.[9] He constructed the initial public library at Lambeth Palace, rebuilt or repaired the archiepiscopal palaces in London and Canterbury and the summerhouse at Croydon. He supported the hospitals in his charge and set a high example in generous giving that others (especially his fellow bishops) could follow. However, Oxford University received the most impressive building gift, with the construction of a theatre for university exercises. The theatre was one of the first big building projects assigned to a young Christopher Wren. Generations of students have Sheldon to thank for the beautiful ceremonial hall where degrees are conferred. Sheldon kept All Souls financially solvent in 1666 with a timely gift. "I beseech you to present my most humble duty to my Lord and aquaint his Grace that his College of Allsouls doth most thankfully acknowledge his great indulgence in suffering us to make our dividend."[10] Sheldon received a petition from one of the great learning societies of his age, the Royal Society:

> In petitioning your Grace to lend your hand to the upholding of the Roy: Soc: by recommending that worke to Sr John C. I faithfully discharged an office putt upon me by some eminent members of that Society, who thinke it wil be no dishonour to your Grace in future times, to have been the Cause of susteming [sustaining?] an institution wch (in the judgment of many Considerable persons) may prove beneficial to the whole world.[11]

Sheldon believed in education and advancement in knowledge of many kinds. He promoted university men and placed them in positions to help the church both internally and externally. With

---

9 MS 224, f. 105.

10 MS Add c 307, f. 152. Warden of All Souls to Miles Smyth, February 3, 1666.

11 MS Tanner 42, f. 29. Sectary of Royal Society to Sheldon, August 19, 1673.

the Royal Society, Sheldon might have enjoyed the idea of a place where ideas of various concerns could be discussed freely, much as he and his friends and colleagues did at Tew.

Another argument could follow that he did much to advance scholarship throughout his life. He read and reviewed the work of Henry Hammond, Robert Sanderson, Jeremy Taylor, Matthew Wren, and many others. Sheldon working with others preserved much of one of his predecessor's work. He authorized others to work on and to publish William Laud's *Summary of Devotion* at the university press. An earlier cleric's unpublished and unfinished work was made public at Sheldon's desire. Richard Hooker's *The Laws of Ecclesiastical Polity* was a standard of Anglican thought in the early seventeenth century. The first four volumes went to the press before the end of Hooker's life. Volumes 5-7 were published later—and in the case of volumes 6 and 7, Sheldon had some influence on how the unpublished volumes were presented to the public. Volumes 6 and 7 focused on the traditional arguments for the historicity of the episcopacy and liturgical traditions over and above new innovations in religion.

The most telling memorial may be to examine what happened to Sheldon's church less than a decade after his death. Sheldon was a great believer and proponent of the traditional Anglican idea of the *via media*. His church allowed freedom of opinion as long as the outward expressions of faith and piety conformed to the established rubrics and rituals of the Church of England. The church during the Restoration was outwardly a uniform body, but internally, differences of opinions and character threatened to split the *via media* asunder. Ultimately, the *via media* failed and the church split along factional and increasingly party lines, as the tumultuous 1680s ushered in the last of the seventeenth-century British revolutions. Sheldon's real legacy may be in the simple fact that under his guidance, the church remained, at least outwardly, uniform, despite internal differences. However, Sheldon was not above using whatever means at his disposal to make those subordinate to his direction obedient.

The Restoration church was, despite the work of its bishops and loyal clerics, never a uniform body. Many within the clerical establishment questioned the practices or chose not to carry out the injunctions for conformity to the full letter of the law. This position evolved into a comprehensive and broad-based vision of the church, open to many interpretations, as opposed to a narrow and rigorously uniform High Church position. The bishops encouraged following ecclesiastical regulations, but they and the clerics who supported them worked against limited local and national support. These groups, which by the end of the century developed into true political factions, changed the face of both the church and state. Both sides used the press and the developing print culture of the late Stuart regime to vilify their opponents and defend their own positions.

The High Church position followed the line that the succession was inviolate and that James II could be counted on to uphold his word and promise to preserve and protect the Church, as established by law. The threat to the church and the state was twofold: papacy and nonconformists in England. For some, the most problematic threat came not from abroad but from homegrown conventicles preaching sedition and republicanism. Politically, these churchmen aligned with the emerging Tory party, working to suppress dissent, ensure and protect the established church, and prevent the exclusion of the duke of York. The Low Churchmen have a reputation of being religious moderates, seeking to unite the divergent Protestant groups in England in the belief that popery led to arbitrary government. These men allied themselves less staunchly than their High Church brethren with the developing Whig position; however, their political views marked them as less moderate. These divisions, like much in the later Stuart period, were not hard and fast. There was considerable use of personal ties to support both sides and family connections were not steadfast indications of support. A good example of this was of the defection of Edward Hyde, Viscount Cornbury, from the Royal Dragoons to the camp of William of Orange on November 12, 1688. His father, Henry Hyde, Second Earl of Clarendon, and his uncle, Laurence Hyde, First Earl of Rochester, were leaders within the High Church and Tory councils.[12]

In this environment of political and religious tumult, the court, church, and parliament learned of the Popish Plot. The discovery of and the fervor surrounding the Popish Plot resulted in James's exile to Scotland, until tempers and suspicion dwindled. Parliamentary records for March 3, 1679 stated,

> Resolved by the Lords Spirtuall and Temporall and Commons in Parliament assembled, That they doe declare; that they are fully satisfied by the [Persons?] they have heard, that there now is, and for diverse yeares last past hath been a horride and treasonable Plott and Conspiracy continued and carried on by those of the Popish Religion for the muthering of his Majesties sacred Person and for subverting the Protestant Religion and the Ancient and established Gouvernment of this Kingdome.[13]

James's northern sojourn allowed him to enforce and shore up the royal position in Scotland to a greater authority than had existed since before the Bishop's War. James was not without supporters and his success in Scotland and as Lord Admiral made compelling arguments for his right to succession. The anonymous author

---

12 Tim Harris, *Revolution*, 284. See also Grant Tapsell, "Laurence Hyde and the Politics of Religion in Later Stuart England," *The English Historical Review* 125, no. 517 (2010): 1414–1448 and Scott Sowerby, "Forgetting the Repealers: Religious Toleration and Historical Amnesia in Later Stuart England," *Past & Present* 215 (2012): 85–123.

13 MS Tanner 38, f. 3

of *A Plea for Succession in Opposition to Popular Exclusion* wrote, "View Him in His Conduct; and He hath, like a cheering Sun, thaw's the Northern World, and overcome the *Scottish Nation*; not with Arms, but with Love and Wisdom; where He is now become, next [to] His Majesty the Pride and Darling of the Age."[14]

Francis Turner, future non-juring bishop of Ely and the chaplain to the Anglicans within James' household, reported to Archbishop Sancroft from Edinburgh in 1680, "upon all occasions, I find, Hee places his Hope altogether upon that [which] we call the Church of England, upon the Episcopal party, & mainly upon the Bishops themselves."[15] James through Turner also desired that Sancroft "take all Opportunitys of Encouraging the King ... to bee."[16] Turner's letter alludes to what was becoming apparent within the hierarchy of the church and a deepening of the split between two wings of the church along political lines. Turner and Sancroft were protégés of Sheldon. Turner was the son of Thomas Turner, Dean of Canterbury, and Sancroft was one of the capable younger men that Sheldon promoted. Both Charles and James expected the bishops to stay true to the Restoration idea that the church supports the king and vice versa.

The removal of the Duke allowed Charles II to let tempers cool down and to call a parliament with the hope of ensuring the succession of his brother to his throne. Charles II refused rather uncharacteristically to be swayed by any person upon the removal of his brother in favor of a Protestant heir. The parliament that sat in the autumn of 1680 was less than amenable to the king's desires. The Commons quickly stated their intentions in a resolution of November 2, 1680:

---

14 Anonymous, *A Plea for Succession in Opposition to Popular Exclusion* (Walter David: London, 1682), 2.

15 MS Tanner 36, f. 31a.

16 MS Tanner 36, f. 31a.

The first was, that the D. of York's being a Papist, and his hopes of coming to the Crown, had given the greatest countenance to the present designs and Conspiracies against the King and the Protestant Religion. Secondly, That in defence of the Kings person and Government, and of the Protestant Religion, the House did declare, That they would stand by his Majesty with their Lives and Fortunes, and that if his Majesty should come by a violent death (which God forbid) they would revenge it utmost upon the Papists. Thirdly, That a Bill should be brought in to disenable the D. of York to inherit the Imperial Crown of England.[17]

Charles II then quickly dissolved the parliament in Westminster and began his own politicking to ensure the next parliament would toe the line. The selection of Oxford as the site of the next parliament was not without precedent. Oxford had a reputation of loyalty to the crown and the colleges exhibited their loyalty to the Stuarts throughout the divisions and strife of the Civil Wars. However, the many contested elections throughout various locations in England ensured that many of the same men returned to parliament with the same agenda—exclusion and naming a new Protestant heir. The commons presented quickly another bill for the exclusion of the Duke of York:

> Presently after, the House taking into debate the means for the securing of the Protestant Religion, and the safety of his Majesties Person, came to a Resolution, that a Bill should be brought in for excluding James D. of York from Inheriting the Imperial Crown of England and Ireland, and all the Dominions and Territories thereto belonging.[18]

---

17 Anonymous, *Historical Collections, Or a Brief Account ... the Last two Parliaments*. (London: Simon Neal, 1681), 27–28.

18 Ibid., 242.

Charles dissolved the short-lived Oxford parliament and determined not to work with one again entering into a period of personal rule. Charles recalled James from Scotland in spring 1682
and thus began the work of the unpopular Committee for Ecclesiastical Promotions. The royal brothers worked to ensure that
those appointed to power within the church supported the king
and his chosen successor. James's former brothers-in-law, Earls
Clarendon and Rochester, worked on the committee and began a
new campaign to enforce conformity in England. This last period
of religious persecution went into effect with the greatest support
of the monarchy for the programs of the church since the heyday
of the Laudians in the 1630s.

The High Church worry that their Whiggish brethren were but
republicans in disguise got a boost with the revelation of the Rye
House Plot in June 1683. The plot, whether real or complete fab-
rication, stated an intention to kill both the king and duke and
to replace them with more "Protestant" successors. Tory propagandists used the plot to discredit their opposition, and several notable MPs went to their deaths for their involvement. One
of the conspirators, Lord William Russell, had a scaffold speech
circulated in his native county of Bedfordshire, which was most
probably written by future bishop and historian, Gilbert Burnett.
Laurence Womock, Bishop of St. David's, reported to Sancroft in
December 1683, "several Sermons & discourses [are] published
... [and] give great Scandal: viz. Consolatory Addresses to the
lady Russell upon the death of her Lord, without taking notice
of his Crime or supposing his Repentance."[19] Men anxious to
prove their loyalty and division from the Whig position sent numerous loyal addresses to the king and the duke stating their dis-
approval and horror at the plot. The Cheshire grand jury's loyal
address stated, "it was high time to manifest our seperacion from

---

19 Grant Tapsell, *The Personal Rule of Charles II* (Woodbridge: Boydell & Brewer, 2007), 103. MS Tanner 34, f. 226. St. David to Canterbury, Ely.

such persons and principles,"[20] such as those involved in the Rye House Plot. Future Bishop of Oxford, Samuel Parker, voiced his concern in a letter of 1681/2 to Edward Stillingfleet, "for it is not all material what men oppose but what they assert, neither does is concern me how zealous men are against the Church of Rome, but what affection the have for the Church of England."[21] This was the concern of the High Church party that overrode much during this period—real affection for the established church, not just anti-Catholic beliefs or rhetoric, was what mattered. The proponents of the High Church position, which melded security of the state to uniformity in religion, supported James and believed in the assurances of protection for their beloved Church of England as established by law.

The last years of Charles II's reign allowed the High Churchmen to feel secure. The great Whig hope, James Scott, Duke of Monmouth, went into exile as a result of the Rye House Plot, and their propagandist wrote decisively against the other side, capably aided by the clever pen of Roger L'Estrange and many others. L'Estrange's first volume of the *Observator* pronounced judgment on the Whig writings as "the Venom of a Club of Common-wealthsmen."[22] The great attack of the Whigs on the Tories dealt with their loyalty to the ceremonies deemed crypto-Catholic in worship and as inviting arbitrary rule in government. The often-vitriolic rhetoric on both sides flaunted the specter of the Civil War, but the cry "41 is come again" was effective from the Tory position. The Tories and their allies in the church argued back from the press and the pulpit.

> But now men are grown presumptuous, self-willed; they are not afraid to speak evil of dignities and things which they understand not. They are not afraid to insinuate as

---

20 Ibid., 114.

21 MS Tanner 36, f. 255.

22 Tapsell, *The Personal Rule of Charles II*, 149.

if the King favoured the Plot, which hath been declared to be against His Majesties person, and the Established Religion. They quarrel the Succession, and they would put by the true and undoubted Heir. They insinuate that His Majesty is no friend to Parliaments, and would Rule us by an Arbitrary power. And as to the Church of England, they accuse it for declining apace to Popery, and approving Popish, Socinian and Pelagian Doctrines ...[23]

Charles II died February 6, 1685, and James took the throne in a far stronger position than many would have believed possible during the height of the Exclusion Crisis. However, the honeymoon between the new monarch and the country proved to be short-lived; within a year, he began to alienate all but his strongest supporters.

At the beginning of his reign, James used the church to distribute ideas and proclamations, and likewise, the clergy preached due obedience and loyalty to the lawful king, regardless of mistaken opinions in religious matters. Francis Turner, raised to the see of Ely, preached the coronation sermon and reminded all, "We have a King who understands that in a Hereditary Monarchy, 'tis the great peculiar advantage of the Prince as well as People, that their Interest is one in the same, their happiness so closely united."[24] James faced down the rebellions of Monmouth and Argyll, securing his crown with a majority of the three kingdoms supporting him.

The Whigs' power base appeared to be broken and James was free to pursue other agendas, one of which was to reduce the penalties for nonconformity both on dissenters and Roman Catholics. In dispensing with the penalties, he alienated his staunch-

---

23 Thomas Long, *A Sermon Against Murmuring* (London: Richard Royston, 1680), 3.

24 Harris, 59–60.

est supporters, the High Churchmen, and their lay Tory allies. High and Low Churchmen began to preach and write against the errors of Catholic teaching. A contemporary account gave the number of small books against Roman Catholicism produced by the Church of England at 228. Protestant dissenters in turn produced three, seeming to be willing to allow the established church to bear the brunt of this fight and argument against the king's religion.[25] James further ostracized the church by issuing in March 1686 his Direction for Preachers, ordering the clergy to avoid espousing political views in preaching, much like his elder brother's declaration of 1662. James was about to come in direct conflict with both wings of the Church of England. James quarreled with the Bishop of London, Henry Compton, in the short-lived parliament of 1685, but events after the Direction for Preachers went into effect made other actions necessary. James Sharp, Dean of Norwich, preached an anti-Catholic sermon at St. Martin in the Fields, London. James wanted Sharp arrested and suspended. Compton refused, and the newly organized Ecclesiastical Commission suspended Compton from his duties as bishop. Compton reacted by being the only bishop to sign the invitation to the Prince of Orange.

The Archbishop of Canterbury, William Sancroft, refused to sit on the committee formed to police the church formed by either royal brother. Sancroft kept his own counsel, but his opinion of the Dutch and the religion of the United Provinces might be glimpsed from a report he received in 1680 from the royal envoy William Carr in Amsterdam:

> I have amongst other Observations I have made in this rich and great Citty taken Especall notice that this place

---

25 Ibid., 199. See also Scott Sowerby, "Opposition to Anti-Popery in Restoration England," *Journal of British Studies* 51, no. 1 (2012): 26–49 and Kate Loveman, "Samuel Pepys and 'Discourses Touching Religion' under James II," *The English Historical Review* 127, no. 524 (2012): 46–82.

hath been the Center or nest where all the Poysoned
Phanaticall People of England, & other places resort to
Either by corospondancye or by making thine Resed-
ence heare. In this Citty it was where first the English
Brownists, Purtaine, Anabaptists, & Prebeterian first
began thine Plotts Planting heare thine Doctrines, then
printed them & Sent them over to be put into Rebellious
practices, from hence went into England.[26]

Monmouth's failed rebellion launched from the United Provinces only reinforced this idea. Many High Churchmen believed it to be a breeding ground of sedition and Whiggish ideology because of its reputation as a safe haven, and therefore
suspect, if not dangerous, even without worrying about differences in theology.

James's second Declaration of Indulgence of 1687 brought the
events of the trial of the Seven Bishops. The High Church party taught a policy of nonresistance to a legitimate monarch, so
James assumed they would be more amenable to his desire to
read the indulgence from the pulpits. The clergy of London high
and low and a number of bishops, including Sancroft, decided
against reading the indulgence in their churches or dioceses.
Seven Bishops, Francis Turner of Ely, Thomas Ken of Bath and
Wells, John Lake of Chichester, Thomas White of Peterborough,
Jonathan Trelawney of Bristol, and William Lloyd of St. Asaph,
petitioned the king to not have to force their clergy to read the
declaration. All six of the later non-juroring bishops gave assent
to the petition, although only four of the six attached their name
to the petition.[27] The bishops insisted that their refusal to obey
was not a disagreement with the dispensing power of the king,
but questioned the validity of the indulgence since parliament

---

26 MS Tanner 37, f. 123.

27 Harris, 260.

proved other similar indulgences invalid. The high-profile disagreement with the bishops led to the declaration's distribution failure. Out of 9000 churches, perhaps 200 read the declaration. London had seven churches read the declaration; Oxford had none.[28] The trial of the bishops proved disastrous and illustrated how deeply James misunderstood his kingdom. It was unique in the period for causing the dissenters, Presbyterian and others, to rally behind the Episcopal leadership of the Church of England. The stage was set and within a year James would flee to Ireland and then to France ushering in the reign of William and Mary. The loyal High Church supporter and Tory, Lord Clarendon, summed the events up thusly: "I think this is the most dismal day I ever saw in my life. God help us: we are certainly a miserable, undone people."[29]

The Parliament that met to confer the crown upon William and Mary used oaths of loyalty and allegiance to cement the new order. Oaths were not unknown in the late seventeenth century political realm. Charles used oaths of allegiance throughout his reign to ensure support and bind his servants to the crown. James used them as well for members of his household, government, and the established church. Each bishop swore an oath of allegiance to the monarch and head of the Church of England upon consecration. For many, the oath was binding until the death of one of the parties caused need for a new oath to be taken. Much had been written about the necessities of oaths throughout the proceeding decades, especially when confronting groups that disavowed the taking of any oaths, such as the Quakers. John Tillotson wrote in *The Lawfulness and Necessity of Oaths* that oaths

> Set God before their eyes, and to have his fear in their
> hearts, whenever they come to take an oath: And to gov-

---

28 Ibid., 261.

29 George Every, *The High Church Party, 1688-1714* (London: SPCK, 1956), 31.

ern and discharge their consciences in this matter by known and approved Rules, and by the Resolutions of pious and wise men; and not by the loose Reasonings and Resolutions of Pamphlets, sent abroad to serve the turns of unpeacable and ill-minded men (whether Atheists, or Papists, or others) on purpose to debauch the Consciences of men by teaching them to play fast and loose with oaths.[30]

Oaths taken by an individual obliged that individual to keep it under penalty of ultimate punishment.

Those who supported William as king argued that James abdicated his crown by fleeing to France, leaving Parliament free to grant the crown and to impose new oaths of loyalty onto the people. A smaller number believed that James was still the legitimate king and therefore their oaths of loyalty bound them to him despite the rapidly changing face of English political life. Those who supported James did so for a variety of personal beliefs and convictions. Six bishops of the Church of England, William Sancroft of Canterbury, Francis Turner of Ely, Thomas Ken of Bath and Wells, William Lloyd of Norwich, Robert Frampton of Gloucester, and Thomas White of Peterborough, lost their clerical sees due to William's will February 1, 1690.

These newly vacant sees found replacements in the Low Churchmen, who had political views and agendas that the new regime found easier to work with. The deprived bishops lived in relative peace and safety, with those remaining in the Church reluctant to persecute men like Sancroft. William Beveridge, a High Churchman, refused the vacant see of Bath and Wells due to his friendship and association with the non-jurors. Bishop of Oxford, Timothy Hall, waited until the last moment to decide to

---

30 John Tillotson, *The Lawfulness, and Obligations of Oaths* (London: Brabazon Alymer, 1681), 35–36.

take the oath. Henry Dodwell became a great mouthpiece for the deprived bishops. He argued in *A Defence of the Deprived Bishops,*

> Then it will not be in Power of Acts of Parliament to drive us from our Principles, and to bring a Scandal on our Religion: Then where our Bishops follow Christ, we shall follow them, and it will not be in the Power of the Worldly Magistrate, or the Gates of Hell itself, to prevail against our Church, and to dissolve the Union between us: Then Magistrates themselves will be more wary of involving Consciences on occasion of their little Worldly Politicks; at least they will not pretend Religion, and the Religion of that very Church which suffers by them for doing so.[31]

The High Churchmen weathered the storm of the 1680s, but lost their exclusive hold on religion in England. Admittance into the universities and political life remained tied to outward Anglican conformity, which would have pleased Sheldon. He would have agreed with the High Churchmen politically, but dividing the church would have been a difficult event for him to countenance. Sheldon's real legacy might be that under his direction and rule, prayer book Anglicanism returned to England and both the High and Low Churchmen used it; as time passed, the prayer books produced in the late seventeenth century are the basis for most modern prayer books within the worldwide Anglican communion today. Sheldon would be pleased by that.

---

31 Henry Dodwell, *A Defence of the Deprived Bishops* (London, 1692), 22.

BIBLIOGRAPHY

PRIMARY SOURCES

Manuscript Sources

Bodleian Library, University of Oxford

Carte Papers
> MS Carte 45, 49, 77, 79

Clarendon Papers
> MS Clarendon 77

Dolben Papers
> MS Add c 303
> MS Add c 304a
> MS Add c 304 b

Sheldon Papers
> MS Add c 305
> MS Add c 307
> MS Add c 308

Tanner Manuscripts
> MS Tanner 36-49, 51, 73, 123-127, 129-141, 145-147, 150

Unnamed Papers
> MS DD All Souls c 146
> MS DD All Souls c 259
> MS Eng bib 1648 d 3 (Sheldon's Bible)
> MS Eng let c 210

Gilbertus Sheldon. 1903. Bucks Pamphlets # 8 1867-1905, 8 43 (11).

Coddrington Library, All Souls College, University of Oxford
> MS 244

British Library, London

Harleian Manuscripts

    MS Harleian 3784, 3785, 6942, 7377

Lambeth Palace Library, London

    AA/AP/Sheldon

    CM VI/1-48 Plague Relief

Printed Sources

Airy, Osmond, Ed. *The Lauderdale Papers*, 3 volumes. London: Camden Society, 1884-1885.

Anonymous. *The Act of Parliament Against Religious Meetings, Proved to be the Bishop's Act.* 1670.

_____. *A Collection of Cases, Lately Written to Recover Dissenters to the Church of England.* Vol. 3, 3rd ed. London, 1718.

_____. *An Elegi On the Death of the Most Reverend Father in God, Gilbert Late Arch-Bishop of Canterbury.* London: John Smith, 1677.

_____. *An Elegiacal Poem, Humbly Suffered to the Memory of the most Reverend Father in god, Gilbert Late Arch-Bishop of Canterbury.* London: D. M., 1677.

_____. *A Letter From a Scholar in Oxford to his Friend in the Countrey.* Oxford, 1647.

Ashmole, Elias. *His Autobiographical and Historical Notes, His Correspondence, and Other Contemporary Sources Relating to his Life and Work.* Edited by C.H. Josten. Oxford: Clarendon Press, 1966.

Baxter, Richard. *The Autobiography of Richard Baxter.* Abridged by J.M. Lloyd Thomas and edited by N.H. Keeble. London: Dent, 1974.

Birch, Thomas, Ed. *A Collection of the State Papers of John Thurloe, Volume 1: 1638-1653.* London, 1742.

Bolde, Thomas. *Rhetorick Restrained.* London, 1660.

Boyle, G.D., Ed. *Characters and Episodes of the Great Rebellion.* Oxford: Clarendon Press, 1889.

Browning, Andrew, Ed. *English Historical Documents 1660-1714.* Vol. 8. London: Eyre & Spottiswoode Ltd., 1953.

_____. *The Book of Common Prayer.* New York: Oxford University Press, 1990.

Burnet, Gilbert. *A History of His Own Times.* Edited by Osmond Airy. Oxford: Clarendon Press, 1897.

_____. *Calendar of State Papers, Domestic Charles I.* London, 1858.

_____. *Calendar of State Papers, Domestic Charles II.* London, 1939.

Charles II. *His Majesties Declaration To all His Loving Subjects, Touching the Causes and Reasons that moved him to dissolve the two last Parliaments.* London: John Bill, Thomas Newcomb, and Henry Hill, 1681.

_____. *Constitutions and Canons Ecclesiastical.* London: John Norton, 1633.

_____. *Constitutions and Canons Ecclesiastical.* London: Robert Barker, 1640.

Crook, John. *Liberty of Conscience Asserted*. London: 1661.

Dodwell, Henry. *A Vindication of the Deprived Bishops*. London, 1692

Evelyn, John. *The Diary of John Evelyn*. Edited by E. S. De Beer. Oxford: The Clarendon Press, 1955.

Fiennes, Nathanael. *A Second Speech of the Honorable Nathanael Fiennes, Touching the Subjects Liberty against the Late Canons, and the New Oath*. London, 1641.

Firth, C.H. and R.S. Rait, Eds. *Acts and Ordinances of the Interregnum*. London, 1911.

Fullwood, Francis. *Toleration not to be Abused by Independents*. London, 1672.

G.S. *Monarchy Triumphing*. London, 1660.

Gardiner, Samuel R., Ed. *The Constitutional Documents of the Puritan Revolution 1625-1660, Third Edition*. Oxford: Clarendon Press, 1906.

Green, Mary Anne Everett, Ed. *Calendar of the Proceeding of the Committee for Compounding, 1643-1660*. Vol. 4, *Cases, July 1650-Dec. 1653*. London: Eyre & Spottiswoode, 1892.

Hall, Thomas. *The Beauty of Magistracy*. London, 1660.

Hewit, John. *Prayers of Intercession for their Use who Mourn in Secret for the Publick Calamities of this Nation*. London, 1659.

Horn, Joyce M., Ed. *Fasti Ecclesia Anglicanae 1541-1851*, vols. 1-11. London: Institute for Historical Research, 1969-2004.

Hyde, Edward, Earl of Clarendon. *Second Thoughts*. London, 1660.

_____. *Characters and Episodes of the Great Rebellion Selected from the History and Autobiography of Edward, Earl of Clarendon.* Oxford: Clarendon Press, 1889.

_____. *A History of the Civil War and Rebellion in England Began in the Year 1641.* Oxford, 1712.

Josselin, Ralph. *The Dairy of Ralph Josselin.* Edited by Alan Macfarlane. London: The British Academy by Oxford University Press, 1976.

Kenyon, J.P., Ed. *The Stuart Constitution 1603-1688.* Cambridge: Cambridge University Press, 1986.

Long, Thomas. *A Sermon Against Murmuring.* London: Richard Royston, 1680.

Milward, John. *The Diary of John Milward, September 1666 to May 1668.* Cambridge: Cambridge University Press, 1938.

Parker, Samuel. *Bp Parker's History of His Own Time.* London: H. Curll, 1728.

_____. *A Discourse of Ecclesiastical Politie: Wherein the Authority of the Civil Magistrate over the Consciences of Subjects in Matters of External Religion is Asserted.* London: John Martyn, 1671.

_____. *A Discourse in Vindication of Bp Bramhall and the Clergy of the Church of England from the Fanatick Charge of Popery.* London: James Collins, 1673.

Patrick, Simon. *A Brief Account of the New Sect of Latitude-Men.* London, 1662.

Pepys, Samuel. *The Diary of Samuel Pepys.* Robert Latham and William Matthews, Eds. Berkeley: University of California Press, 1970-83.

_____. *Reasons of the Present Judgement of the University of Oxford.* Oxford, 1647.

Pope, Walter. *The Life of the Right Reverend Father in God Seth Lord Bishop of Salisbury.* London: William Kebelwhite, 1697.

Sanderson, Robert. *Reasons of the Present Judgement of the University of Oxford.* Oxford, 1647.

Sheldon, Gilbert. *David's Deliverance.* London: Timothy Garthwait, 1660.

Sudbury, John. *A Sermon Preached at the Consecration of the Right Reverend Fathers in God, Gilbert Lord Bishop of London, Humphry Lord Bishop of Sarum, George Lord Bishop of Worcester, Robert Lord Bishop of Lincolne, George Lord Bishop of St. Asasph.* London: R. Royston, 1660.

Tillotson, John. *The Lawfulness, and Obligation of Oaths, A Sermon Preach'd at the Assises held at Kingston upon Thames, July 21, 1681.* London: Brabazon Aylmer, 1681.

_____. *The Protestant Religion Vindicated.* London: Brabazon Aylmer, 1680.

Tomkins, Thomas. *The Inconveniences of Toleration, Or an Answer to a Late Book, Intitled, A Proposition Made to the King and Parliament, for the Safety and Happiness of the King and of the Kingdom.* London: W. Garret, 1667.

Underhill, Edward B., Ed. *Tracts on Liberty of Conscience and Persecution 1614-1661.* New York: Burt Franklin, 1966.

Ussher, James, Archbishop of Armagh. *The Bishop of Armaghes Direction.* London, 1660.

Walker, John. *An Attempt towards the Recovering of the Numbers and Sufferings of the Clergy of the Church of England, Heads of*

Colleges, Fellows, Scholars, &c. who were Sequester'd, Harass'd, &c in the Late Times of the Grand Rebellion: Occasion'd by the Ninth Chapter (Now the Second Volume) of Dr. Calamy's Abridgement of the Life of Mr. Baxter. London: W.S. for J. Nicholson, 1714.

Ward, Thomas. *Some Queries to the Protestants Concerning the English Reformation.* London, 1687.

Wolseley, Sir Charles. *Liberty of Conscience.* London, 1668.

Wood, Anthony à. *A History of the Visitation of the University of Oxford by a Parliamentary Commission in the Years 1647, 1648.* Abridged. Oxford: J.H. Parker, London: J.G. and F. Rivington, 1837.

SECONDARY SOURCES

Abbott, William M. "James Ussher and 'Ussherian' Episcopacy, 1640-1656: The Primate and His Reduction Manuscript." *Albion* 22 (1990): 237–259.

Abernathy, George R. "Clarendon and the Declaration of Indulgence." *Journal of Ecclesiastical History* 11 (1960): 55–73.

Addelshaw, G.W.O. *The High Church Tradition: A Study in the Liturgical Thought of the Seventeenth Century.* London: Faber and Faber, Ltd., 1941.

Allen, David. "Political Clubs in Restoration England." *Historical Journal* 19 (1976): 561–580.

Atherton, Ian. "Cathedrals, Laudianism, and the British Churches." *The Historical Journal* 53, no. 4 (2010): 895–918.

Atkins, Jonathan M. "Calvinist Bishops, Church Unity, and the Rise of Arminianism." *Albion* 18 (1986): 411–427.

Bangs, Carl. "All the Best Bishoprics and Deaneries: The Enigma of Arminian Politics." *Church History* 42 (1973): 5–16.

Barnard, Toby. *The English Republic 1649-1660, Second Edition.* London: Longman Ltd., 1997.

Bayne, Peter. "English Puritanism: Its Character and History." In *Documents Relating to the Settlement of the Church of England by the Act of Uniformity in 1662.* Rev. George Gould, Ed. London: W. Kent and Co., 1862.

Beddard, R. A. "An Unpublished Memoir of Archbishop Sheldon." *The Bodleian Library Record X* (1978-1982): 40–51.

_____. "Wren's Mausoleum for Charles I and the Cult of the Royal Martyr." *Architectural History* 27 (1984): 36–49.

Bosher, Robert S. *The Making of the Restoration Settlement: The Influence of the Laudians 1649-1662.* New York: Oxford University Press, 1951.

Brockliss, L.W.B. *The University of Oxford: A History.* Oxford: Oxford University Press, 2016.

Brown, Louise Fargo. *The Political Activity of the Baptists and Fifth Monarchy Men in England During the Interregnum.* Washington DC: The American Historical Association, 1912.

Bulman, William J. *Anglican Enlightenment: Orientalism, Religion, and Politics in England and its Empire, 1648-1714.* Cambridge: Cambridge University Press, 2015.

Burrows, Montagu. *Worthies of All Souls: Four Centuries of English History.* London: Macmillan and Co., 1874.

Cairns, Alan. *Dictionary of Theological Terms*, 2nd ed. Belfast: Ambassador-Emerald International, 1998.

Cary, Henry. *Memorials of the Great Civil War in England from 1642 to 1652.* London: Henry Colburn, 1842.

Chadwick, Henry, Consulting Ed. *Not Angels but Anglicans: The History of Christianity in the British Isles.* Norwich: Canterbury Press, 2000.

Champion, J.A.I. *The Pillars of Priestcraft Shaken: The Church of England and its Enemies, 1660-1730.* Cambridge: Cambridge University Press, 1992.

Clark, G.N. *The Later Stuarts 1660-1714.* Oxford: Clarendon Press, 1934.

Collins, Jeffrey R. "The Restoration Bishops and the Royal Supremacy." *Church History* 68 (1999): 549–580.

Collinson, Patrick. *From Cranmer to Sancroft.* London: Hambledon Continuum, 2006.

Como, David R. *Blown by the Spirit: Puritanism and the Emergence of an Antinomian Underground in Pre-Civil War England.* Stanford: Stanford University Press, 2004.

Cust, Richard. *Charles I: A Political Life.* Harlow, UK: Pearson Longman Ltd., 2005.

Davies, Horton. *Worship and Theology in England: From Cranmer to Baxter to Fox, 1534-1690.* Grand Rapids: William B. Eerdmans Publishing Co., 1996.

Davies, Julian. *The Caroline Captivity of the Church: Charles I and the Remoulding of Anglicanism 1625-1641.* Oxford: Clarendon Press, 1992.

De Krey, Gary S. "Between Revolutions: Re-Appraising the Restoration in Britain." *History Compass* 6 (2008): 1–36.

Donald, Peter. *An Uncounselled King: Charles I and the Scottish Troubles, 1637-1641.* Cambridge: Cambridge University Press, 1990.

Dutton, Christopher and Judith Maltby, Eds. *Religion in Revolutionary England.* Manchester: Manchester University Press, 2006.

Echard, L. *An Appendix to the Three Volumes of Mr. Archdeacon Echard's History of England Consisting of Several Explanations and Amendments as well as New and Curious Additions to that History.* London: Jacob Tonson, 1720.

Every, George. *The High Church Party 1688-1718.* London: Church History Society (SPCK), 1956.

Feiling, Keith. *A History of the Tory Party 1640-1714.* Oxford: Clarendon Press, 1924.

Fincham, Kenneth and Stephen Taylor. "Vital Statistics: Episcopal Ordination and Ordinands in England, 1646-60." *The English Historical Review* 126, no. 519 (2011): 319–344.

_____. Ed. *The Early Stuart Church, 1603-1642.* Stanford: Stanford University Press, 1993.

Fincham, Kenneth, Stephen Taylor and Peter Lake. "The Ecclesiastical Policy of James I." *Journal of British Studies* 24 (1985): 169–207.

Fincham, Kenneth, Stephen Taylor and Nicholas Tyacke. *Altars Restored: The Changing Face of English Religious Worship, 1547-c. 1700.* Oxford: Oxford University Press, 2007.

Fissel, Mark. *The Bishops' Wars: Charles I's campaigns against Scotland, 1638-1640.* Cambridge: Cambridge University Press, 1994.

Foster, Elizabeth Read. *The House of Lords, 1603-1649: Structure, Procedure, and the Nature of Its Business.* Chapel Hill: The University of North Carolina Press, 1983.

Foster, Gavin. "Ignoring "The Tempest": Pepys, Dryden, and the Politics of Spectating in 1667." *The Huntington Library Quarterly* 63 (2000): 5–22.

Gardiner, S.R. *History of the Great Civil War,* 4 Volumes. London: Longman's, Green, and Co., 1905.

Gentles, Ian. *The English Revolution and the Wars in the Three Kingdoms 1638-1652.* Harlow, UK: Pearson Longman, 2007.

Gilliam, Elizabeth and W.J. Tighe. "To 'Run with the Time' Archbishop Whitgift, the Lambeth Articles, and the Politics of Theological Ambiguity in Late Elizabethan England." *Sixteenth Century Journal* 23 (1992): 325–340.

Greaves, Richard L. *Deliver us From Evil: The Radical Underground in Britain, 1660-1663.* Oxford: Oxford University Press, 1986.

_____. *Enemies Under His Feet: Radicals and Nonconformists in Britain, 1664-1677.* Stanford: Stanford University Press, 1990.

Green, I.M. "The Persecution of 'Scandalous' and 'Malignant' Parish Clergy during the Civil War." *English Historical Review* 94 (1979): 507–531.

_____. *The Re-Establishment of the Church of England 1660-1663.* Oxford: Oxford University Press, 1978.

Green, S.J.D. and Peregrine Horden, Eds. *All Souls under the "Ancien Regime": Politics, Learning, and the Arts, c. 1600-*

1850. Oxford: Oxford University Press, 2007.

Greenspan, Nicole. "Charles II, Exile, and the Problem of Allegiance." *The Historical Journal* 54, no. 1 (2011): 73–103.

Gregory, Jeremy, Ed. *The Oxford History of Anglicanism*. Vol. 2, *Establishment and Empire, 1662-1829*. Oxford: Oxford University Press, 2017.

_____. *Restoration, Reformation, and Reform, 1660-1828: The Archbishops of Canterbury and their Diocese*. Oxford: Clarendon Press, 2000.

Groot, Jerome de. *Royalist Identities*. Houndmills, UK: Palgrave Macmillan, 2004.

Goldie, Mark and John Spurr. "Politics and the Restoration Parish: Edward Fowler and the Struggle for St. Giles Cripplegate." *English Historical Review* 109 (1994): 572–596.

Gorski, Phillip S. *The Disciplinary Revolution: Calvinism and the Rise of the State in Early Modern Europe*. Chicago: University of Chicago Press, 2003.

Hardarce, Paul H. "The Genesis of the Declaration of Breda, 1657-1660." *A Journal of Church and State* 15 (1973): 65–82.

Harris, Tim. "The Bawdy House Riots of 1668" in *Historical Journal* 29 (1986): 537–556.

_____. *London Crowds in the Reign of Charles II: Propaganda and Politics from the Restoration to the Exclusion Crisis*. Cambridge: Cambridge University Press, 1987.

_____. *Politics Under the Later Stuarts: Party Conflict in a Divided Society 1660-1715*. London: Longman Group, Ltd, 1993.

_____. *Restoration: Charles II and his Kingdoms*. London: Penguin Books, 2005.

_____. *Revolution: The Great Crisis of the British Monarchy 1685-1714*. London: Penguin Books, 2006.

Harris, Tim, Paul Seaward and Mark Goldie, Eds. *The Politics of Religion in Restoration England*. Oxford: Basil Blackwell Press, 1990.

Harrington, Melanie. "The Earl of Derby and His Tenants: Sales of Royalist Land during the Interregnum Revisited." *The Economic History Review* 64, no. 4 (2011): 1195–1217.

Henson, H. Hensley. *Studies in English Religion in the Seventeenth Century*. London: John Murray, 1903.

Hibbard, Caroline M. *Charles I and the Popish Plot*. Chapel Hill: The University of North Carolina Press, 1983.

Hirst, Derek. "The Place of Principle." *Past and Present* 92 (1981): 79–99.

Hill, Christopher. *The Century of Revolution 1603-1714, Second Edition*. New York: W.W. Norton and Company, 1980.

_____. *A World Turned Upside Down*. London: Penguin Books Ltd., 1973.

Hirschberg, D.R. "The Government and Church Patronage in England, 1660-1760." *Journal of British Studies* 20 (1980): 109–139.

Holmes, Clive. *Why was Charles I executed?* London: Hambledon and London, 2007.

Hughes, Ann. *The Causes of the English Civil War*. Houndmills, UK: Palgrave Macmillan, 1998.

Hutton, Ronald. *Charles II: King of England, Scotland, and Ireland.* Oxford: Clarendon Press, 1989.

_____. *The Restoration: A Political and Religious History of England and Wales, 1658-1667.* Oxford: Oxford University Press, 1985.

_____. *The Royalist War Effort 1642-1646.* London: Routledge Press, 2003.

"Illustrations of the State of the Church during the Great Rebellion." In *The Theologian and Ecclesiastic,* vols. 6-13. London: Joseph Masters, 1849-1852.

Johnston, Warren. "The Anglican Apocalypse in Restoration England." *Journal of Ecclesiastical History* 55 (2004): 467–501.

Jones, J.R. *Charles II: Royal Politician.* London: Allen & Unwin, Ltd., 1987.

_____. Ed. *The Restored Monarchy 1660-1688.* Totowa, NJ: Rowman and Littlefield, 1979.

Kaplan, Lawrence. "English Civil War Politics and Religious Settlement." *Church History* 41 (1972): 307–325.

Keeble, N. H. *The Restoration: England in the 1660's.* Oxford: Blackwell Publishing, 2002.

Kenyon, John. *The Civil Wars of England.* London: Phoenix Giant, 1996.

King, Peter. "The Episcopate during the Civil Wars, 1642-1649." *English Historical Review* 83 (1968): 523–537.

Kishlansky, Mark. "Mission Impossible: Charles I, Oliver Cromwell and the Regicide." *The English Historical Review* 125, no. 515 (2010): 844–874.

Knights, Mark. *Representation and Misrepresentation in Later Stuart Britain: Partisanship and Political Culture.* Oxford: Oxford University Press, 2005.

Lake, Peter and Michael Questier, Eds. *Conformity and Orthodoxy in the English Church, c. 1560-1660.* Woodbridge, UK: The Boydell Press, 2000.

Lehmberg, Stanford. *English Cathedrals: A History.* London: Hambledon and London, 2005.

Lettinga, Neil. "Covenant Theology Turned Upside Down: Henry Hammond and Caroline Anglican Moralism: 1643-1660." *Sixteenth Century Journal* 24 (1993): 653–669.

Lindley, Keith. *Popular Politics and Religion in Civil War London.* Hants: Scolar Press, 1997.

Loveman, Kate. "Samuel Pepys and 'Discourses Touching Religion' under James II." *The English Historical Review* 127, no. 524 (2012): 46–82

Macaulay, Lord Thomas B. *A History of England.* London: George Routledge and Sons, Ltd., 1849.

Macdonald, Alan R. "James VI and I, the Church of Scotland, and British Ecclesiastical Convergence." *Historical Journal* 48 : 885–903.

Macinnes, Allan I. *The British Revolution 1629-1660.* Houndmills, UK: Palgrave Macmillan, 2005.

Marsh, Christopher. "'Common Prayer' in England 1560-1640: The View from the Pew." *Past and Present* 171 (2001): 66–94.

Maltby, Judith. "Suffering and Surviving: The Civil Wars, the Commonwealth and the formation of 'Anglicanism', 1642-

1660." In *Anglicanism and the Western Christian Tradition: Continuity, Change and the Search for Communion.* Edited by Stephen Platten. Norwich: Canterbury Press, 2008.

McCullough, Peter. "Making Dead Men Speak: Laudianism, Print, and the Works of Lancelot Andrewes, 1626-1642." *Historical Journal* 41 (1998): 401–424.

McGregor, J.F. and B. Reay, Eds. *Radical Religion in the English Revolution.* Oxford: Oxford University Press, 1984.

Mensing, Raymond C. *Toleration and Parliament, 1660-1714.* Washington, D.C: University Press of America, Inc., 1979.

Miller, John. *After the Civil Wars: English Politics and Government in the Reign of Charles II.* Harlow, UK: Pearson Education Ltd., 2000.

_____. *The Restoration and the England of Charles II, Second Edition.* Harlow, UK: Addison Wesley Longman Ltd., 1997.

Millstone, Noah. "Evil Counsel: The Propositions to Bridle the Impertinency of Parliament and the Critique of Caroline Government in the Late 1620s." *Journal of British Studies* 50, no. 4 (2011): 813–839.

Milton, Anthony, Ed. *The Oxford History of Anglicanism.* Vol. 1, *Reformation and Identity, c. 1520-1662.* Oxford: Oxford University Press, 2017.

_____. *Catholic and Reformed: The Roman and Protestant Churches in English Protestant Thought, 1600-1640.* Cambridge: Cambridge University Press, 1995.

_____. "Licensing, Censorship, and Religious Orthodoxy in Early Stuart England." *Historical Journal* 41 (1998): 625–651.

Moorman, J.R.H. *A History of the Church of England*, 3rd ed. Harrisburg, PA: Morehouse Publishing, 1980.

More, Paul E. and Frank L. Cross, Eds. *Anglicanism: The Thought and Practice of the Church of England, Illustrated from the Religious Literature of the Seventeenth Century.* London: SPCK, 1935.

Morrill, John. "The Attack on the Church of England in the Long Parliament, 1640-1642." In *History, Society and the Churches: Essays in Honour of Owen Chadwick.* Edited by Derek Beales and Geoffrey Best . Cambridge: Cambridge University Press, 1985.

Overton, J. H. *Life in the English Church 1660-1714.* London: Longmans, Green and Co., 1885.

_____. *Oxford Dictionary of National Biography.* Oxford: Oxford University Press, 2004-2010.

Peacey, Jason. "Print, Publicity, and Popularity: The Projecting of Sir Balthazar Gerbier, 1642-1662." *Journal of British Studies* 51, no. 2 (2012): 284–307.

Pestana, Carla G. *Protestant Empire: Religion and the Making of the British Atlantic World.* Philadelphia: University of Pennsylvania Press, 2009.

Pocock, Nicholas. "The Restoration Settlement of the English Church." *English Historical Review* 1 (1886): 677–698.

Prior, Charles A. "Ecclesiology and Political Thought in England, 1580-c. 1630." *Historical Journal* 48 (2005): 855–884.

Quantin, Jean-Louis. *The Church of England and Christian Antiquity: The Construction of a Confessional Identity in the 17th Century.* Oxford: Oxford University Press, 2009.

Raffe, Alasdair. "Presbyterians and Episcopalians: The Formation of Confessional Cultures in Scotland, 1660-1715." *The English Historical Review* 125, no. 514 (2010): 570–598.

Raylor, Timothy. "The Anglican Attack on Hobbes in Paris, 1651." *The Historical Journal* 53, no. 1 (2010): 153–164.

Read, Elizabeth Foster. *The House of Lords 1603-1649*. Chapel Hill: The University of North Carolina Press, 1983.

Rose, Jacqueline. "Kingship and Counsel in Early Modern England." *The Historical Journal* 54, no. 1 (2011): 47–71.

Rosenheim, James M. *The Townshends of Raynham: Nobility in Transition in Restoration and Early Hanoverian England*. Middletown, CT: Wesleyan University Press, 1989.

Royle, Trevor. *The British Civil War: The Wars of Three Kingdoms 1638-1660*. New York: Palgrave Macmillan, 2004.

Russell, Conrad. *The Causes of the English Civil War*. Oxford: Clarendon Press, 1990.

_____. *The Crisis of Parliaments: English History 1509-1660*. Oxford: Oxford University Press, 1971.

_____. *The Fall of the British Monarchies 1637-1642*. Oxford: Clarendon Press, 1991.

Salamon, N. *The Lives of English Bishops from the Restauration to the Revolution*. London: J. Roberts, 1733.

Schwartz, Hillel. "Arminianism and the English Parliament, 1624-1629." *Journal of British Studies* 12 (1973): 41–68.

Seaward, Paul. *The Cavalier Parliament and the Reconstruction of the Old Regime, 1661-1667*. Cambridge: Cambridge University Press, 1989.

Schoenfeld, Maxwell. *The Restored House of Lords*. The Hague: Mouton & Co., 1967.

Shagan, Ethan. "Beyond Good and Evil: Thinking with Moderates in Early Modern England." *Journal of British Studies* 49, no. 3 (2010): 488–513.

Shapiro, B. J. "Latitudinarianism and Science in Seventeenth-Century England." *Past and Present* 40 (1968): 16–41.

Sharpe, Kevin. "Religion, Rhetoric, and Revolution in Seventeenth-Century England." *The Huntington Library Quarterly* 57 (1994): 255–299.

Shedd, John A. "Legalism over Revolution: The Parliamentary Committee for Indemnity and Property Confiscation Disputes, 1647-1655." *Historical Journal* 43 (2000): 1093–1107.

Smith, Geoffrey. *The Cavaliers in Exile, 1640-1660*. New York: Palgrave Macmillan, 2003.

Sowerby, Scott. "Forgetting the Repealers: Religious Toleration and Historical Amnesia in Later Stuart England." *Past & Present* 215 (2012): 85–123.

———. "Opposition to Anti-Popery in Restoration England." *Journal of British Studies* 51, no. 1 (2012): 26–49.

Spaeth, Donald A. *The Church in an Age of Danger: Parsons and Parishioners, 1660-1740*. Cambridge: Cambridge University Press, 2000.

Spalding, James C. and Maynard F. Brass. "Reduction of Episcopacy as a Means to Unity in England, 1640-1662." *Church History* 30 (1961): 414–432.

Spellman, W.M. *The Latitudinarians and the Church of England, 1660-1700.* Athens: University of Georgia Press, 1993.

Spurr, John. "The Church of England, Comprehension and the Toleration Act of 1689" in *English Historical Review* 104 (1989): 927–946.

_____. *England in the 1670s 'This Masquerading Age.'* Oxford: Blackwell Publishers Ltd., 2000.

_____. *English Puritanism.* London: Palgrave Macmillan, 1998.

_____. "'Latitudinarianism' and the Restoration Church." *Historical Journal* 31 (1988): 61–82.

_____. "A Profane History of Early Modern Oaths." *Transactions of the Royal Historical Society* 11 (2001): 37–63.

_____. "'Rational Religion' in Restoration England." *Journal of the History of Ideas* 49 (1988): 563–585.

_____. *The Restoration Church of England, 1649-1689.* New Haven: Yale University Press, 1991.

Sommerville, C. John. "Interpreting Seventeenth-Century English Religion as Movements." *Church History* 69 (2000): 749–769.

Staley, Vernon. *The Life and Times of Gilbert Sheldon.* London: Wells, Gardner, Darton & Co., 1914.

Stater, Victor L. *Noble Government: The Stuart Lord Lieutenancy and the Transformation of English Politics.* Athens: University of Georgia Press, 1994.

Steere, Dan. "'For the Peace of Both, for the Humour of Neither': Bishop Joseph Hall Defends the Via Media in an

Age of Extremes, 1601-1656." *Sixteenth Century Journal* 27 (1996): 749–765.

Sutch, Victor. *Gilbert Sheldon: Architect of Anglican Recovery.* The Hague: Martinus Nijhoff, 1973.

Sutherland, James. *The Restoration Newspaper and Its Development.* Cambridge: Cambridge University Press, 1986.

Swatland, Andrew. *The House of Lords in the Reign of Charles II.* Cambridge: Cambridge University Press, 1996.

Sykes, Norman. *From Sheldon to Secker: Aspects of English Church History 1660-1768.* Cambridge: Cambridge University Press, 1959.

Tapsell, Grant. "Laurence Hyde and the Politics of Religion in Later Stuart England." *The English Historical Review* 125, no. 517 (2010): 1414–1448.

_____. *The Personal Rule of Charles II.* Woodbridge, UK: Boydell & Brewer, 2007.

Trevelyan, G. M. *England under the Stuarts.* London: Routledge, 2002.

Trevor-Roper, Hugh. *Archbishop Laud 1573-1645.* 2nd ed. Hamden, CT: Archon Books, 1963.

_____. *Catholics, Anglicans, and Puritans.* London: Seeker & Warburg, Ltd., 1987.

Tyacke, Nicholas. "Anglican Attitudes: Some Recent Writings on English Religious History, from the Reformation to the Civil War." *Journal of British Studies* 35 (1996): 139–167.

_____. *Anti-Calvinists: The Rise of English Arminianism, c. 1590-1640.* Oxford: Clarendon Press, 1987.

_____. *Aspects of English Protestantism c. 1530-1700.* Manchester: Manchester University Press, 2001.

_____. Ed. *England's Long Reformation 1500-1800.* London: University College London Press, 1998.

_____. Ed. *The History of the University of Oxford.* Vol. 4, *Seventeenth-Century Oxford.* Oxford: Clarendon Press, 1997.

Vallance, Edward. "Oaths, Casuistry, and Equivocation: Anglican Responses to the Engagement Controversy." *Historical Journal* 44 (2001): 59–77.

_____. "Preaching to the Converted: Religious Justification for the English Civil War." *The Huntington Library Quarterly* 65 (2002): 395–419.

Walsham, Alexandra. *Charitable Hatred: Tolerance and Intolerance in England, 1500-1700.* Manchester: Manchester University Press, 2006.

Watts, Michael. *The Dissenters.* Vol. 1. Oxford: Clarendon Press, 1978.

Williams, M.R.F. "Between King, Faith and Reason: Father Peter Talbot (SJ) and Catholic Royalist Thought in Exile." *The English Historical Review* 127, no. 528 (2012): 1063–1099.

Winship, Michael P. "Defining Puritanism in Restoration England: Richard Baxter and Other Respond to "A Friendly Debate"." *The Historical Journal* 54, no. 3 (2011): 689–715.

Wood, A. Harold. *Church Unity Without Uniformity.* London: The Epworth Press, 1963.

APPENDIX

Seventeenth Century Bishops and Restoration Deans,
a Partial List

* Denotes elevation to an episcopal see
** Identifies those removed as NJ 1 Feb. 1690

Canterbury
Archbishops
William Laud 1633-1645, William Juxon 1660-1663, Gilbert
Sheldon 1663-1677, William Sancroft 1678-90**, John
Tillotson 1691-94, Thomas Tension 1695-1715
Deans
Thomas Turner 1643-1672, John Tillotson 1672-1689, John
Sharp 1689-91*

York
Archbishops
John Williams 1641-1650, Accepted Frewen 1660-1664,
Richard Sterne 1664-1683, John Dolben 1683-1686, Thomas
Lamplugh 1688-1691, John Sharp 1691-1714
Deans
Richard Marsh 1660-1663, William Sancroft 1664, Robert
Hitch 1664-1677, Tobias Wickham 1677-1697

London
Bishops
William Laud 1628-1633, William Juxon 1633-1660, Gilbert
Sheldon 1660-1663, Humphrey Henchman 1663-1675, Henry
Compton 1675-1715
Deans
Matthew Nicholas 1660-1661, John Barwick 1661-1664,
William Sancroft 1664-1678*, John Tillotson 1689-1691*,
William Sherlock 1691-1707

Oxford
Bishops
Robert Skinner 1641-1663, William Paule 1663-1665, Walter
Blandford 1665-1671, Nathaniel Crew 1671-74, Henry
Compton 1674-1675, John Fell 1676-1686, Samuel Parker
1686-1688, Timothy Hall 1688-1690, John Hough 1690-1699
Deans
George Morley 1660*, John Fell 1660-1686*, John Massey (RC)
1686-1688, Henry Aldrich 1689-1710

Ely
Bishops
Matthew Wren 1638-1667, Benjamin Lany 1667-1675, Peter
Gunning 1675-1684, Francis Turner 1684-1690**, Simon
Patrick 1691-1707
Deans
Richard Love 1660-1661, Henry Ferne 1661-1662, Edward
Martin 1662, Francis Wiliford 1662-1667, Robert Mapletoft
1667-1677, John Spencer 1677-1693

Norwich
Bishops
John Hall 1641-1656, Edward Reynolds 1660-1675, Anthony
Sparrow 1676-1685, William Lloyd 1685-1690**, John Moore
1691-1707
Deans
John Crofts 1660-1670, Herbert Astley 1670-1681, John
Sharp 1681-1689

Salisbury
Bishops
Brian Duppa 1641-1660, Humphrey Henchman 1660-1663,
John Earles 1663-1665, Alexander Hyde 1665-1667, Seth Ward
1667-1689, Gilbert Burnet 1689-1715
Deans
Richard Bayley 1635-1667, Ralph Brideoke 1667-1675*,
Thomas Pierce 1675-1691

Bath and Wells
Bishops
William Peirs 1632-1670, Robert Creyghton 1670-1672,
Peter Mews 1673-1684, Thomas Ken 1685-1690**, (William
Beveridge refused in 1691), Richard Kidder 1691-1703
Deans of Wells
Robert Creyghton 1660-70*, Ralph Bathurst 1670-1704

Worcester
Bishops
John Prideaux 1641-1650, George Morley 1660-1662, John
Gauden 1662, John Earles 1662-1663, Robert Skinner 1663-
1670, Walter Blandford 1671-1685, William Thomas 1683-
1689, Edward Stillingfleet 1689-1699
Deans
John Oliver 1660-1661, Thomas Warmestry 1661-65, William
Thomas 1665-1683, George Hicks 1683-1690

Rochester
Bishops
John Warner 1638-1666, John Dolben 1666-1683, Francis
Turner 1683-84, Thomas Sprat 1684-1713
Deans
Benjamin Lany 1660*, Nathaniel Hardy 1661-1670, Peter Mews
1670-1673*, Thomas Lamplugph 1673-1676*, John Castilion
1676-1688

Chicester
Bishops
Brian Duppa 1638-1641, Henry King 1642-1669, Peter
Gunning 1670-1675, Ralph Brideoke 1675-1678, Guy Carleton
1678-1685, John Lake 1685-1689, Simon Patrick 1689-1691
Deans
Joseph Henshaw 1660-1663*, Joseph Gulston 1663-1669,
Nathaniel Crew1669-1671, Thomas Ladbrook 1671-1672,
George Stradling 1672-1688, Francis Hawkins 1688-99

Winchester
Bishops
Walter Curle 1632-1647, Brian Duppa 1660-1662, George
Morley 1662-1684, Peter Mews 1684-1706
Deans
Alexander Hyde 1660-1665*, William Clark 1666-1679,
Richard Meggot 1679-1692

Bristol
Bishops
Thomas Howell 1644-1646, Gilbert Ironsides 1661-1671, Guy
Carleton 1671-1679*, William Gulston 1679-1684, John Lake
1684-1685*, Gilbert Ironsides 1689-1691*
Deans
Henry Glenham 1660-1667, Richard Towgood 1667-1683,
Samuel Crossman 1683-1684, Richard Thompson 1684-1685,
William Levett 1685-1694

Gloucester
Bishops
Godfrey Goodman 1624-1656, William Nicholson 1661-1672,
John Pritchett 1672-1681
Robert Frampton 1681-1690**, Edward Fowler 1691-1714
Deans
William Brough 1644-1671, Thomas Vyner 1671-1673, Robert
Frampton 1673-1681*, Thomas Marshall 1681-1685, William
Jane 1685-1707

Peterborough
Bishops
John Towers 1639-1649, Benjamin Lany 1660-1663*, Joseph
Henshaw 1663-1679, William Lloyd 1679-1685*, Thomas
White 1685-1690**, Richard Cumberland 1691-1718
Deans
John Cosin 1640-1660*, Edward Rainbow 1660-1664*, James
Dupont 1664-1679, Simon Patrick 1679-1689*

Lincoln
Bishops
Thomas Winniffe 1642-1654, Robert Sanderson 1660-1663,
Benjamin Lany 1663-1667*, William Fuller 1667-1675, Thomas
Barlow 1675-1691, Thomas Tenison 1692-1695*
Deans
Michael Honywood 1660-1681, Daniel Brevint 1681-1695

Lichfield and Coventry
Bishops
Accepted Frewen 1644-1660*, John Hackett 1661-1670,
Thomas Wood 1671-1692, William Lloyd 1692-1699*
Deans of Lichfield
William Paule 1661-1663*, Thomas Wood 166416-71*,
Matthew Smallwood 1671-1683, Lancelot Addison 1683-1703
Carlisle
Bishops
James Ussher 1642-1652, Richard Sterne 1660-1664*, Edward
Rainbow 1664-1684, Thomas Smith 1684-1702
Deans
Guy Carleton 1660-1672*, Thomas Smith 1672-84*, Thomas
Musgrave 1684-86, William Grahme 1686-1704

Chester
Bishops
John Bridgeman 1619-1652, Brian Walton 1660-1661, Henry
Ferne 1662, George Hall 1662-1668, John Wilkins 1668-1672,
John Pearson 1673-1686, Thomas Cartwright 168616-89, N.
Stratford 1689-1707
Deans
Henry Bridgeman 1660-1682*, James Arderne 1682-1691

Durham
Bishops
Thomas Morton 1632-1659, John Cosin 1660-1672, Nathaniel
Crew 1674-1721
Deans

John Barwick 1660-1661, John Sudbury 1661-1684, Denis Granville 1684-1690**

Sodor and Man
Richard Parr 1635-1643, Samuel Rutter 1661-1663, Isaac Barrow 1663-1670*, Henry Bridgeman 1671-1682, John Lake 1682-1684*, Baptist Levinz 1685-1693

Bangor
Bishops
William Roberts 1637-1665, Robert Morgan 1666-1673, Humphrey Lloyd 1673-1689, Humphrey Humphreys 1689-1701

Exeter
Bishops
Ralph Brownrigg 1642-1659, John Gauden 1660-1662, Seth Ward 1662-1667*, Anthony Sparrow 1667-1676*, Thomas Lamplugh 1676-1688*, Jonathan Trelawney 1689-1707

Hereford
Bishops
George Coke 1636-1646, Nicholas Monk 1661, Herbert Croft 1662-1691, Gilbert Ironsides 1691-1701

Llandaff
Bishops
Hugh Lloyd 1660-1667, Francis Davis 1667-1675, William Lloyd 1675-1679*, William Beaw 1679-1707

Peculiar Deaneries

Chapel Royal, London
Sheldon 7 June 1660, Morley 2 Oct 1663, Croft, H. 7 Feb 1668, Blandford, W. 5 April 1669,
Compton, H. 15 July 1675

Westminster
John Earles 1660-1662*, John Dolben 1662-1683, Thomas Sprat
1683-1713

Windsor
Bruno Ryves 1660-1677, John Durrell 1677-1683, Francis
Turner 1683-1684*, Gregory Hascard

www.ingramcontent.com/pod-product-compliance
Lightning Source LLC
Chambersburg PA
CBHW022004090426
42741CB00007B/880